THE SIXTH GUN

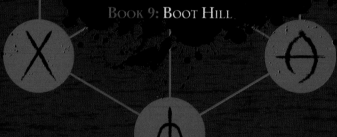

BOOK 9: BOOT HILL

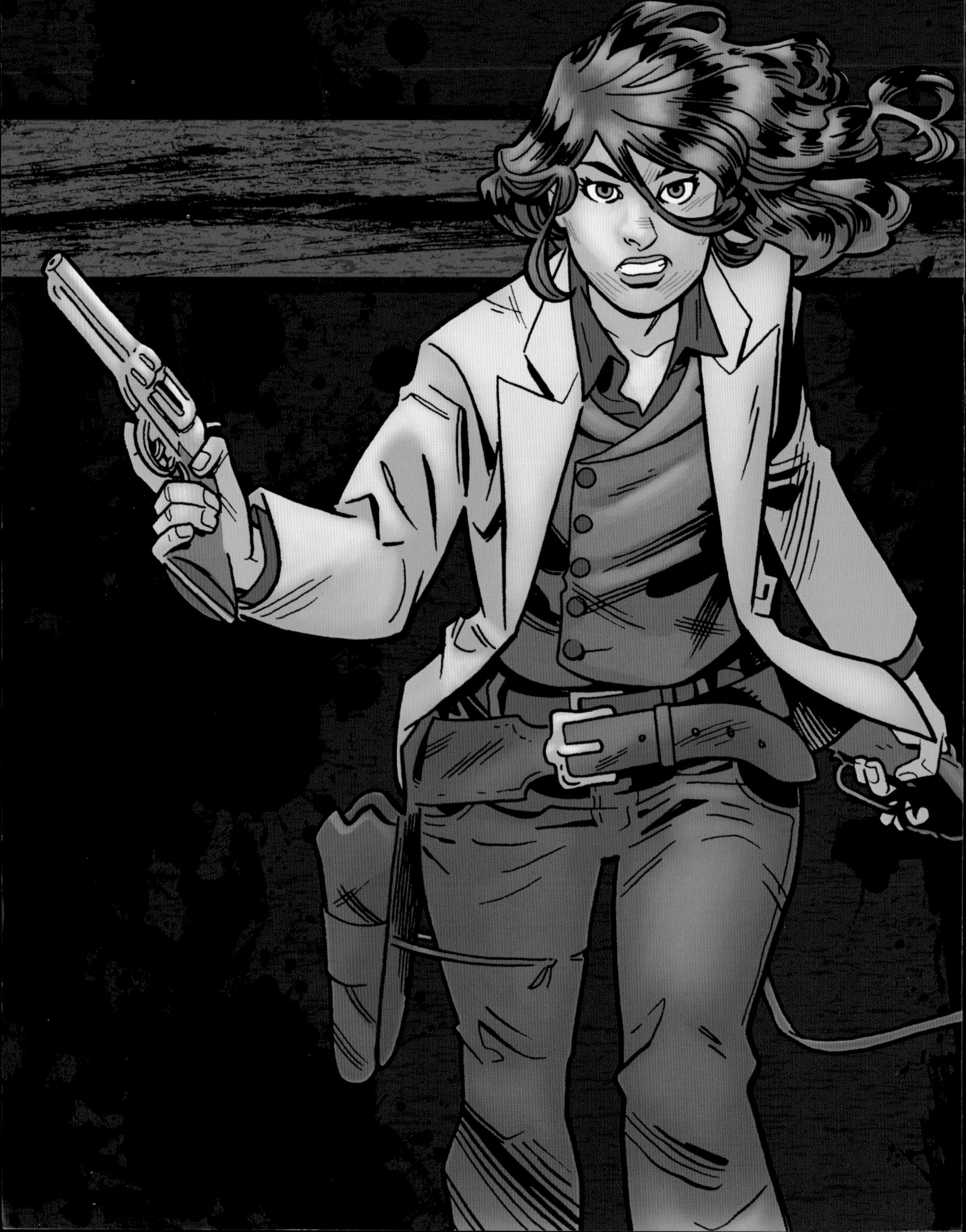

THE SIXTH GUN

BOOK 9: BOOT HILL

WRITTEN BY
CULLEN BUNN

ILLUSTRATED BY
BRIAN HURTT

COLORED BY
BILL CRABTREE

LETTERED BY
CRANK!

EDITED BY
CHARLIE CHU

DESIGNED BY
KEITH WOOD

ONI PRESS

AN ONI PRESS PUBLICATION

THE SIXTH GUN™
BY CULLEN BUNN & BRIAN HURTT

PUBLISHED BY ONI PRESS, INC.

JOE NOZEMACK *publisher*

JAMES LUCAS JONES *editor in chief*

ANDREW MCINTIRE *v.p. of marketing & sales*

RACHEL REED *publicity coordinator*

TROY LOOK *director of design & production*

HILARY THOMPSON *graphic desinger*

JARED JONES *digital art technician*

ARI YARWOOD *managing editor*

CHARLIE CHU *senior editor*

ROBIN HERRERA *editor*

BESS PALLARES *editorial assistant*

BRAD ROOKS *director of logistics*

JUNG LEE *logistics associate*

This volume collects issues #48-50 of the Oni Press series,
The Sixth Gun.

Oni Press, Inc.
1305 SE Martin Luther King Jr. Blvd.
Suite A
Portland, OR 97214
USA

onipress.com
facebook.com/onipress
twitter.com/onipress
onipress.tumblr.com
instagram.com/onipress

cullenbunn.com • @cullenbunn
brihurtt.com • @brihurtt
@crabtree_bill
@ccrank

First edition: October 2016

ISBN: 978-1-62010-299-2
eISBN: 978-1-62010-300-5

Library of Congress Control Number: 2016934336

10 9 8 7 6 5 4 3 2 1

Printed in China

✦ **BECKY MONTCRIEF** - A brave young woman who, until recently, wielded the Sixth Gun.

✦ **DRAKE SINCLAIR** - A treasure hunter with a bleak past.

✦ **NIDAWI** - Former host of the spirit of Screaming Crow.

✦ **NAHUEL** - A hunter and warrior who is sworn to protect Nidawi.

✦ **BILLJOHN O'HENRY** - A bounty hunter, who was killed at the Battle of the Maw. He was a true friend to Becky Montcrief, and Drake Sinclair.

✕ **BROTHER ROBERTO VARGAS** - A priest of the Sword of Abraham who was trapped in the Spirit World.

✦ **GRISELDA** - The Grey Witch who has stolen the Six and thrown open the gates of the Apocalypse.

✦ **GENERAL OLIANDER BEDFORD HUME** - A sadistic Confederate General who called the Six into our world.

✦ **JESUP SUTTER** - A former Pinkerton who has been transformed into a killing machine by Griselda.

CHAPTER
ONE

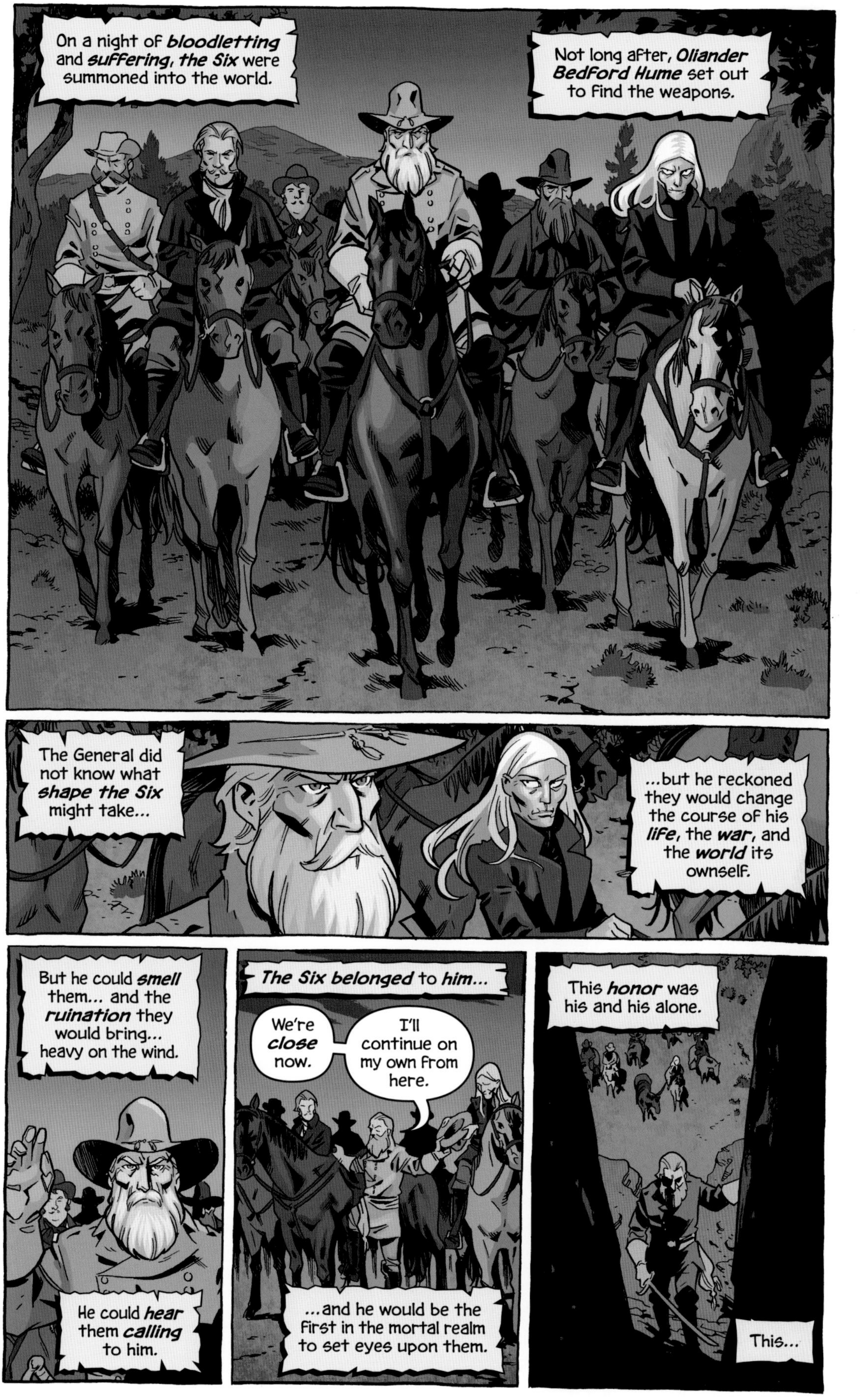
On a night of bloodletting and suffering, the Six were summoned into the world.
Not long after, Oliander Bedford Hume set out to find the weapons.
The General did not know what shape the Six might take...
...but he reckoned they would change the course of his life, the war, and the world its ownself.
But he could smell them... and the ruination they would bring... heavy on the wind.
He could hear them calling to him.
The Six belonged to him...
We're close now.
I'll continue on my own from here.
...and he would be the first in the mortal realm to set eyes upon them.
This honor was his and his alone.
This...

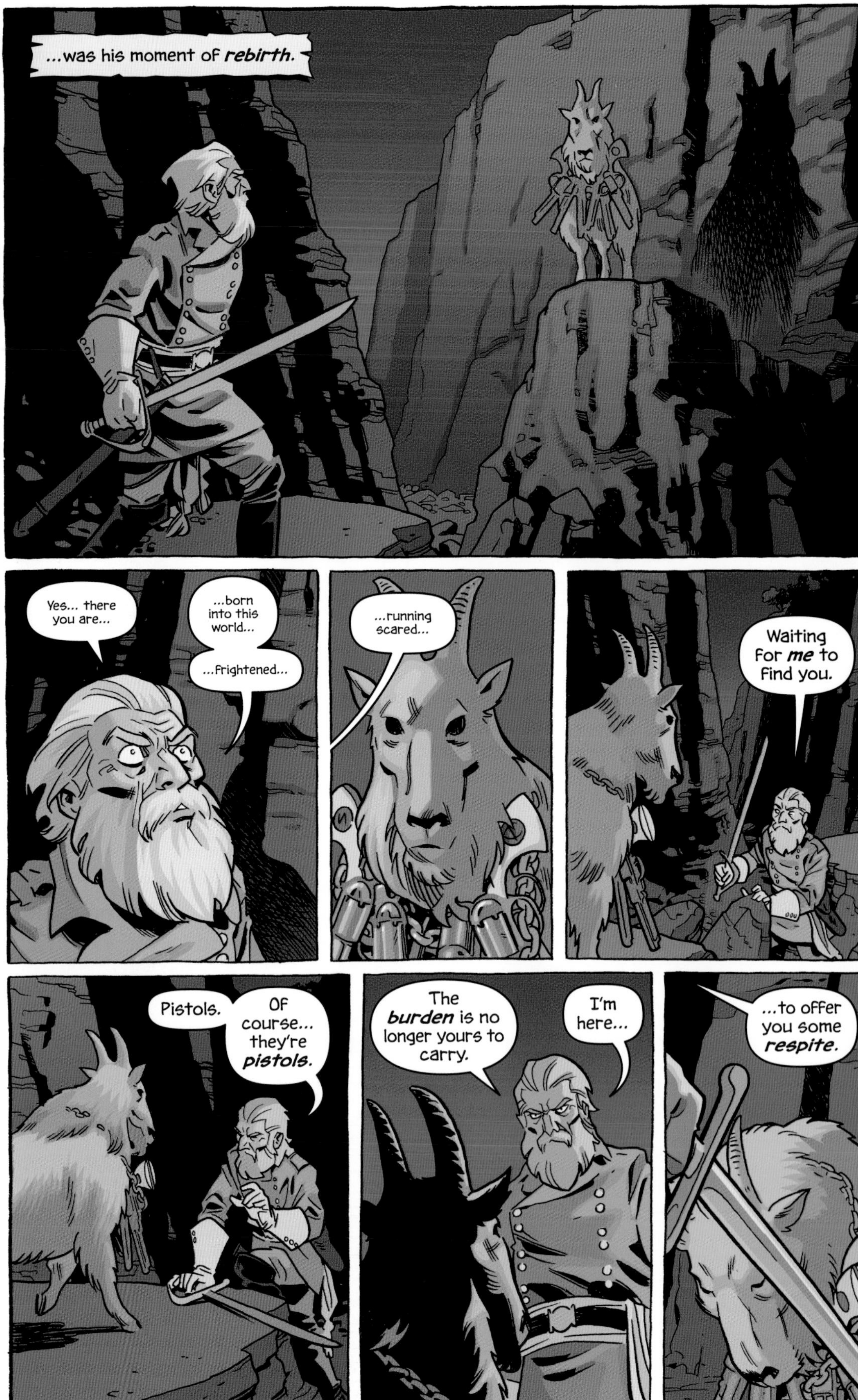
...was his moment of rebirth.
Yes... there you are...
...born into this world...
...frightened...
...running scared...
Waiting for me to find you.
Pistols.
Of course... they're pistols.
The burden is no longer yours to carry.
I'm here...
...to offer you some respite.

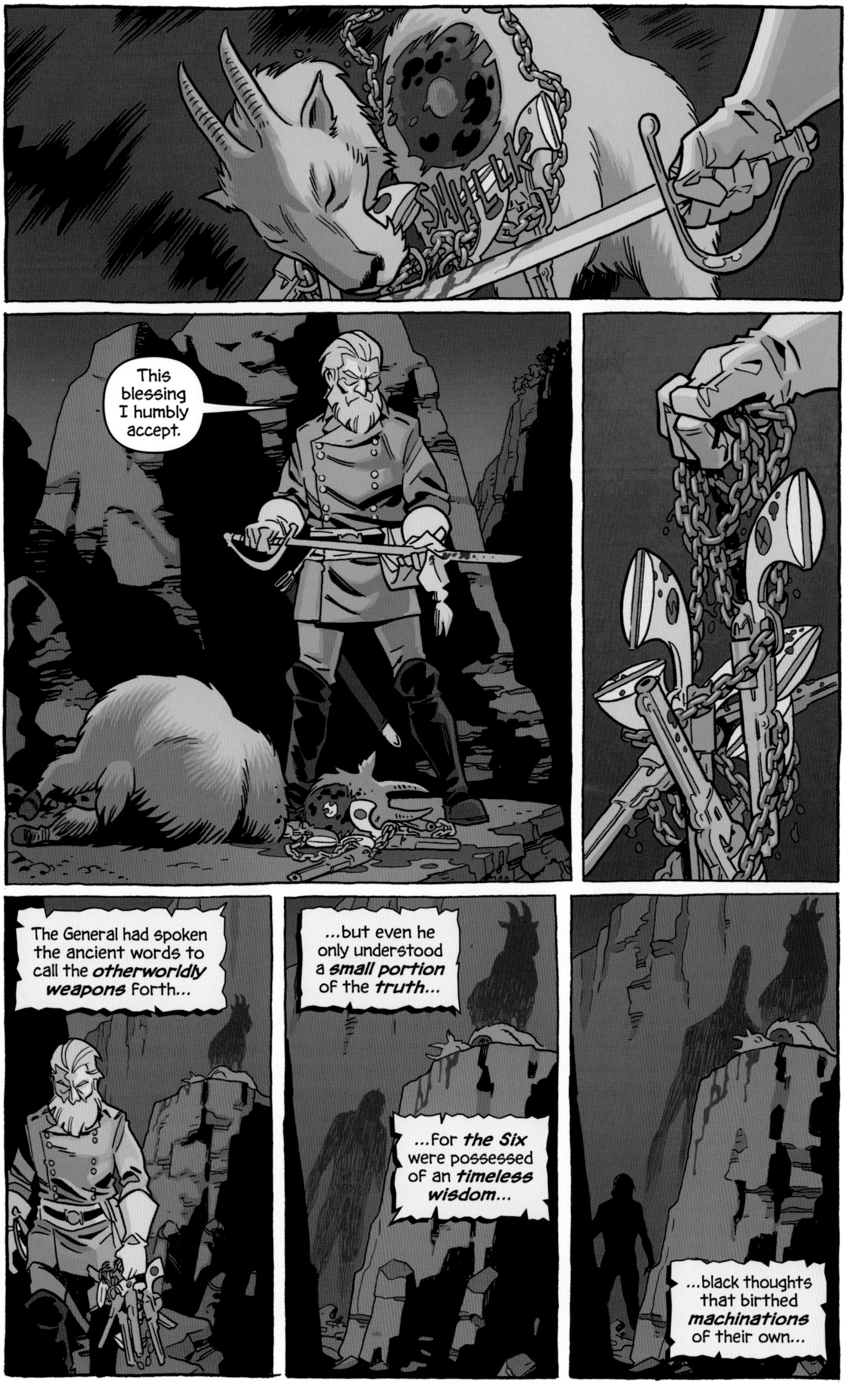
This blessing I humbly accept.
The General had spoken the ancient words to call the otherworldly weapons forth...
...but even he only understood a small portion of the truth...
...for the Six were possessed of an timeless wisdom...
...black thoughts that birthed machinations of their own...

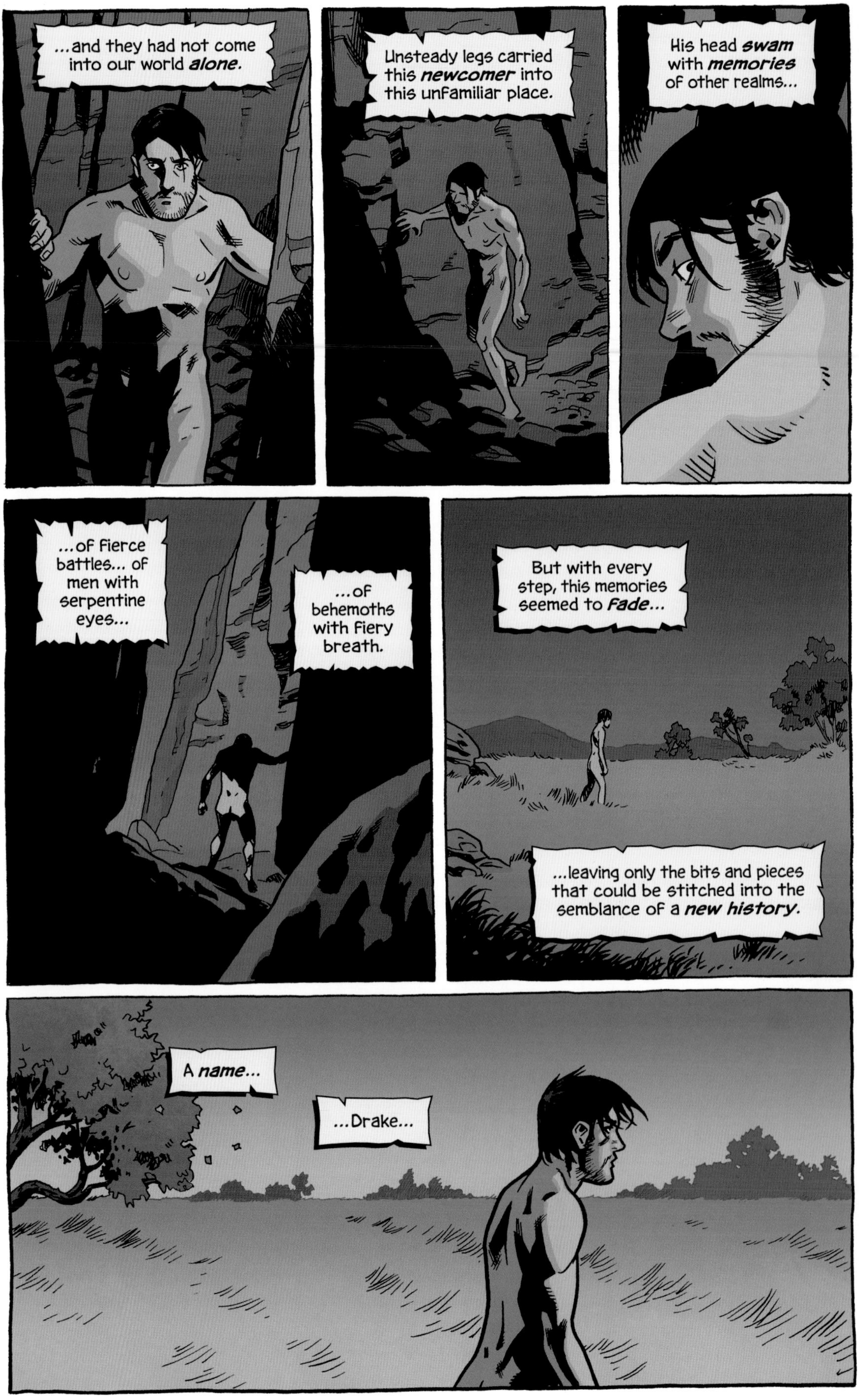
...and they had not come into our world alone.
Unsteady legs carried this newcomer into this unfamiliar place.
His head swam with memories of other realms...
...of fierce battles... of men with serpentine eyes...
...of behemoths with fiery breath.
But with every step, this memories seemed to fade...
...leaving only the bits and pieces that could be stitched into the semblance of a new history.
A name...
...Drake...

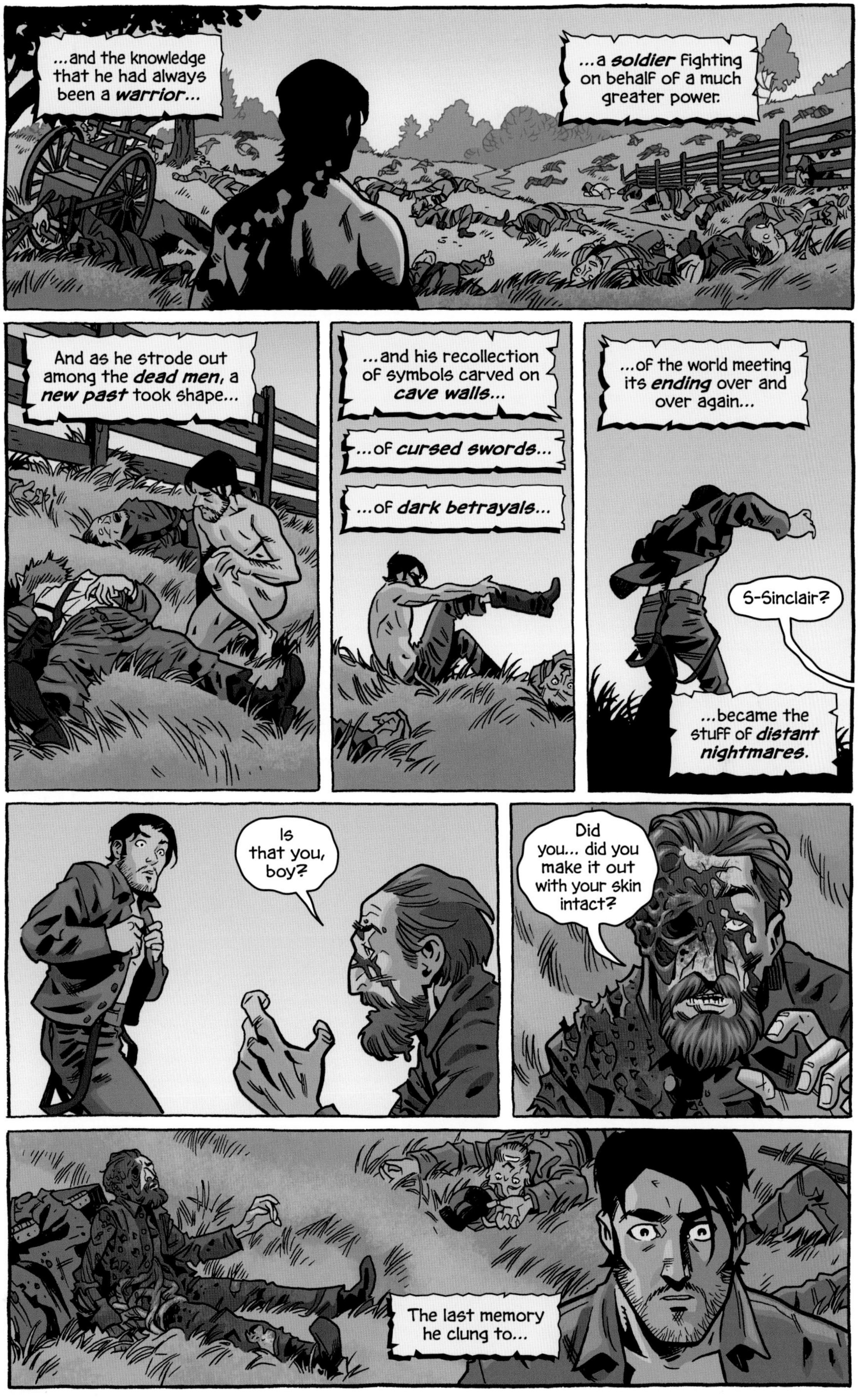
...and the knowledge that he had always been a *warrior*...
...a *soldier* fighting on behalf of a much greater power.
And as he strode out among the *dead men*, a *new past* took shape...
...and his recollection of symbols carved on *cave walls*...
...of *cursed swords*...
...of *dark betrayals*...
...of the world meeting its *ending* over and over again...
S-Sinclair?
...became the stuff of *distant nightmares*.
Is that you, boy?
Did you... did you make it out with your skin intact?
The last memory he clung to...

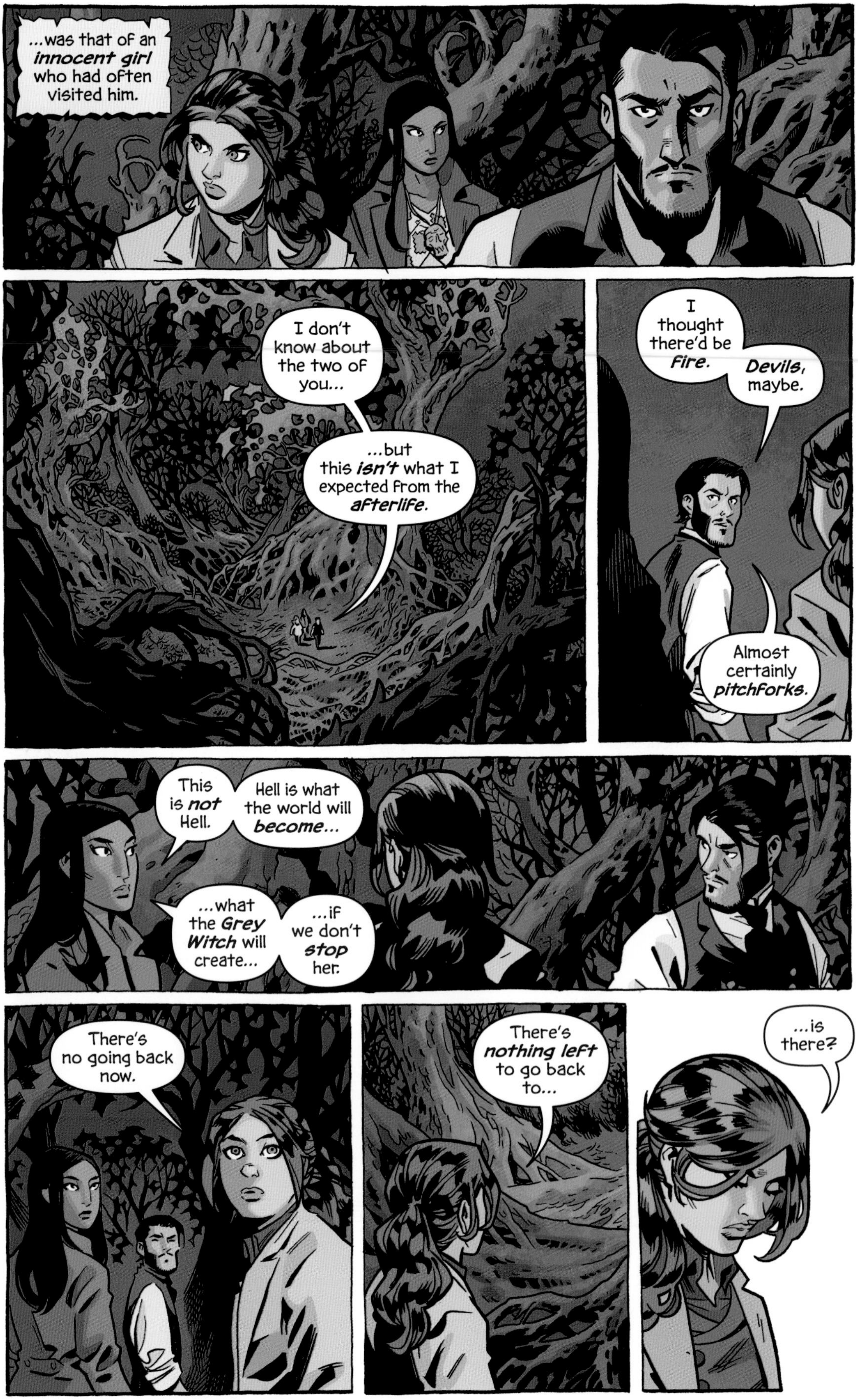
...was that of an *innocent girl* who had often visited him.
I don't know about the two of you...
...but this *isn't* what I expected from the *afterlife.*
I thought there'd be *fire.*
Devils, maybe.
Almost certainly *pitchforks.*
This is *not* Hell.
Hell is what the world will *become*...
...what the *Grey Witch* will create...
...if we don't *stop* her.
There's no going back now.
There's *nothing left* to go back to...
...is there?

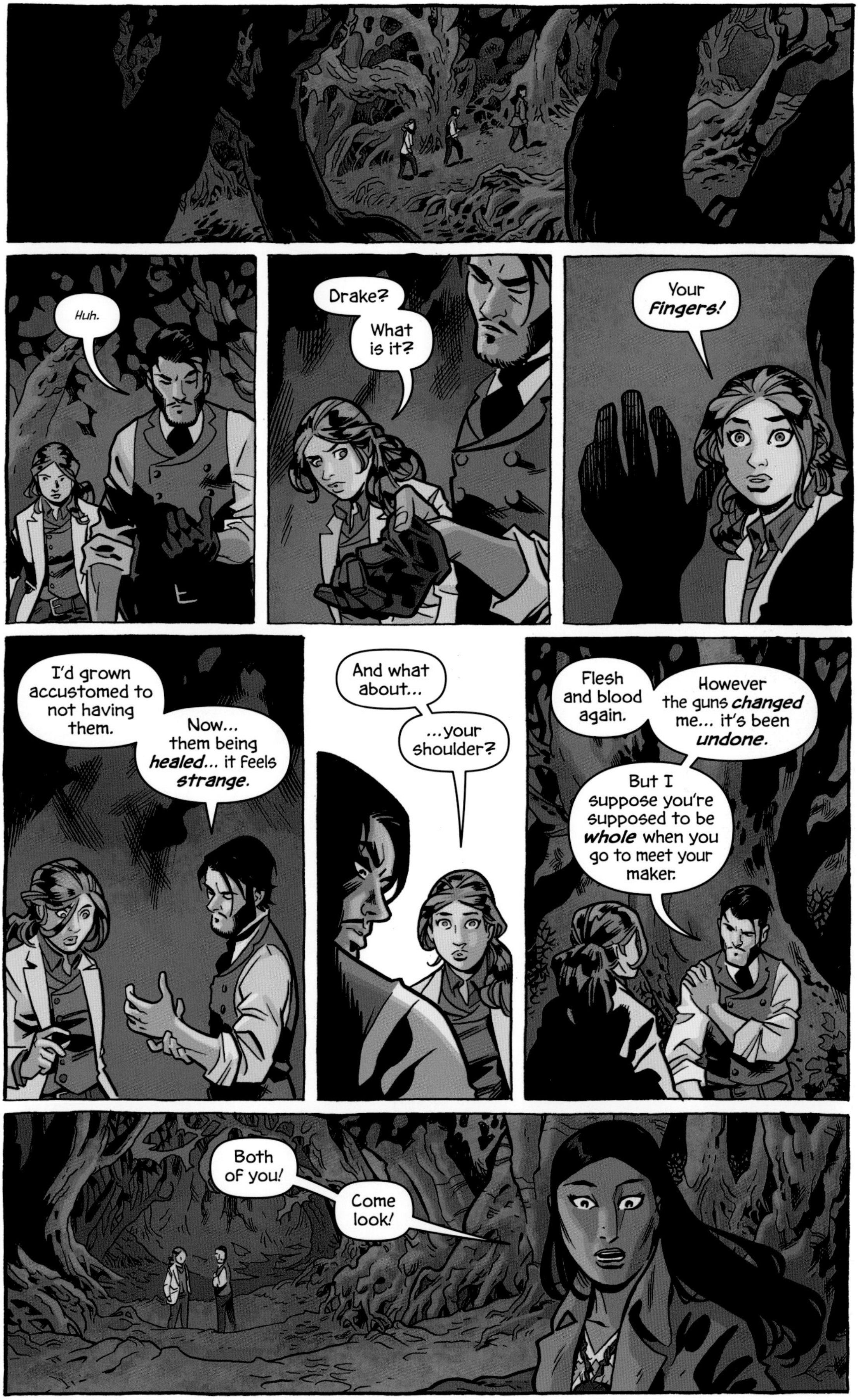
Huh.
Drake?
What is it?
Your fingers!
I'd grown accustomed to not having them.
Now... them being healed... it feels strange.
And what about...
...your shoulder?
Flesh and blood again.
However the guns changed me... it's been undone.
But I suppose you're supposed to be whole when you go to meet your maker.
Both of you!
Come look!

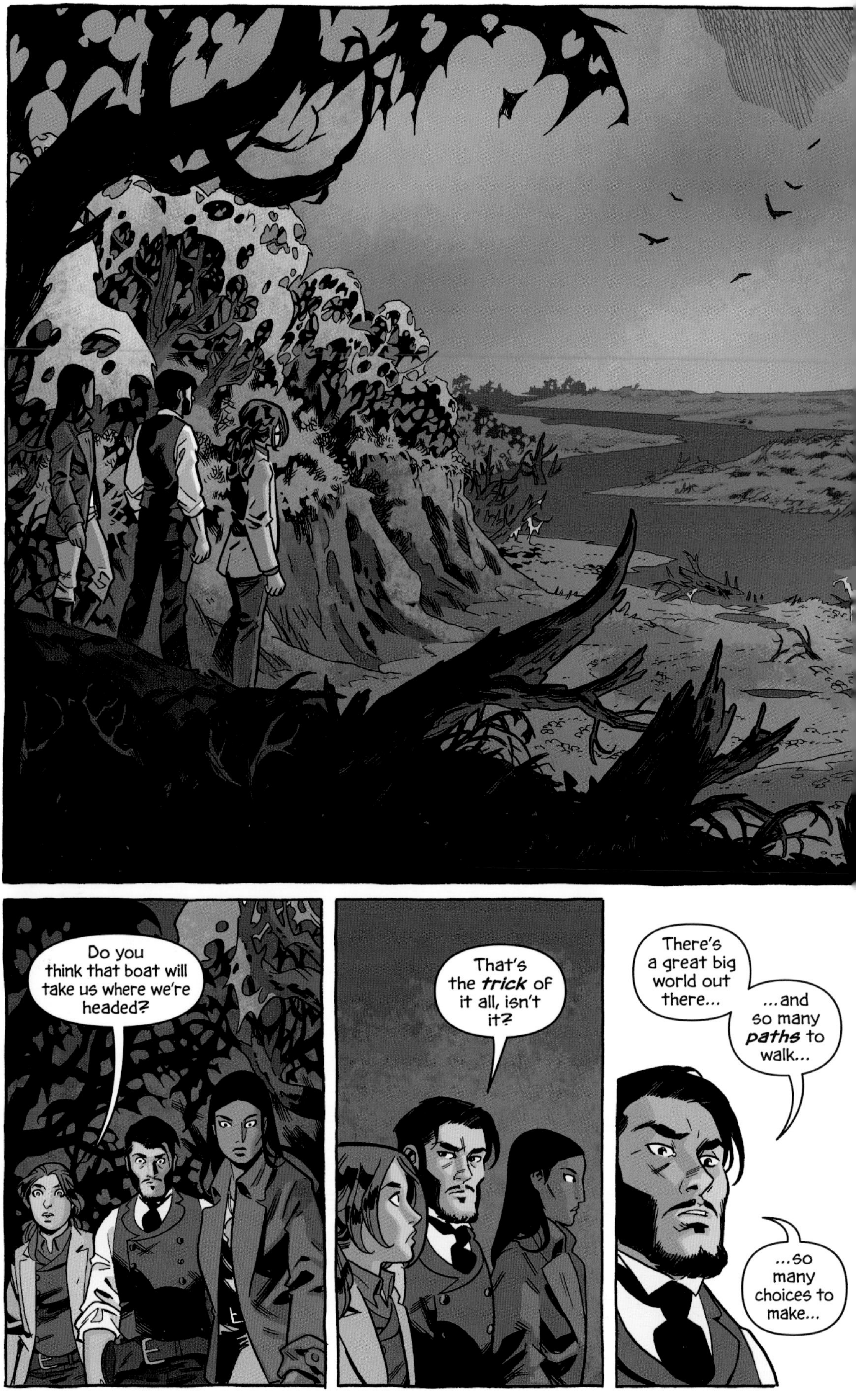
Do you think that boat will take us where we're headed?
That's the *trick* of it all, isn't it?
There's a great big world out there...
...and so many *paths* to walk...
...so many choices to make...

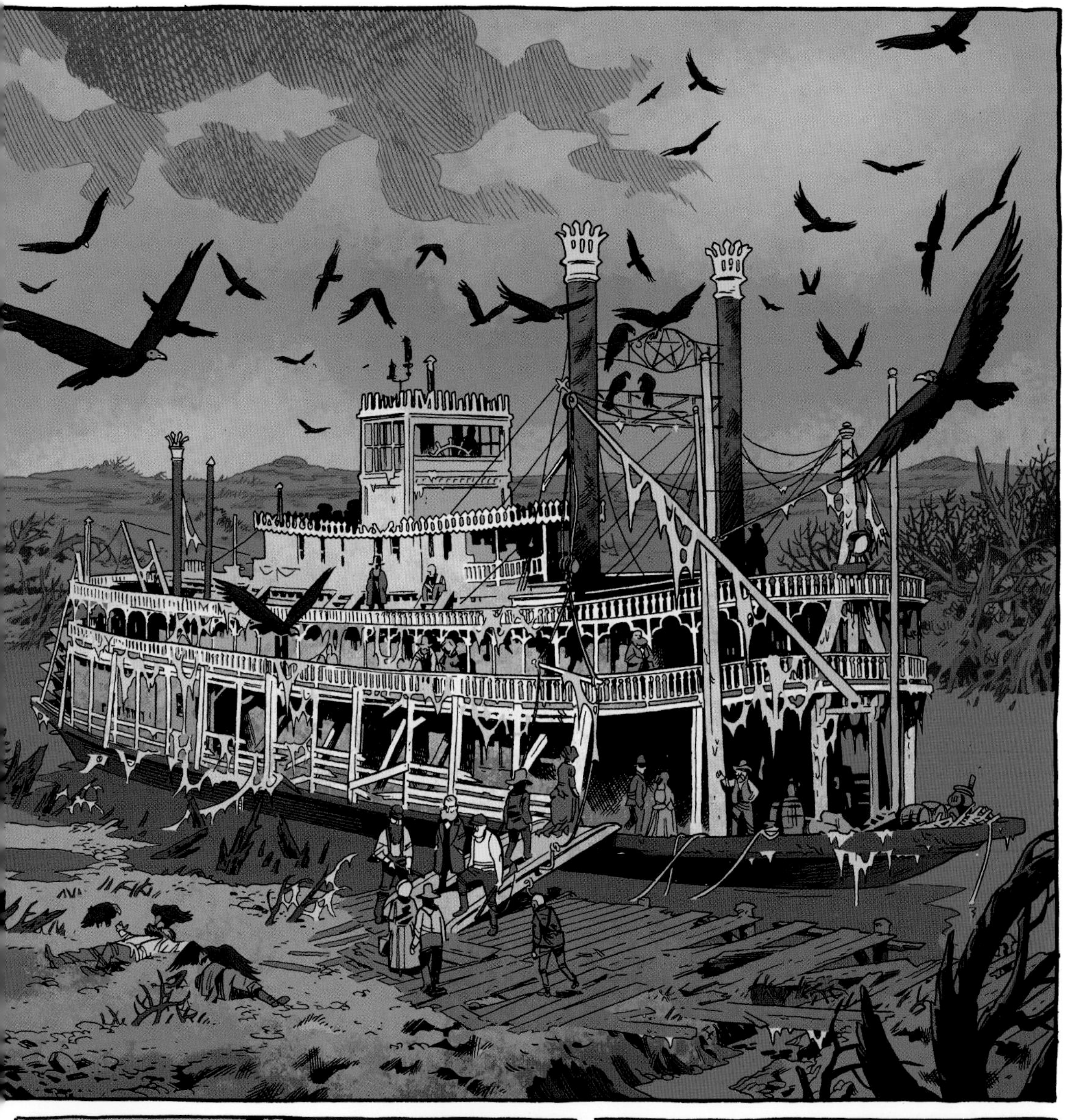

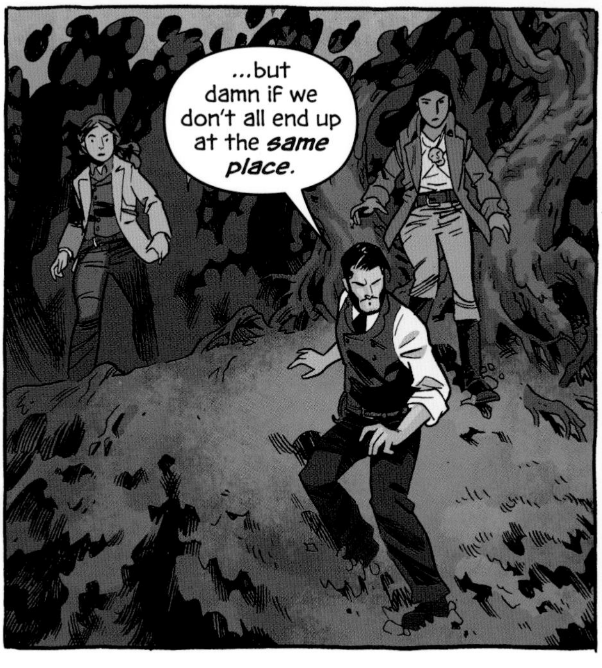

...but damn if we don't all end up at the *same place*.

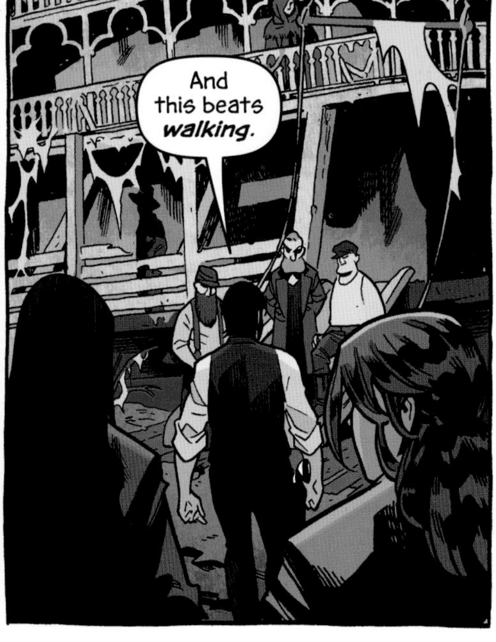

And this beats *walking*.

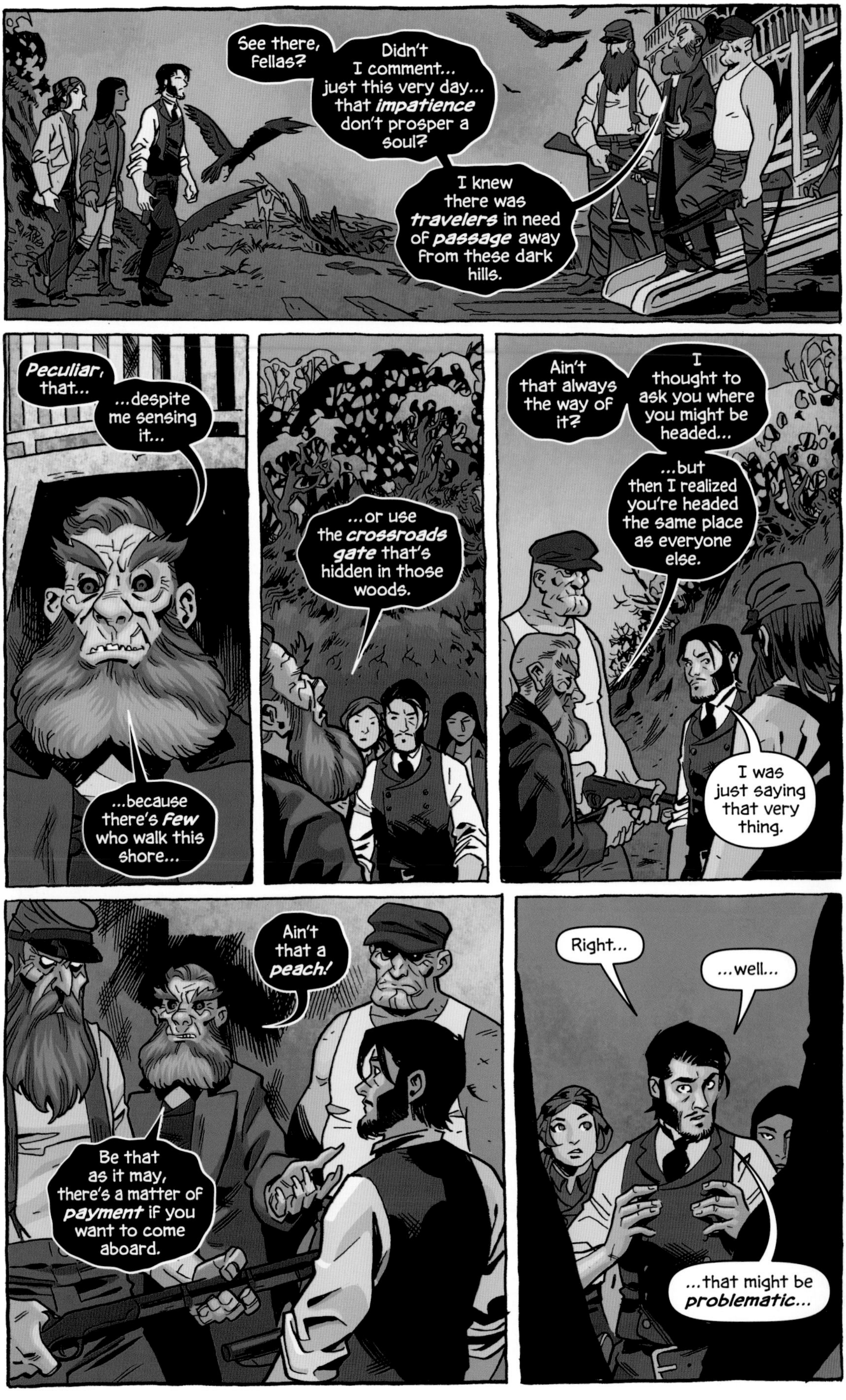
See there, fellas?
Didn't I comment... just this very day... that impatience don't prosper a soul?
I knew there was travelers in need of passage away from these dark hills.
Peculiar, that...
...despite me sensing it...
...because there's few who walk this shore...
...or use the crossroads gate that's hidden in those woods.
Ain't that always the way of it?
I thought to ask you where you might be headed...
...but then I realized you're headed the same place as everyone else.
I was just saying that very thing.
Ain't that a peach!
Be that as it may, there's a matter of payment if you want to come aboard.
Right...
...well...
...that might be problematic...

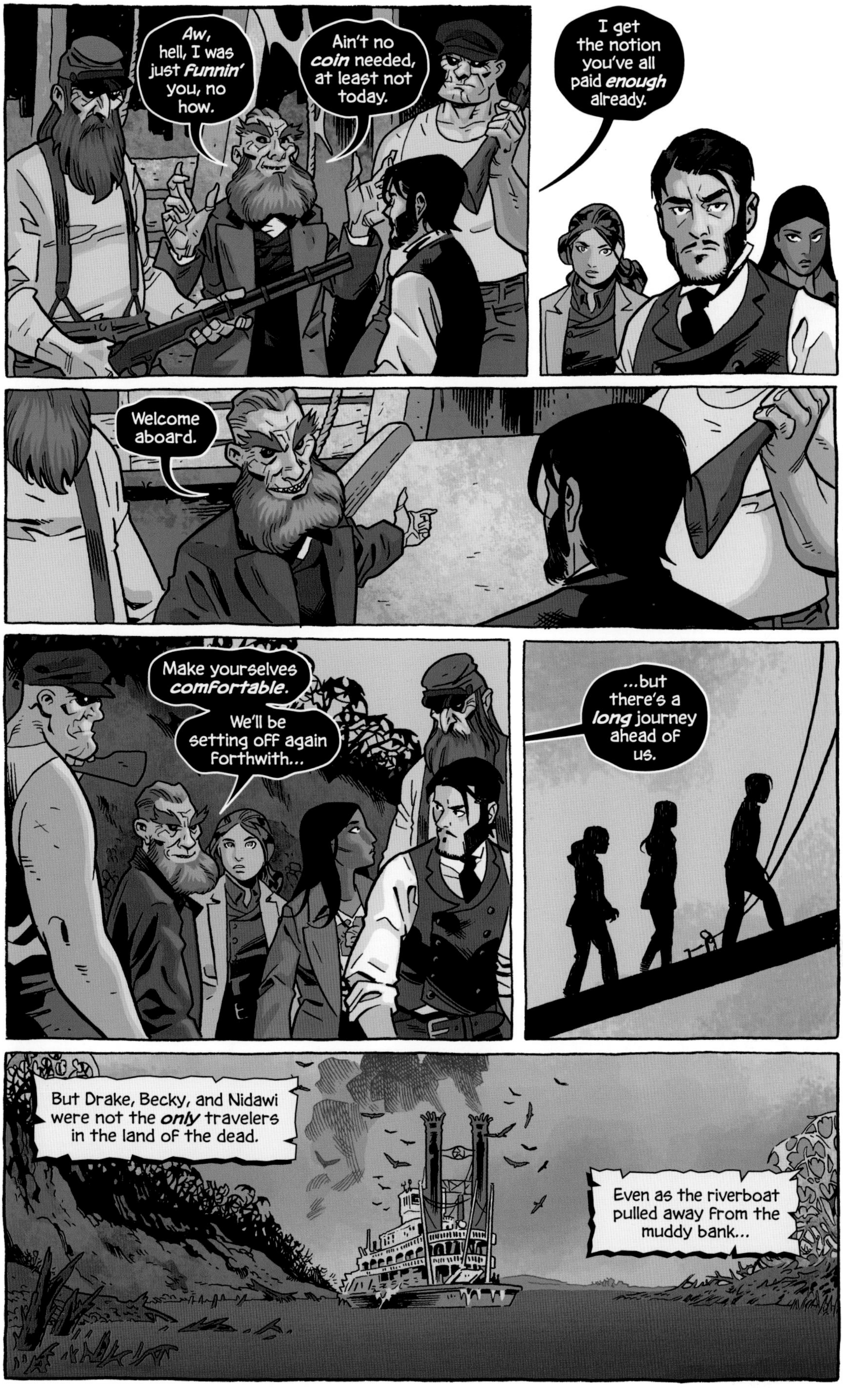

Aw, hell, I was just *funnin'* you, no how.
Ain't no *coin* needed, at least not today.
I get the notion you've all paid *enough* already.
Welcome aboard.
Make yourselves *comfortable.*
We'll be setting off again forthwith...
...but there's a *long* journey ahead of us.
But Drake, Becky, and Nidawi were not the *only* travelers in the land of the dead.
Even as the riverboat pulled away from the muddy bank...

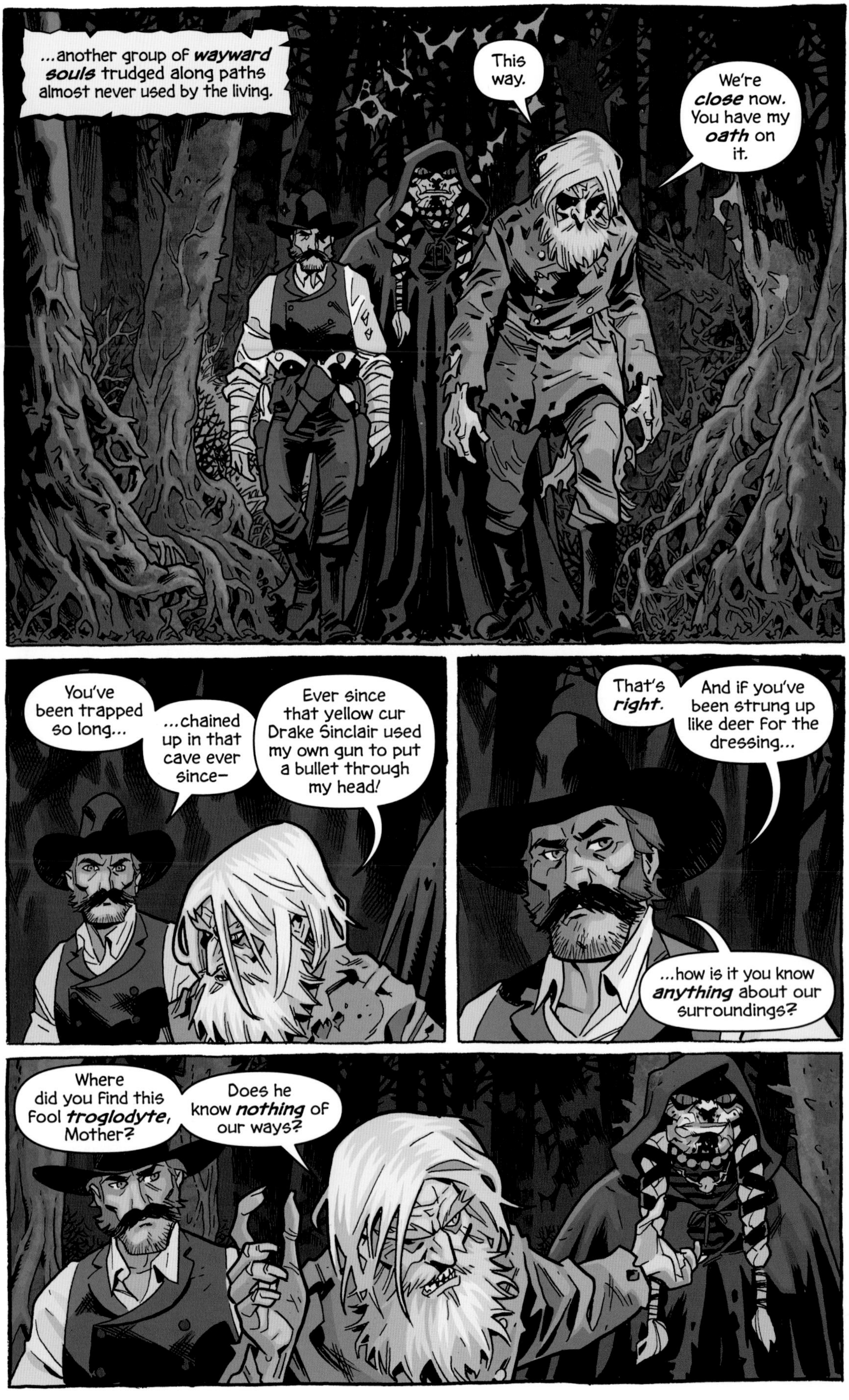
...another group of *wayward souls* trudged along paths almost never used by the living.
This way.
We're *close* now. You have my *oath* on it.
You've been trapped so long...
...chained up in that cave ever since–
Ever since that yellow cur Drake Sinclair used my own gun to put a bullet through my head!
That's *right*.
And if you've been strung up like deer for the dressing...
...how is it you know *anything* about our surroundings?
Where did you find this fool *troglodyte*, Mother?
Does he know *nothing* of our ways?

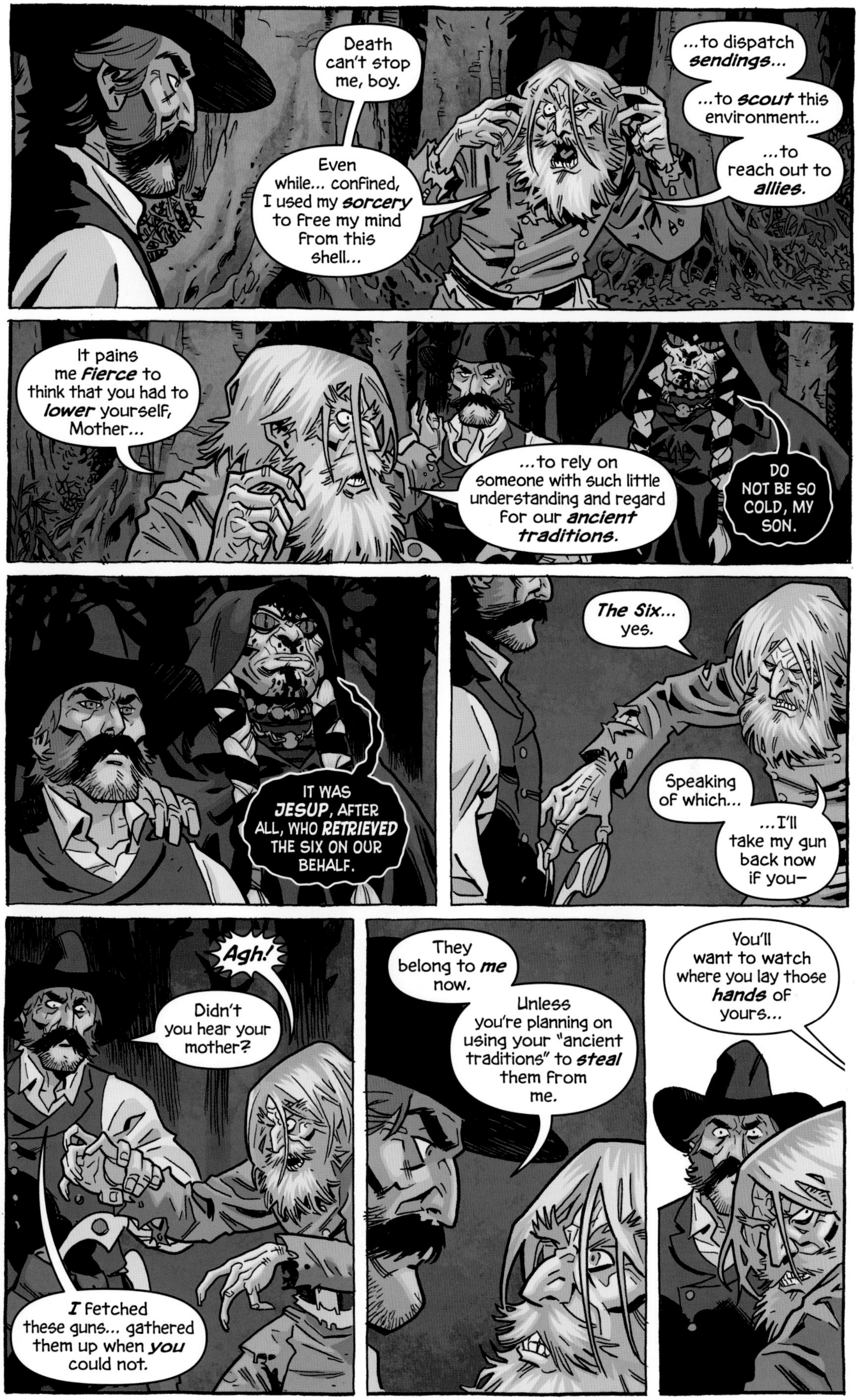
Death can't stop me, boy.
Even while... confined, I used my sorcery to free my mind from this shell...
...to dispatch sendings...
...to scout this environment...
...to reach out to allies.
It pains me Fierce to think that you had to lower yourself, Mother...
...to rely on someone with such little understanding and regard for our ancient traditions.
DO NOT BE SO COLD, MY SON.
IT WAS JESUP, AFTER ALL, WHO RETRIEVED THE SIX ON OUR BEHALF.
The Six... yes.
Speaking of which...
...I'll take my gun back now if you—
Agh!
Didn't you hear your mother?
I fetched these guns... gathered them up when you could not.
They belong to me now.
Unless you're planning on using your "ancient traditions" to steal them from me.
You'll want to watch where you lay those hands of yours...

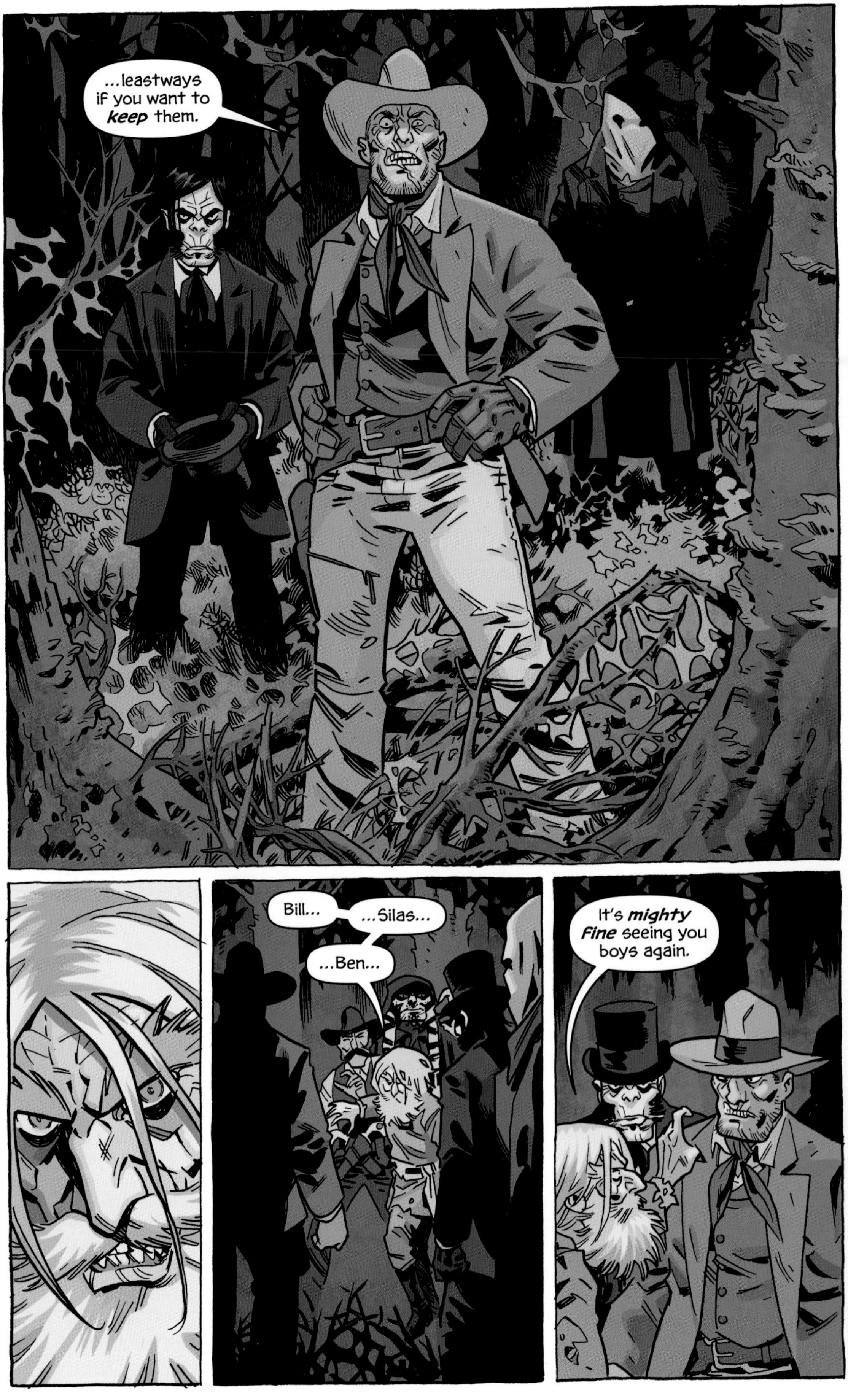
...leastways if you want to *keep* them.
Bill...
...Silas...
...Ben...
It's *mighty fine* seeing you boys again.

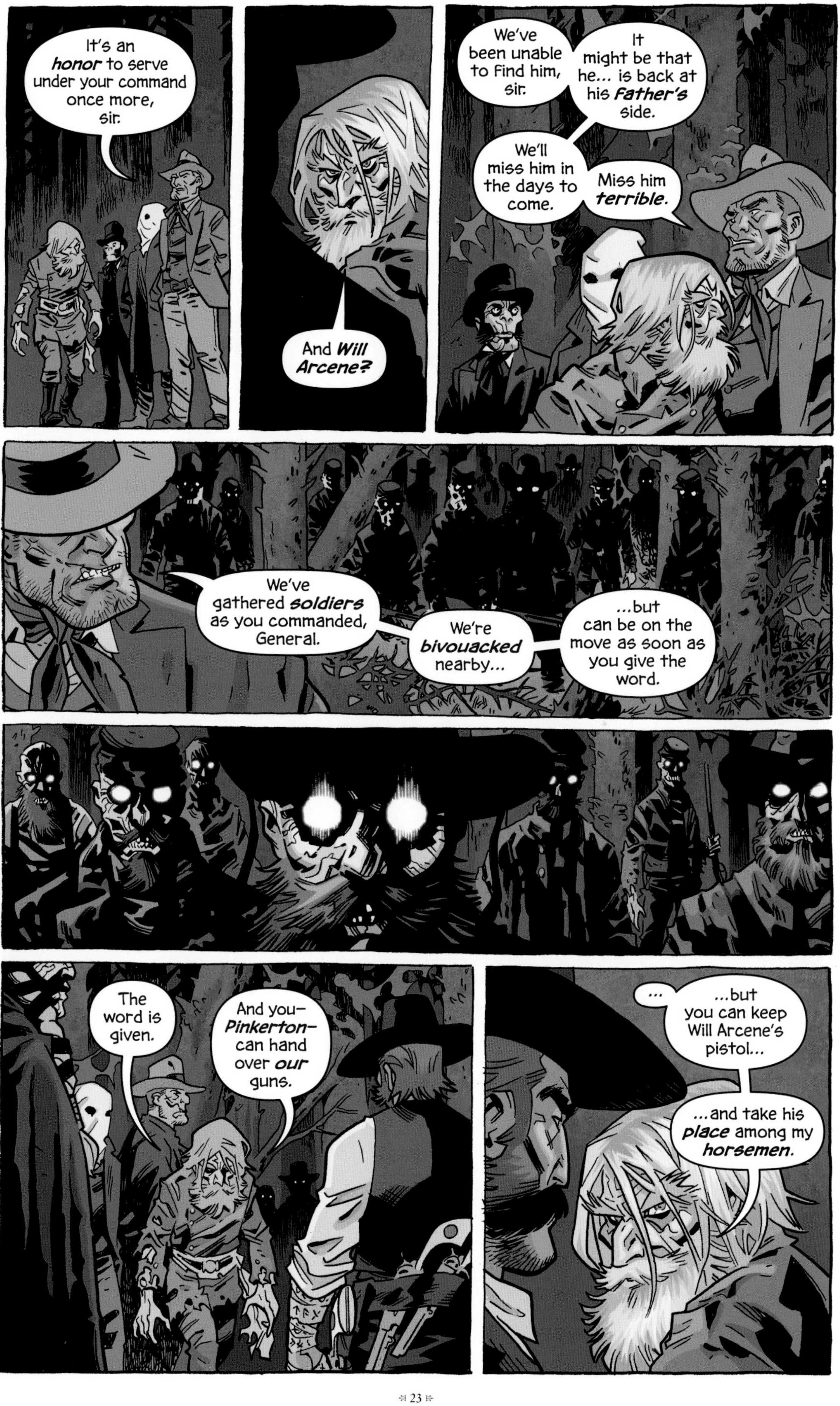

It's an honor to serve under your command once more, sir.
And Will Arcene?
We've been unable to find him, sir.
It might be that he... is back at his father's side.
We'll miss him in the days to come.
Miss him terrible.
We've gathered soldiers as you commanded, General.
We're bivouacked nearby...
...but can be on the move as soon as you give the word.
The word is given.
And you—Pinkerton—can hand over our guns.
...
...but you can keep Will Arcene's pistol...
...and take his place among my horsemen.

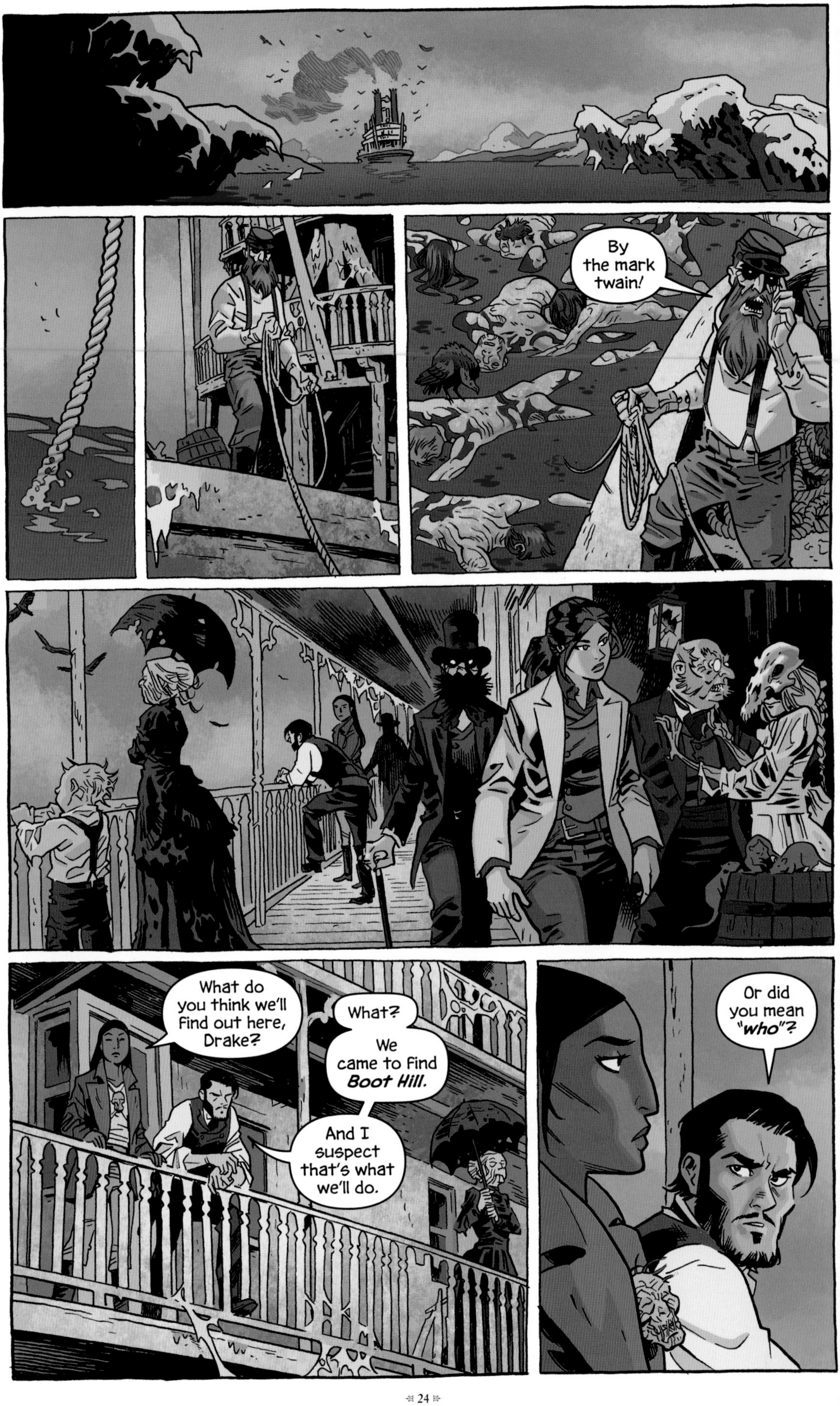
By the mark twain!
What do you think we'll find out here, Drake?
What?
We came to find *Boot Hill.*
And I suspect that's what we'll do.
Or did you mean *"who"*?

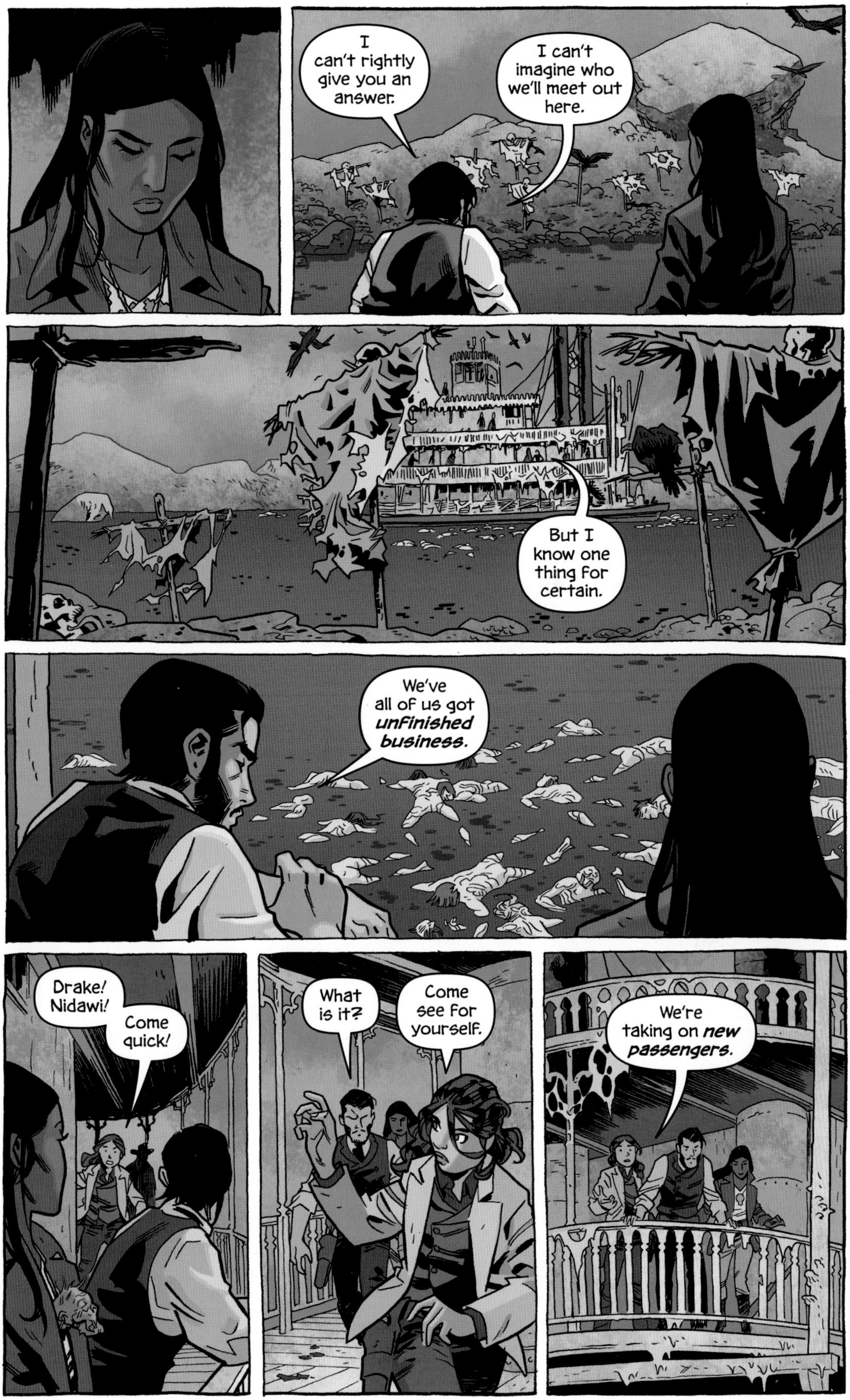
I can't rightly give you an answer.
I can't imagine who we'll meet out here.
But I know one thing for certain.
We've all of us got *unfinished business.*
Drake! Nidawi!
Come quick!
What is it?
Come see for yourself.
We're taking on *new passengers.*

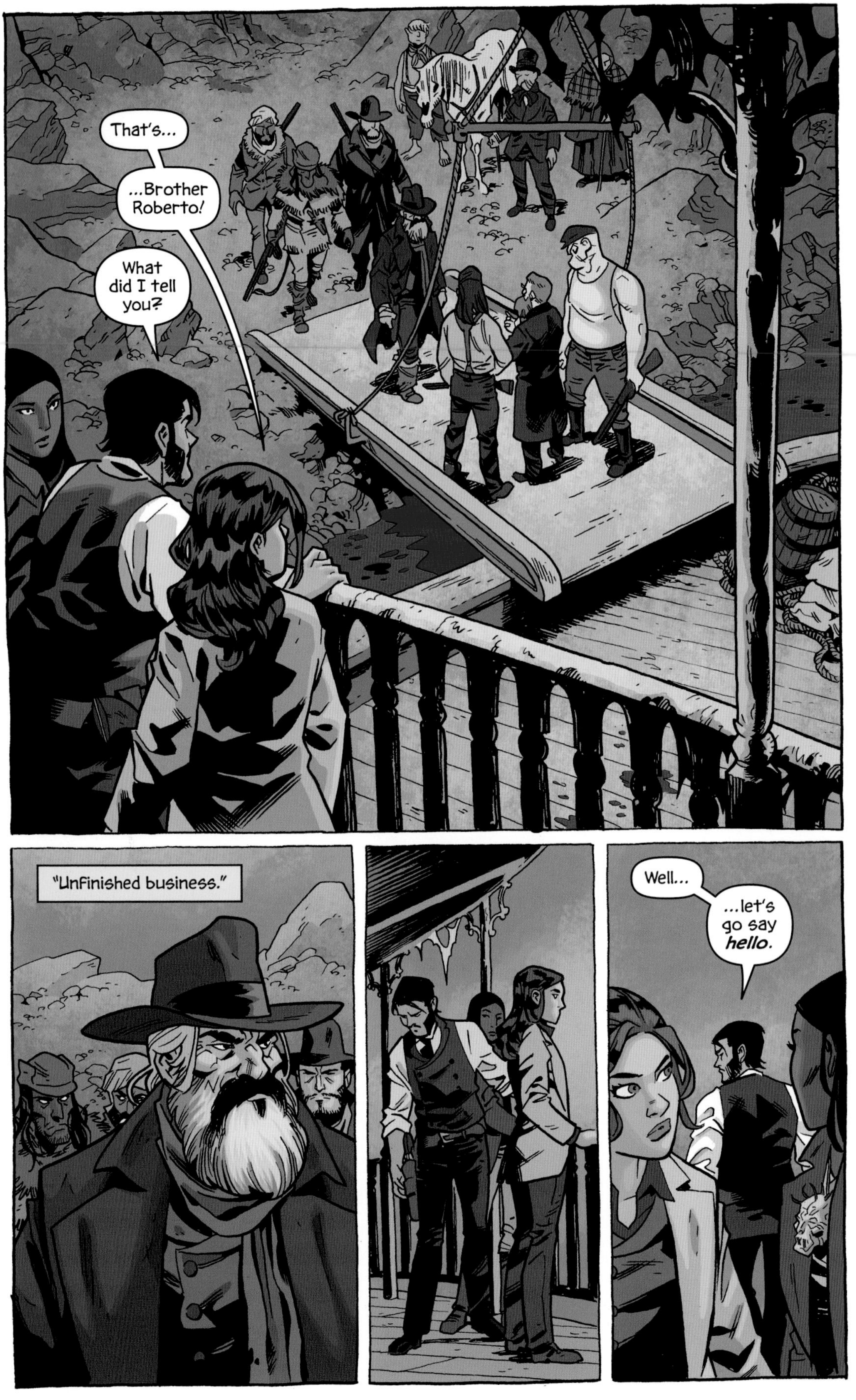
That's...
...Brother Roberto!
What did I tell you?
"Unfinished business."
Well...
...let's go say *hello*.

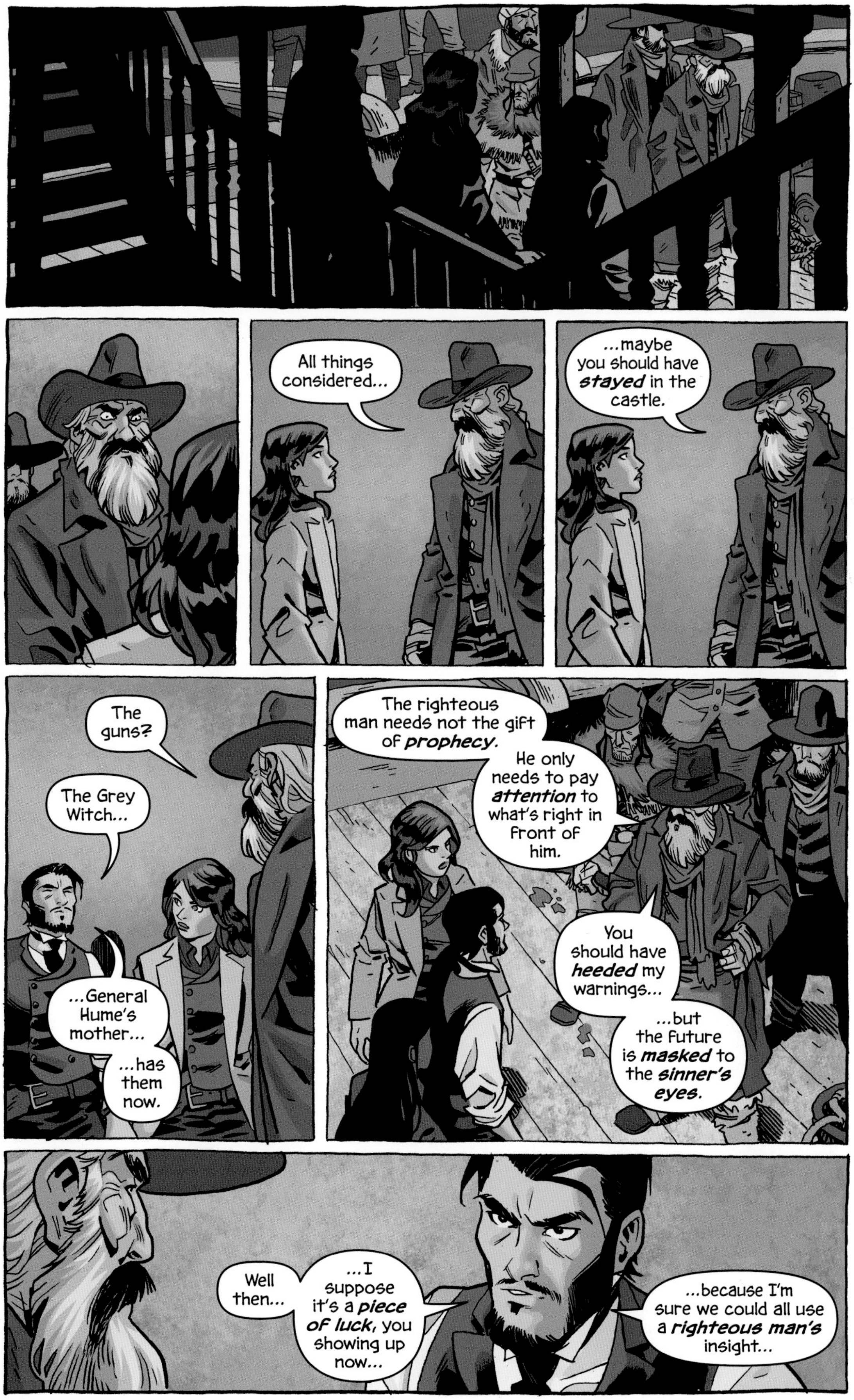

All things considered...
...maybe you should have *stayed* in the castle.
The guns?
The Grey Witch...
...General Hume's mother...
...has them now.
The righteous man needs not the gift of *prophecy.*
He only needs to pay *attention* to what's right in front of him.
You should have *heeded* my warnings...
...but the future is *masked* to the *sinner's eyes.*
Well then...
...I suppose it's a *piece of luck*, you showing up now...
...because I'm sure we could all use a *righteous man's* insight...

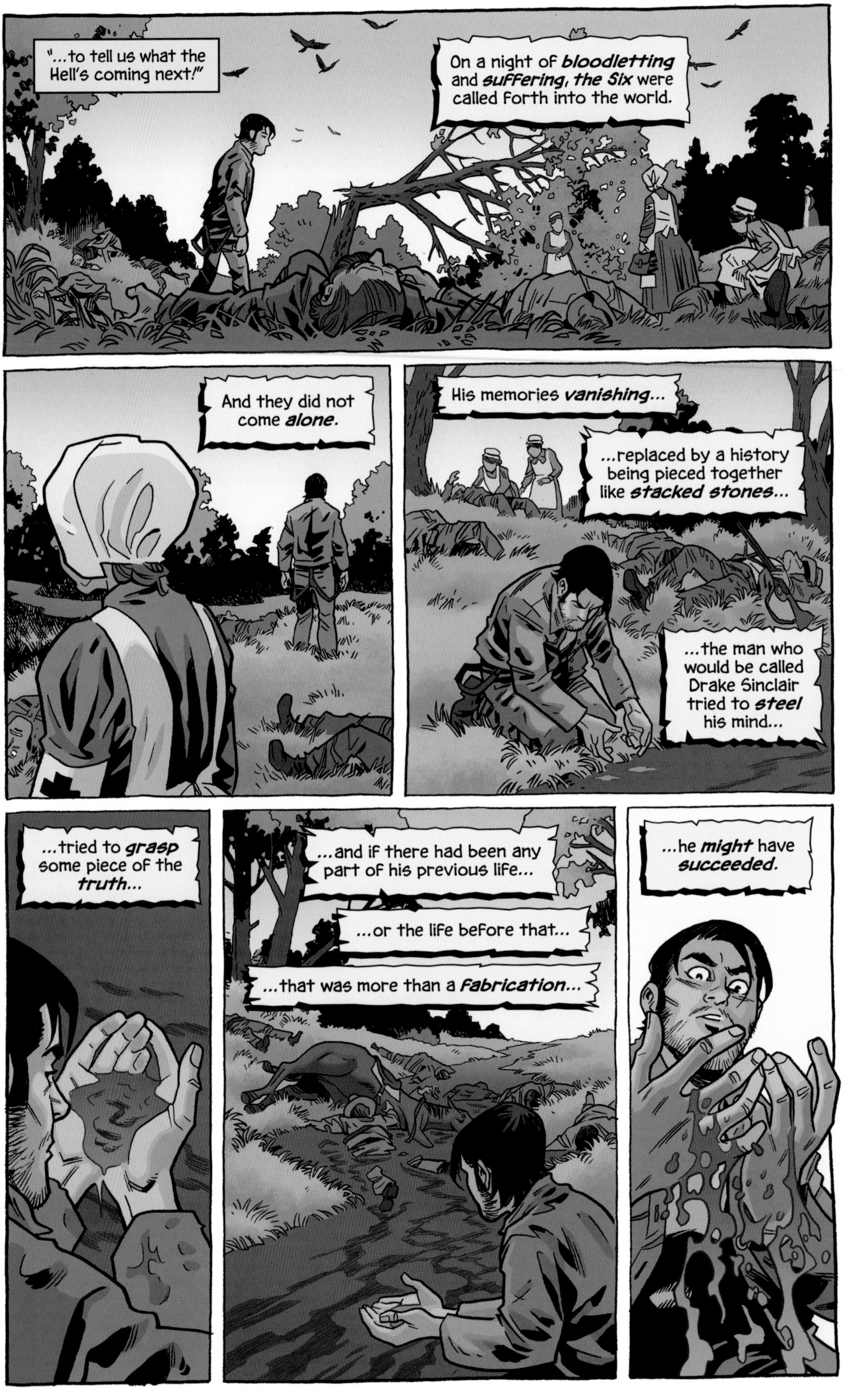
"...to tell us what the Hell's coming next!"
On a night of bloodletting and suffering, the Six were called forth into the world.
And they did not come alone.
His memories vanishing...
...replaced by a history being pieced together like stacked stones...
...the man who would be called Drake Sinclair tried to steel his mind...
...tried to grasp some piece of the truth...
...and if there had been any part of his previous life...
...or the life before that...
...that was more than a fabrication...
...he might have succeeded.

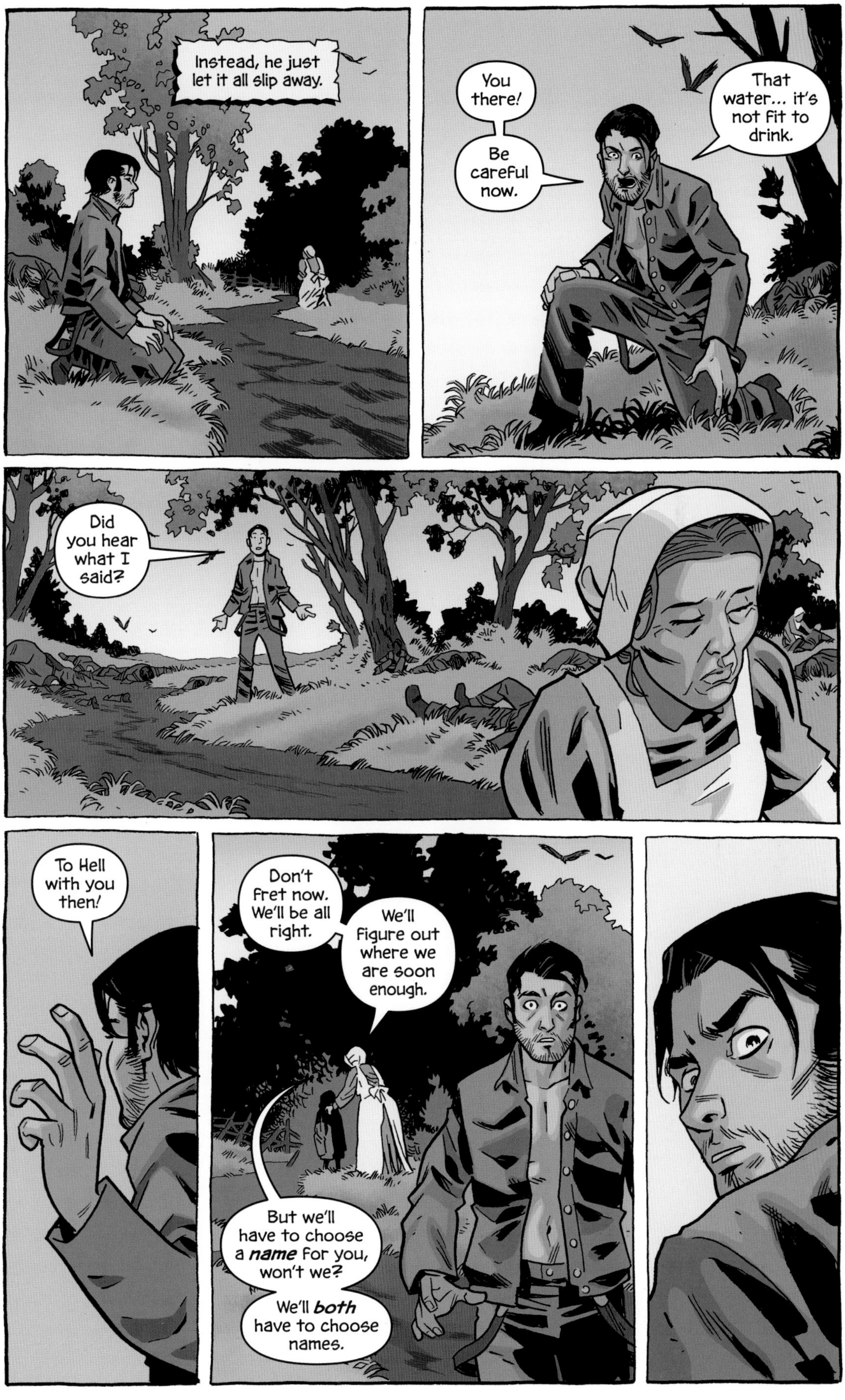
Instead, he just let it all slip away.
You there!
Be careful now.
That water... it's not fit to drink.
Did you hear what I said?
To Hell with you then!
Don't fret now. We'll be all right.
We'll figure out where we are soon enough.
But we'll have to choose a *name* for you, won't we?
We'll *both* have to choose names.

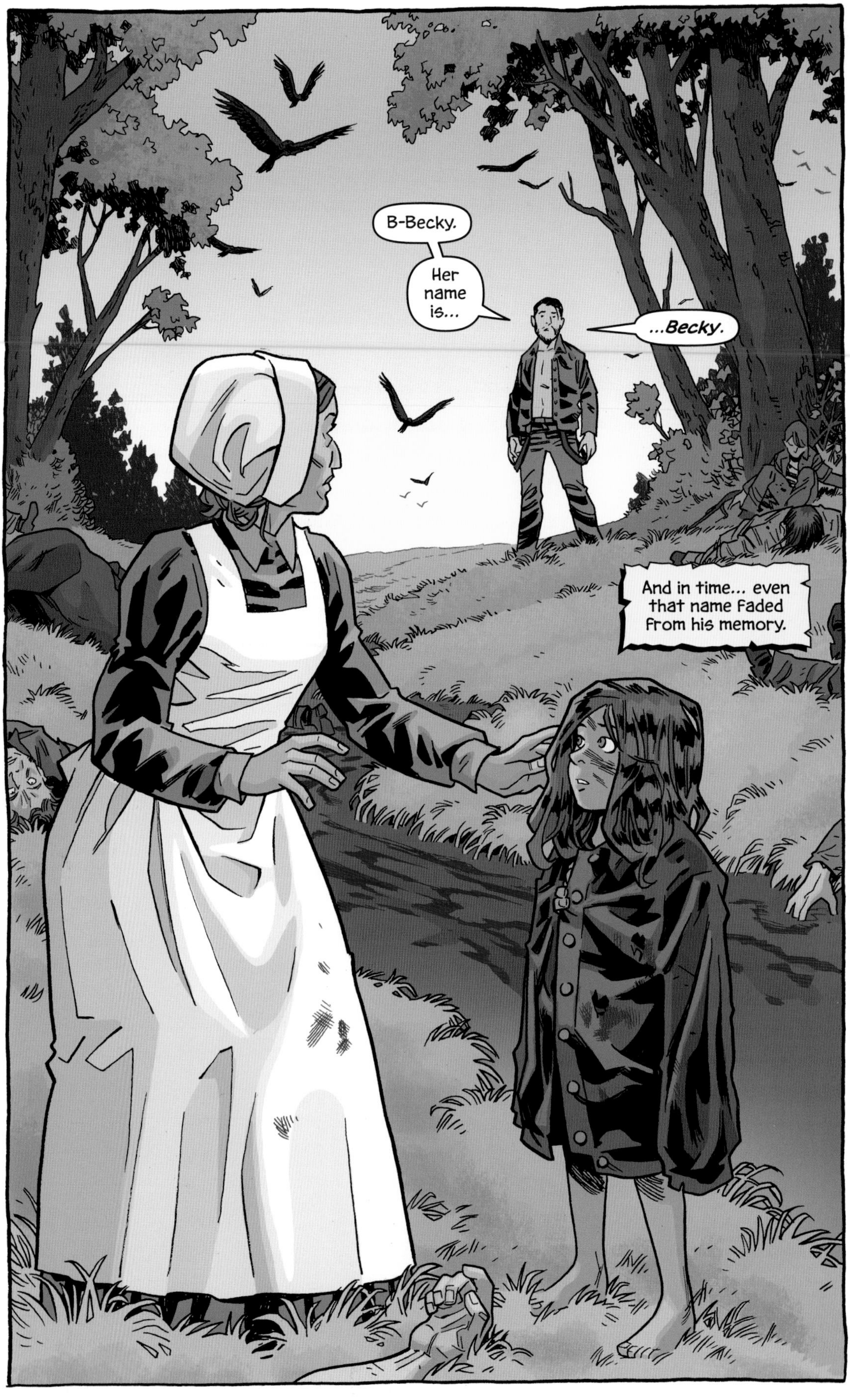
B-Becky.
Her name is...
...Becky.
And in time... even that name faded from his memory.

CHAPTER TWO

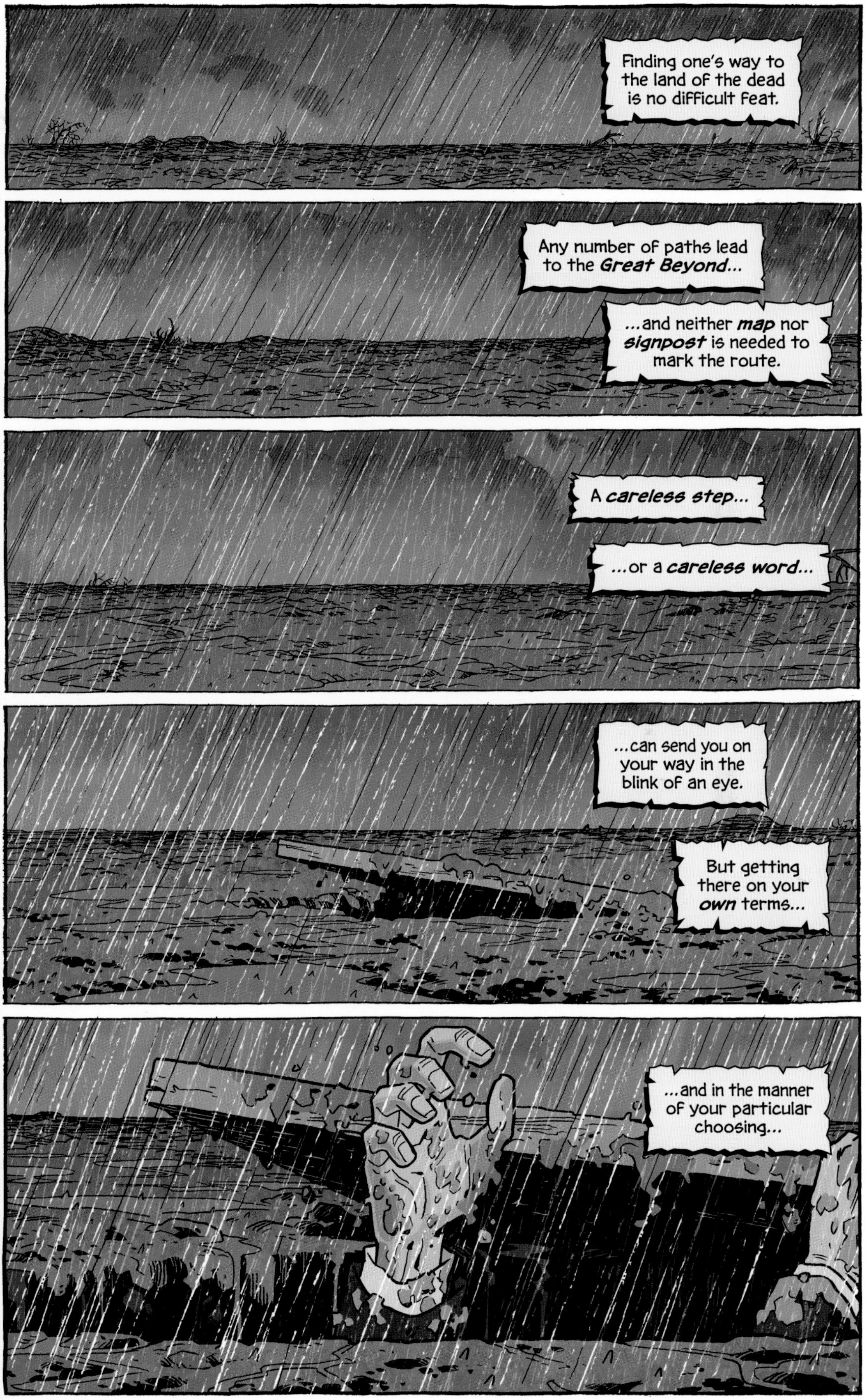
Finding one's way to the land of the dead is no difficult feat.
Any number of paths lead to the *Great Beyond*...
...and neither *map* nor *signpost* is needed to mark the route.
A *careless step*...
...or a *careless word*...
...can send you on your way in the blink of an eye.
But getting there on your *own* terms...
...and in the manner of your particular choosing...

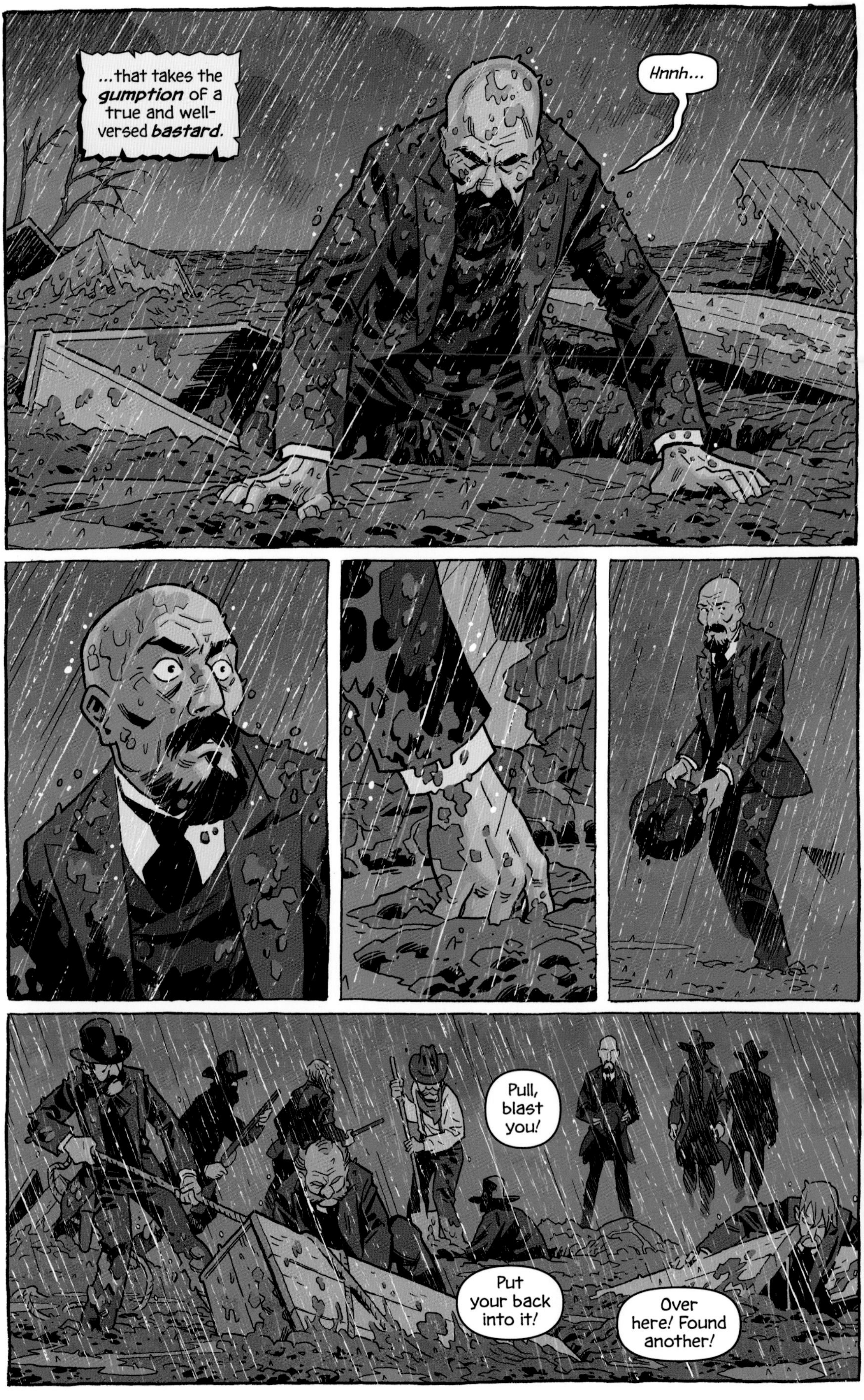
...that takes the *gumption* of a true and well-versed *bastard.*
Hnnh...
Pull, blast you!
Put your back into it!
Over here! Found another!

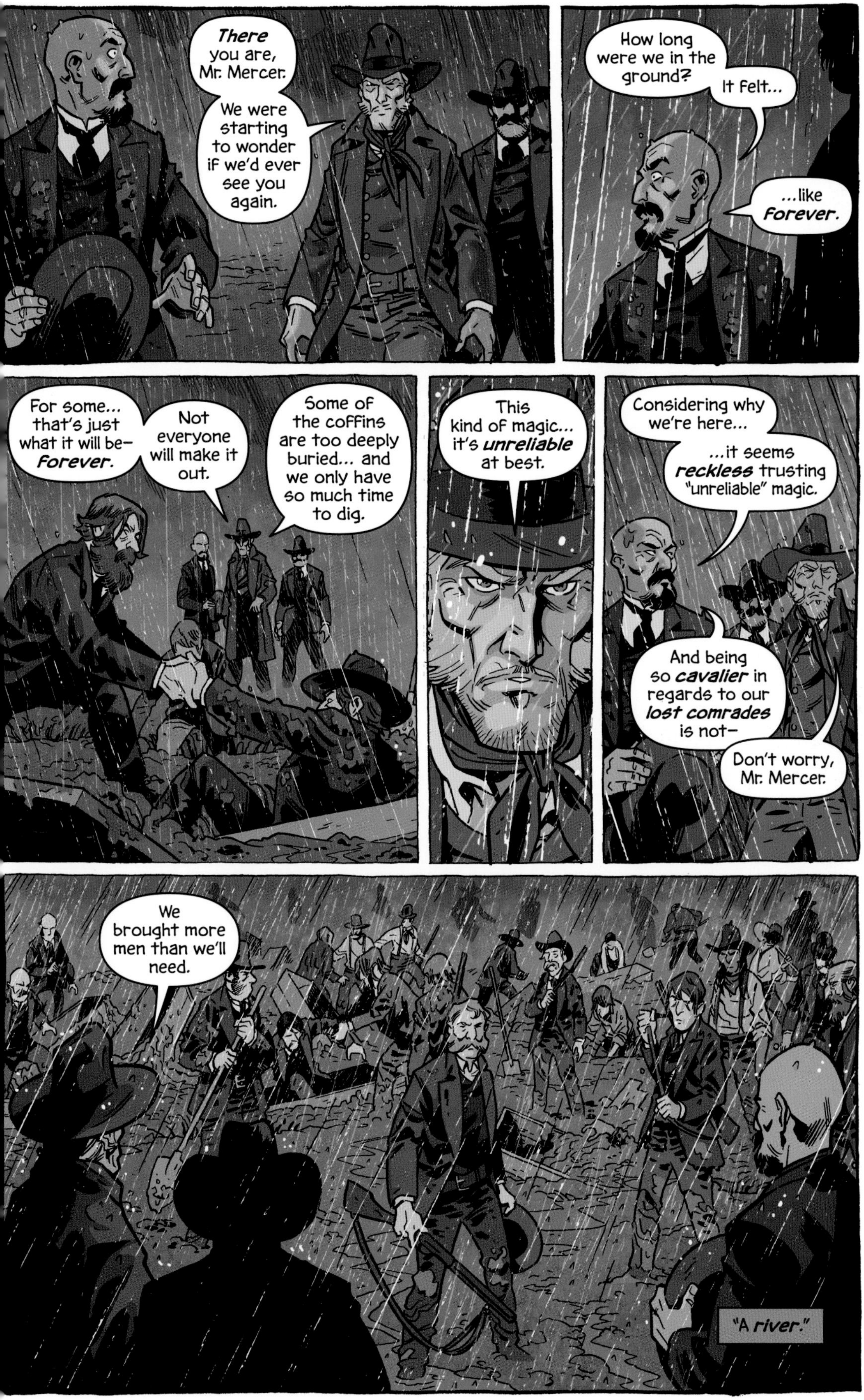

There you are, Mr. Mercer.
We were starting to wonder if we'd ever see you again.
How long were we in the ground?
It felt...
...like *forever*.
For some... that's just what it will be– *forever*.
Not everyone will make it out.
Some of the coffins are too deeply buried... and we only have so much time to dig.
This kind of magic... it's *unreliable* at best.
Considering why we're here...
...it seems *reckless* trusting "unreliable" magic.
And being so *cavalier* in regards to our *lost comrades* is not–
Don't worry, Mr. Mercer.
We brought more men than we'll need.
"A *river*."

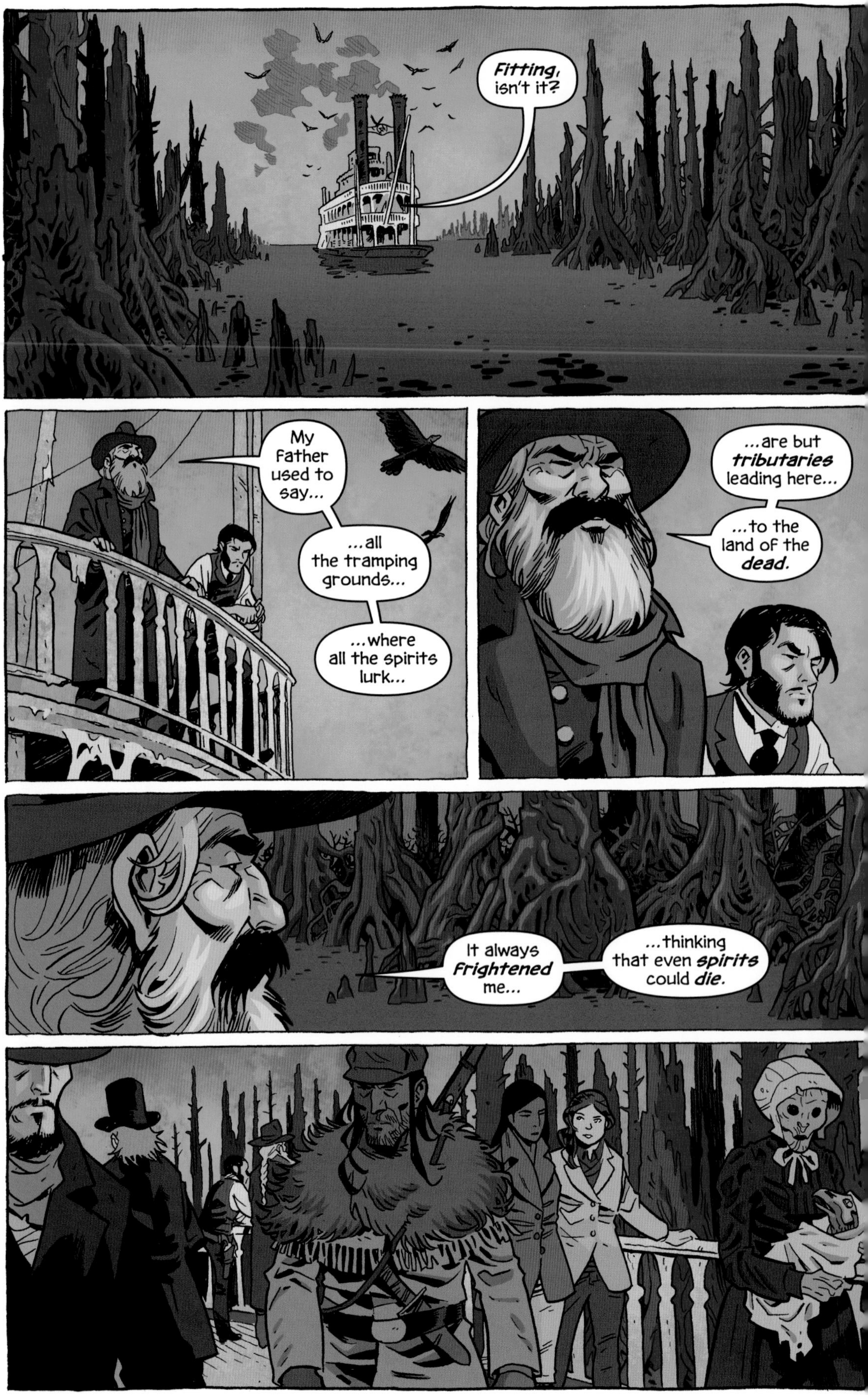

Fitting, isn't it?
My father used to say...
...all the tramping grounds...
...where all the spirits lurk...
...are but tributaries leading here...
...to the land of the dead.
It always frightened me...
...thinking that even spirits could die.

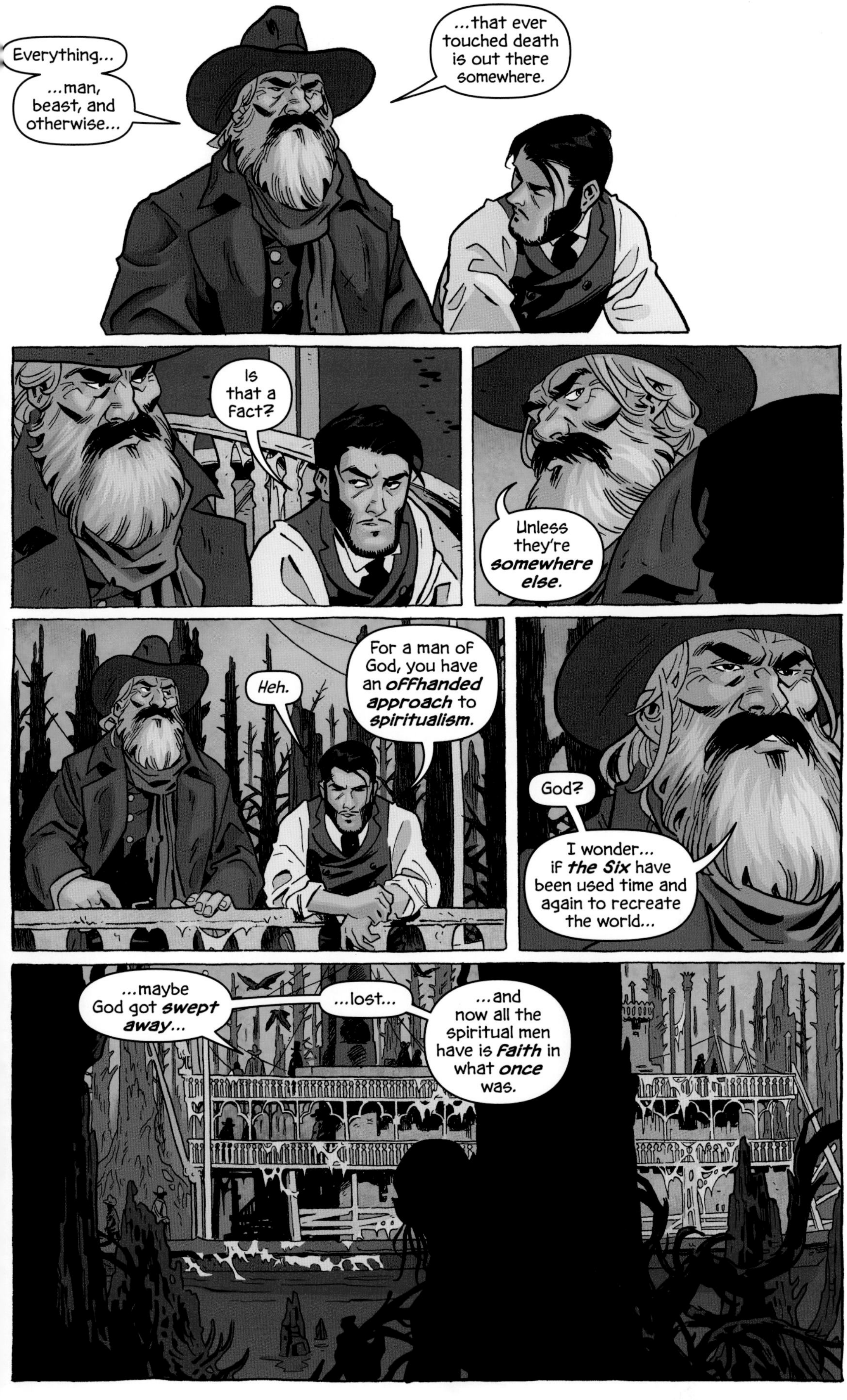
Everything...
...man, beast, and otherwise...
...that ever touched death is out there somewhere.
Is that a fact?
Unless they're *somewhere else*.
Heh.
For a man of God, you have an *offhanded approach* to *spiritualism*.
God?
I wonder... if *the Six* have been used time and again to recreate the world...
...maybe God got *swept away*...
...lost...
...and now all the spiritual men have is *Faith* in what *once* was.

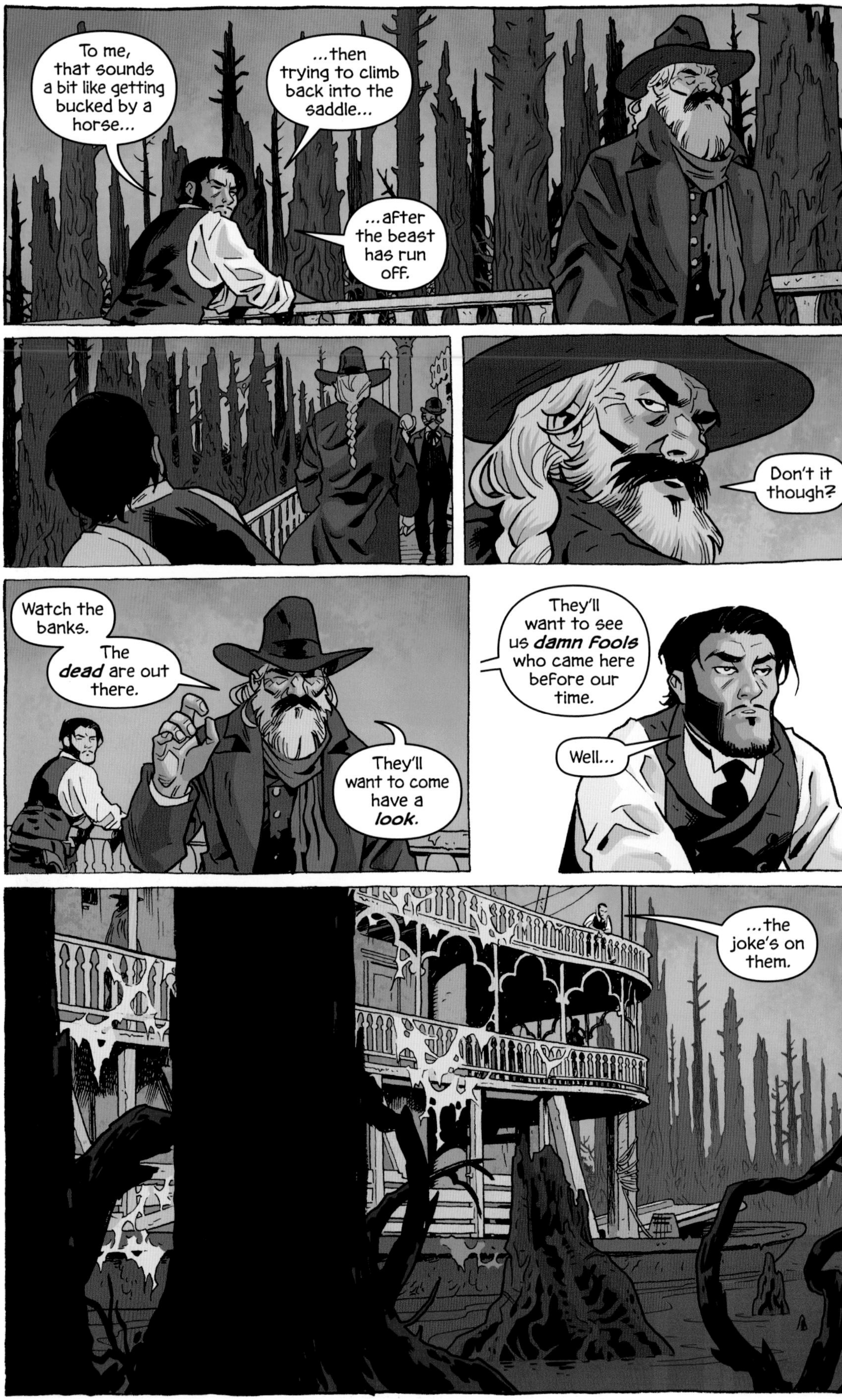

To me, that sounds a bit like getting bucked by a horse...
...then trying to climb back into the saddle...
...after the beast has run off.
Don't it though?
Watch the banks.
The *dead* are out there.
They'll want to come have a *look*.
They'll want to see us *damn fools* who came here before our time.
Well...
...the joke's on them.

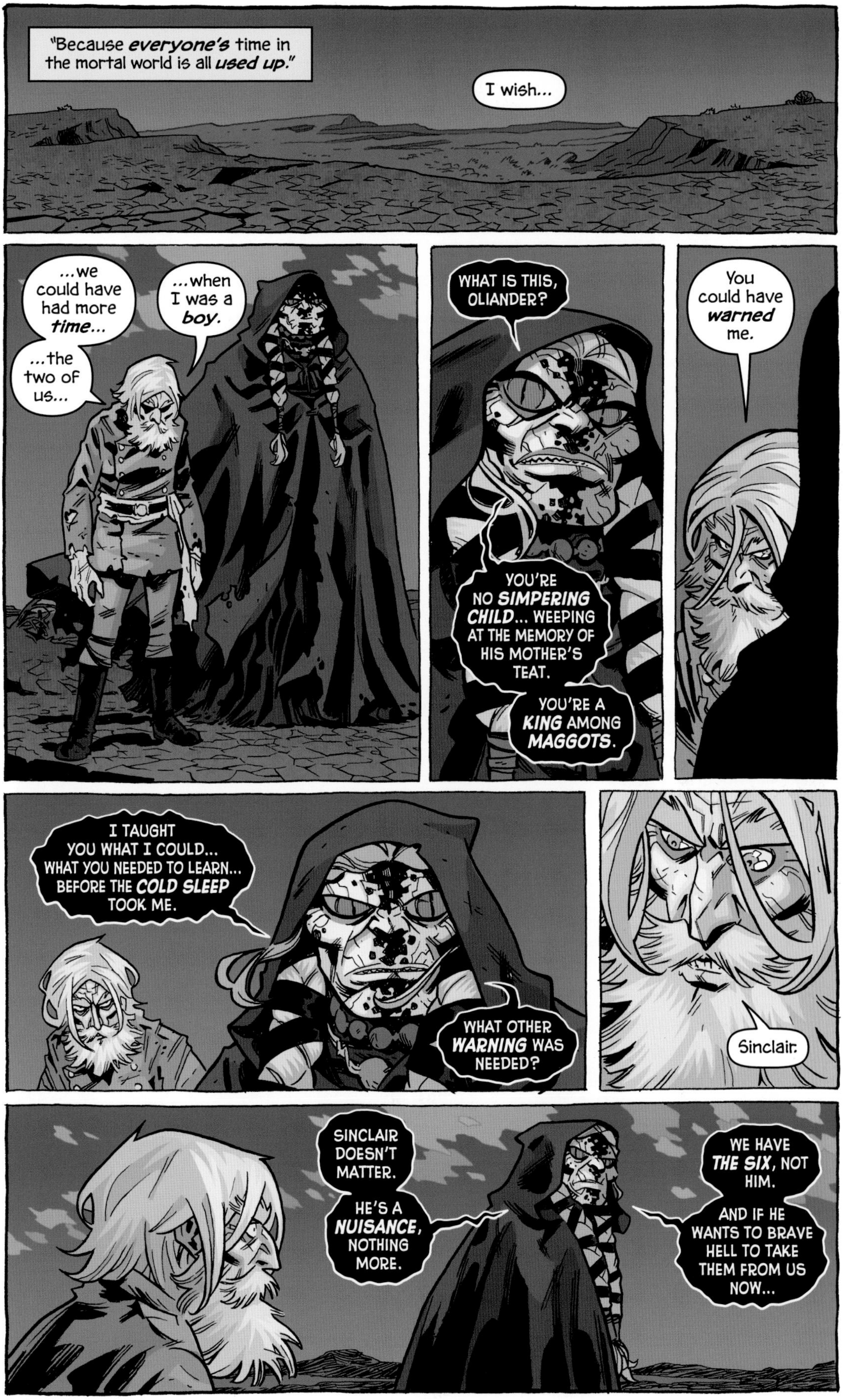
"Because everyone's time in the mortal world is all used up."
I wish...
...we could have had more time...
...the two of us...
...when I was a boy.
WHAT IS THIS, OLIANDER?
YOU'RE NO SIMPERING CHILD... WEEPING AT THE MEMORY OF HIS MOTHER'S TEAT.
YOU'RE A KING AMONG MAGGOTS.
You could have warned me.
I TAUGHT YOU WHAT I COULD... WHAT YOU NEEDED TO LEARN... BEFORE THE COLD SLEEP TOOK ME.
WHAT OTHER WARNING WAS NEEDED?
Sinclair.
SINCLAIR DOESN'T MATTER.
HE'S A NUISANCE, NOTHING MORE.
WE HAVE THE SIX, NOT HIM.
AND IF HE WANTS TO BRAVE HELL TO TAKE THEM FROM US NOW...

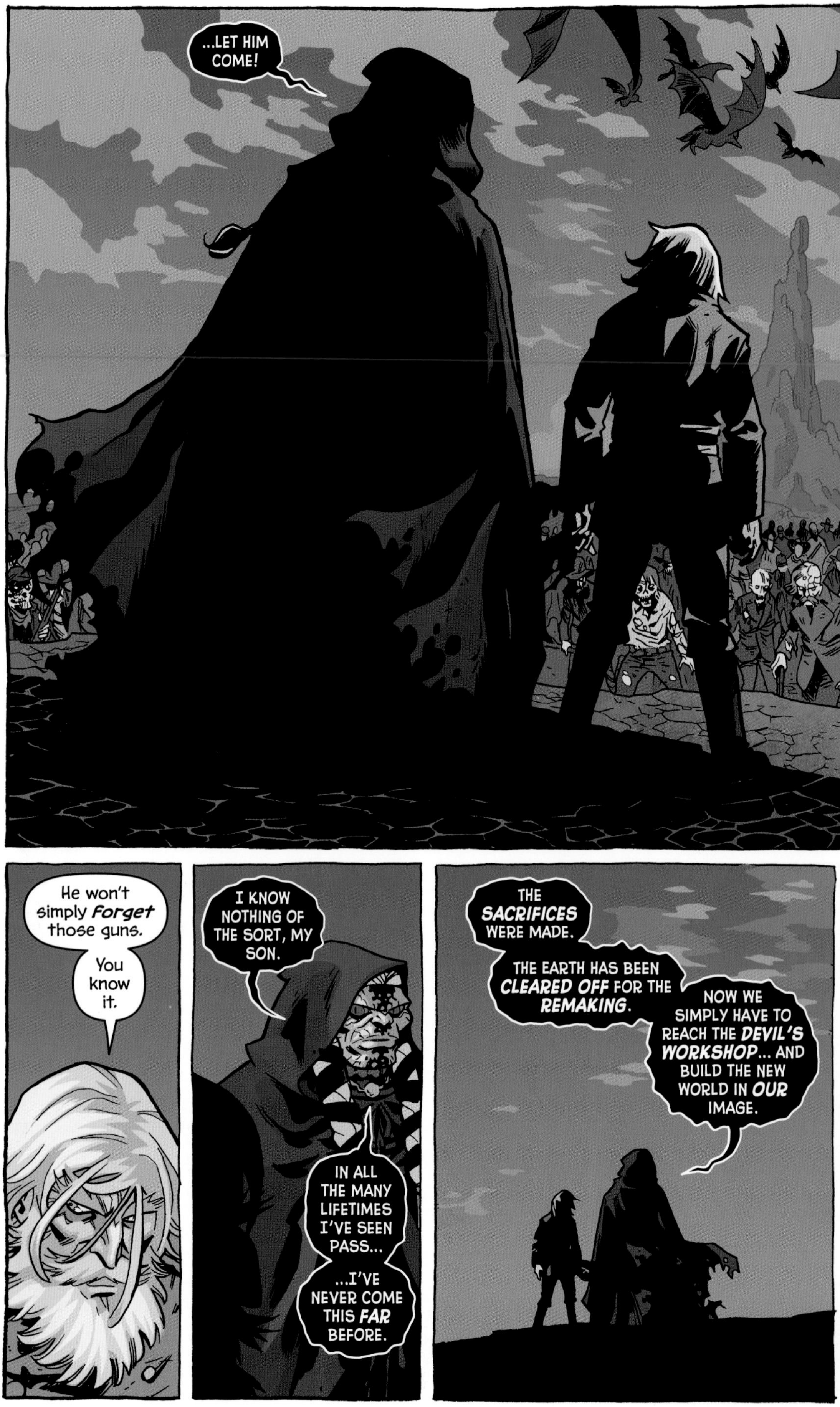
...LET HIM COME!
He won't simply *Forget* those guns.
You know it.
I KNOW NOTHING OF THE SORT, MY SON.
IN ALL THE MANY LIFETIMES I'VE SEEN PASS...
...I'VE NEVER COME THIS *FAR* BEFORE.
THE *SACRIFICES* WERE MADE.
THE EARTH HAS BEEN *CLEARED OFF* FOR THE *REMAKING*.
NOW WE SIMPLY HAVE TO REACH THE *DEVIL'S WORKSHOP*... AND BUILD THE NEW WORLD IN *OUR* IMAGE.

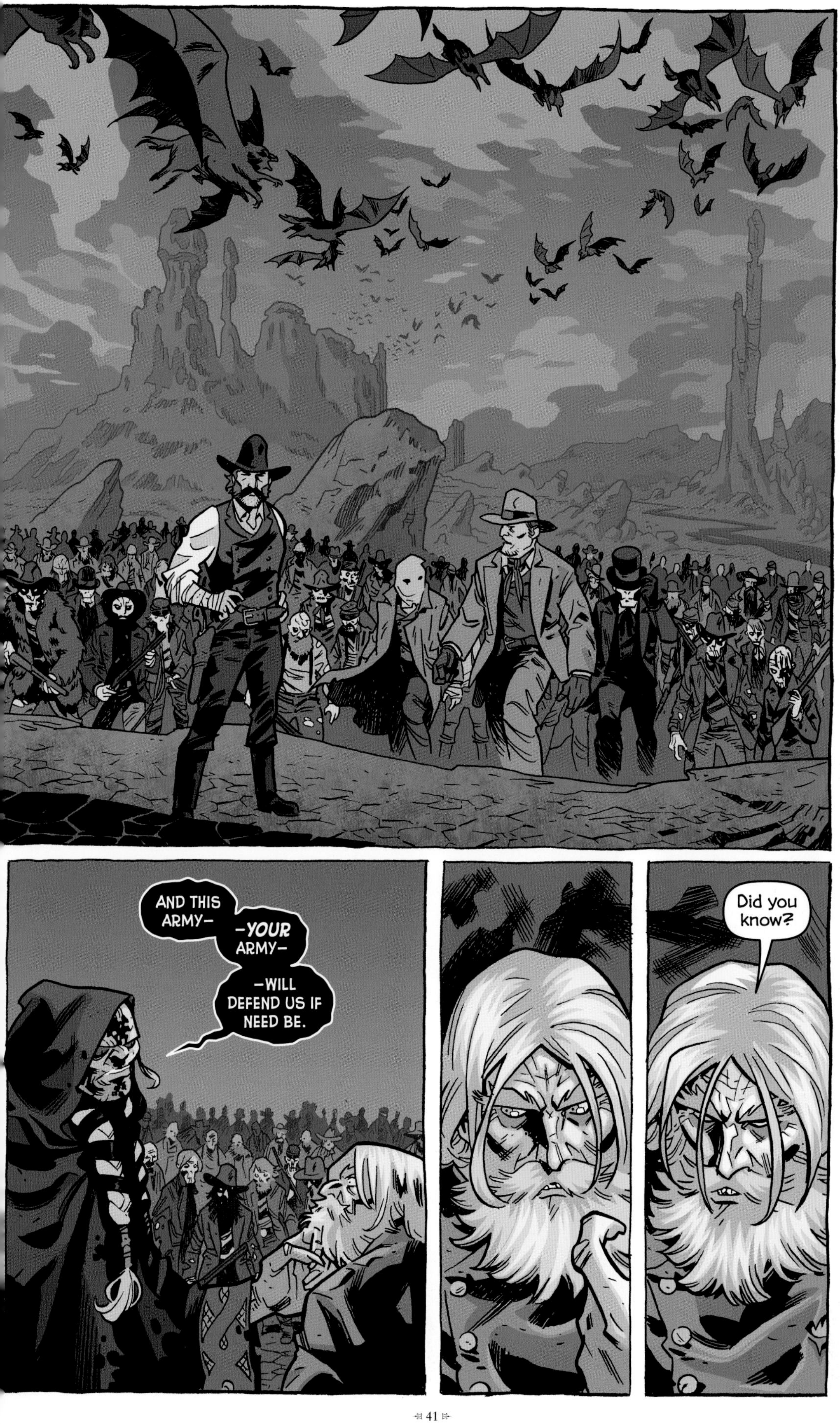
AND THIS ARMY–
–YOUR ARMY–
–WILL DEFEND US IF NEED BE.
Did you know?

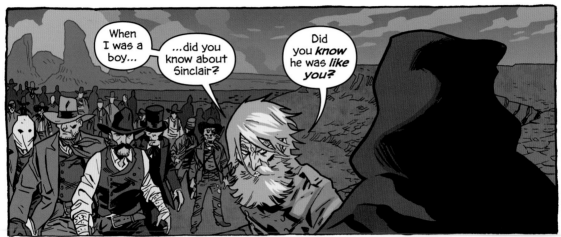

When I was a boy...

...did you know about Sinclair?

Did you *know* he was *like you?*

HE'S *NOT* LIKE ME.

I HAVE SEEN THE BIRTH OF COUNTLESS WORLDS.

SO, TOO, HAS SINCLAIR.

N-no.

He's just a man.

I'VE *SEEN* HIM. I'VE *KILLED* HIM.

PERHAPS HE WAS A *NATURAL CREATURE* ONCE... BUT *NO LONGER.*

Why?

The guns are meant to recreate reality...

Why would—

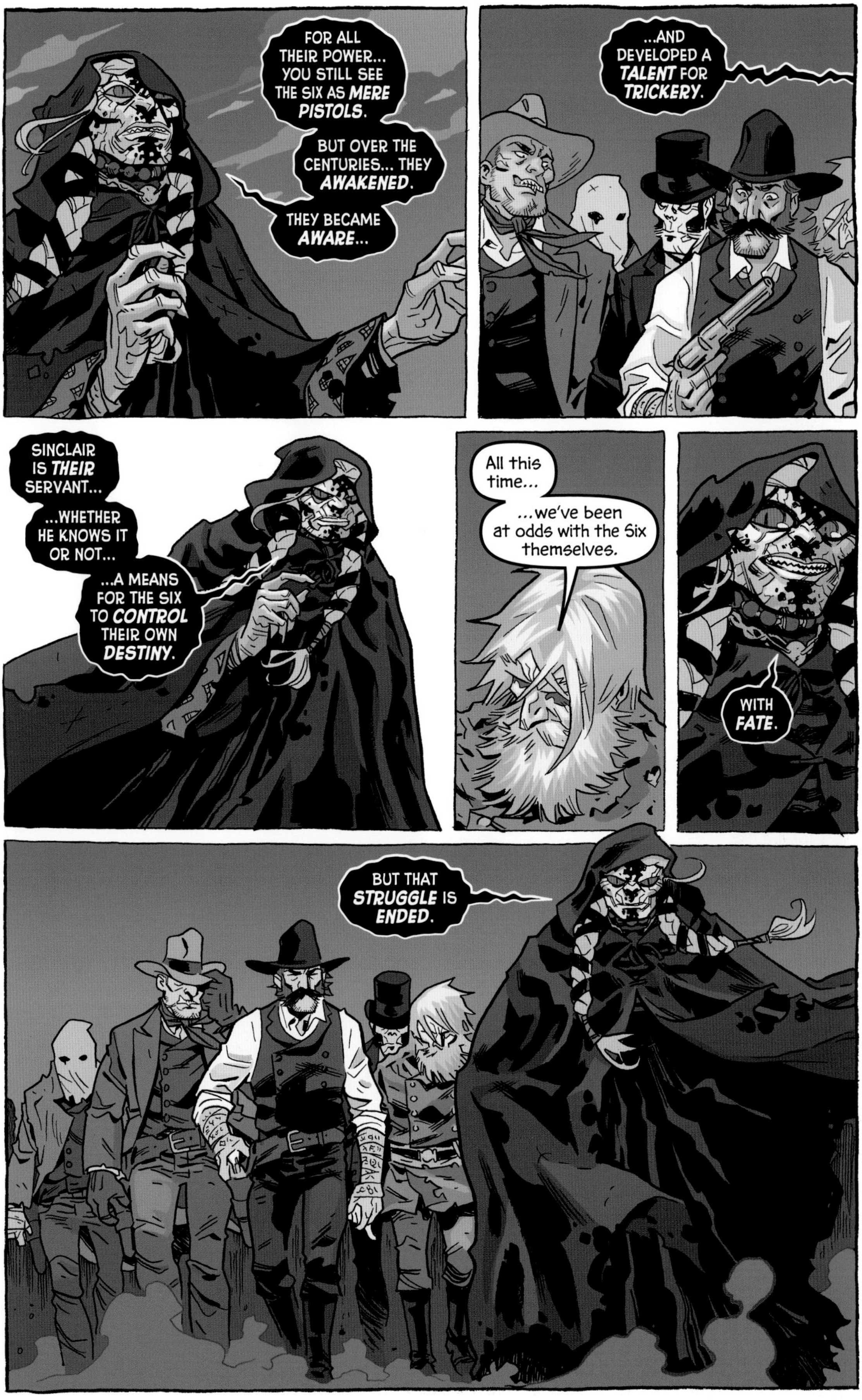
FOR ALL THEIR POWER... YOU STILL SEE THE SIX AS MERE PISTOLS.
BUT OVER THE CENTURIES... THEY AWAKENED.
THEY BECAME AWARE...
...AND DEVELOPED A TALENT FOR TRICKERY.
SINCLAIR IS THEIR SERVANT...
...WHETHER HE KNOWS IT OR NOT...
...A MEANS FOR THE SIX TO CONTROL THEIR OWN DESTINY.
All this time...
...we've been at odds with the Six themselves.
WITH FATE.
BUT THAT STRUGGLE IS ENDED.

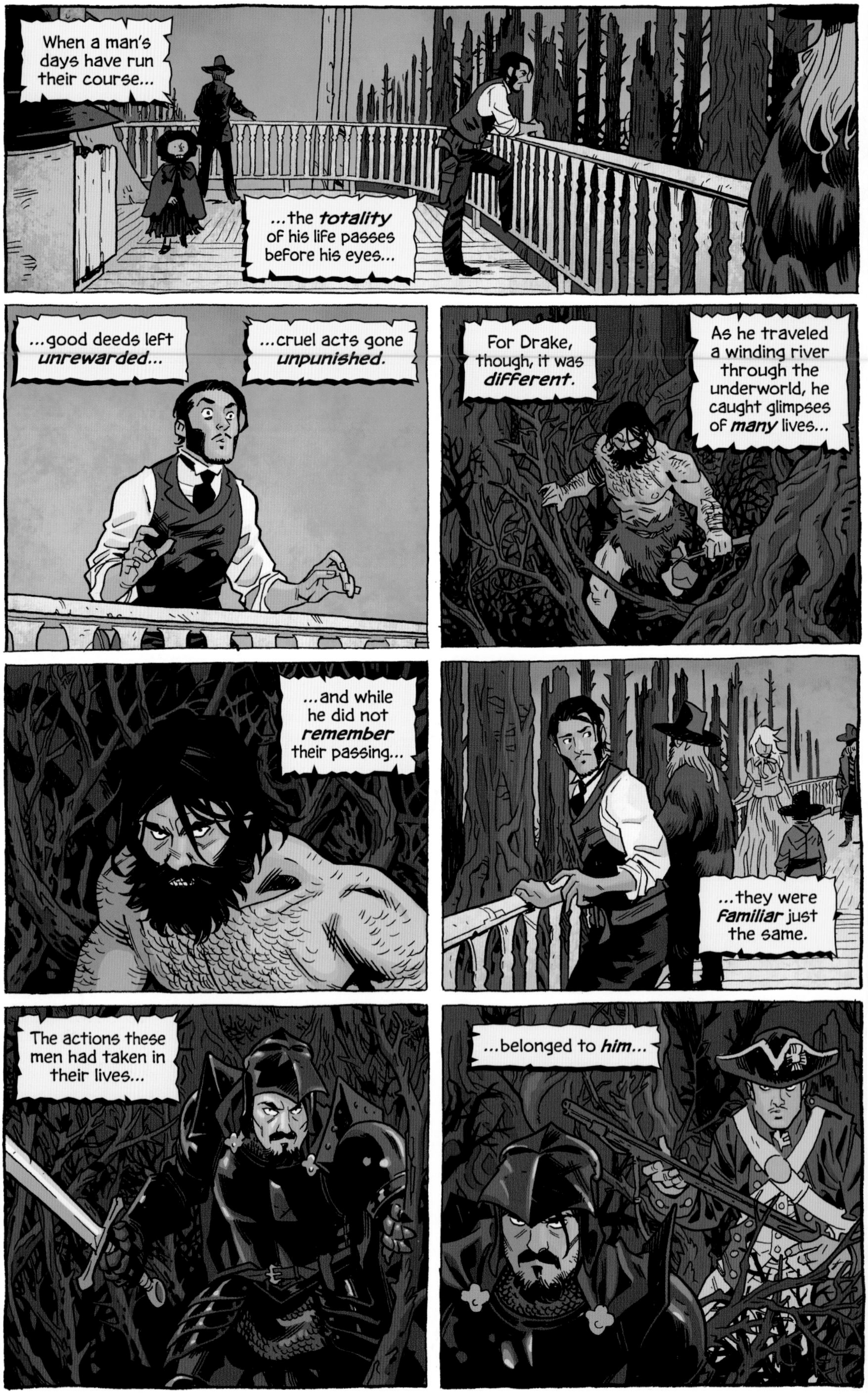
When a man's days have run their course...
...the *totality* of his life passes before his eyes...
...good deeds left *unrewarded*...
...cruel acts gone *unpunished*.
For Drake, though, it was *different*.
As he traveled a winding river through the underworld, he caught glimpses of *many* lives...
...and while he did not *remember* their passing...
...they were *familiar* just the same.
The actions these men had taken in their lives...
...belonged to *him*...

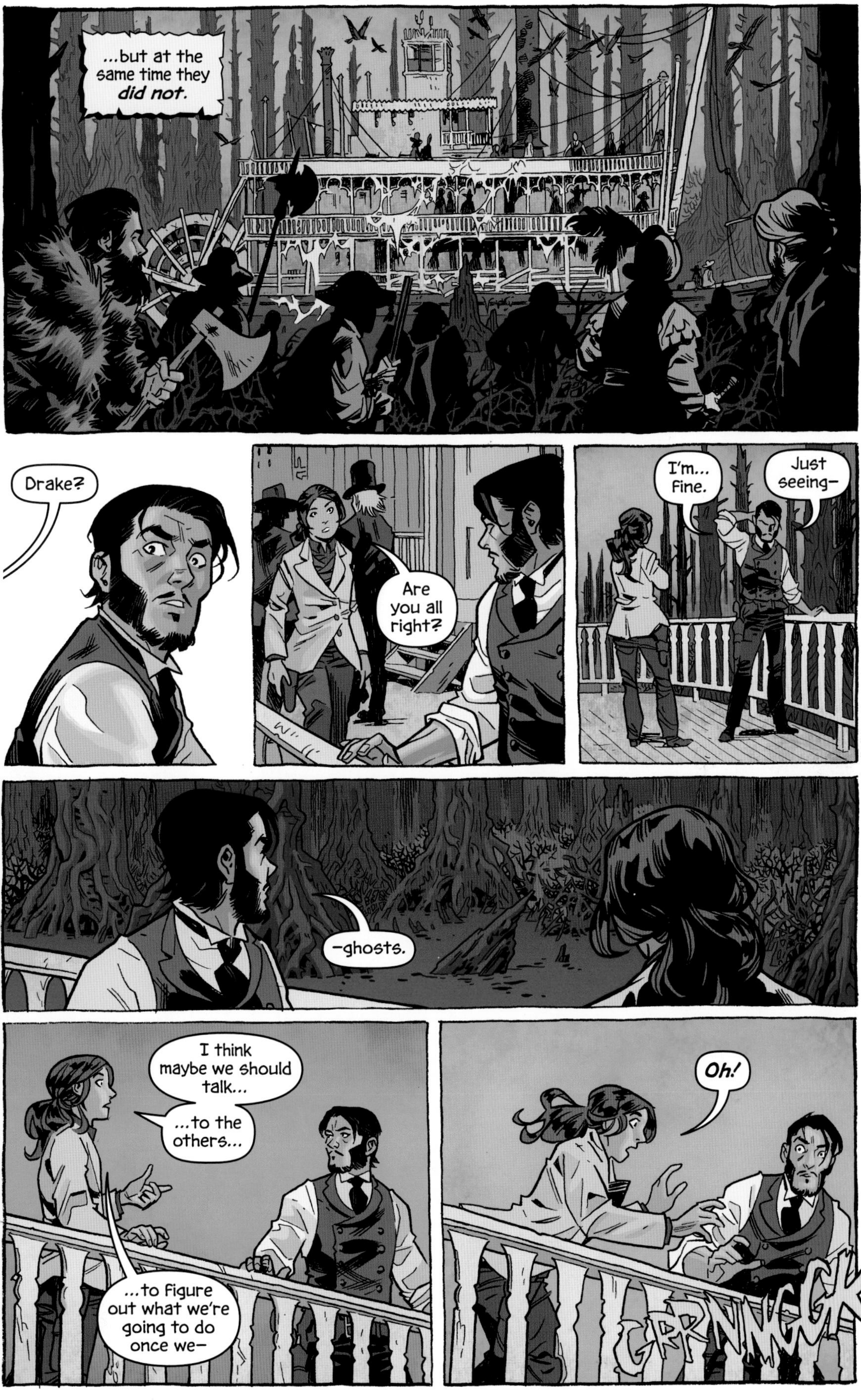

...but at the same time they *did not.*
Drake?
Are you all right?
I'm... fine.
Just seeing–
–ghosts.
I think maybe we should talk...
...to the others...
...to figure out what we're going to do once we–
Oh!
GRRNNGK

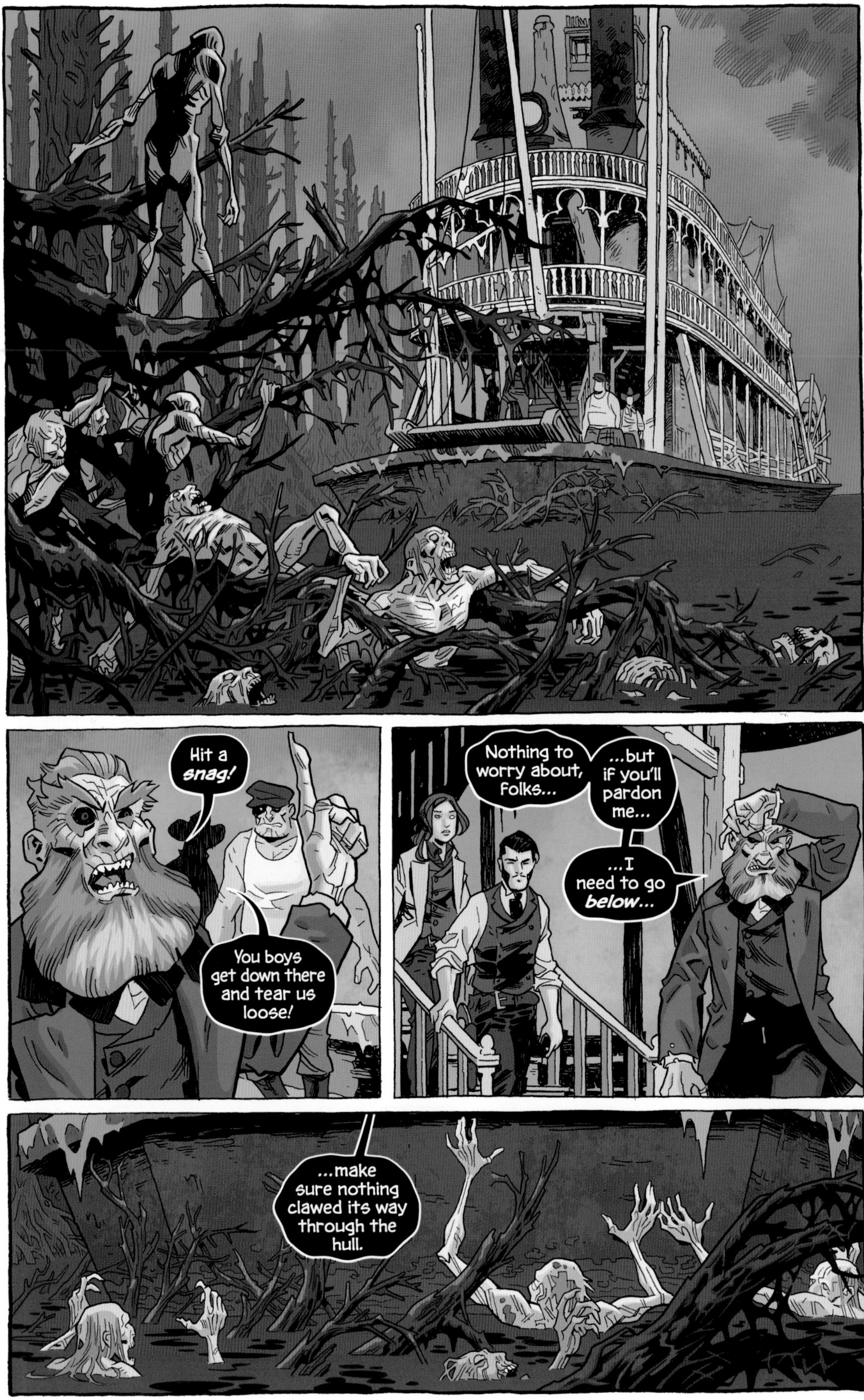
Hit a snag!
You boys get down there and tear us loose!
Nothing to worry about, folks...
...but if you'll pardon me...
...I need to go below...
...make sure nothing clawed its way through the hull.

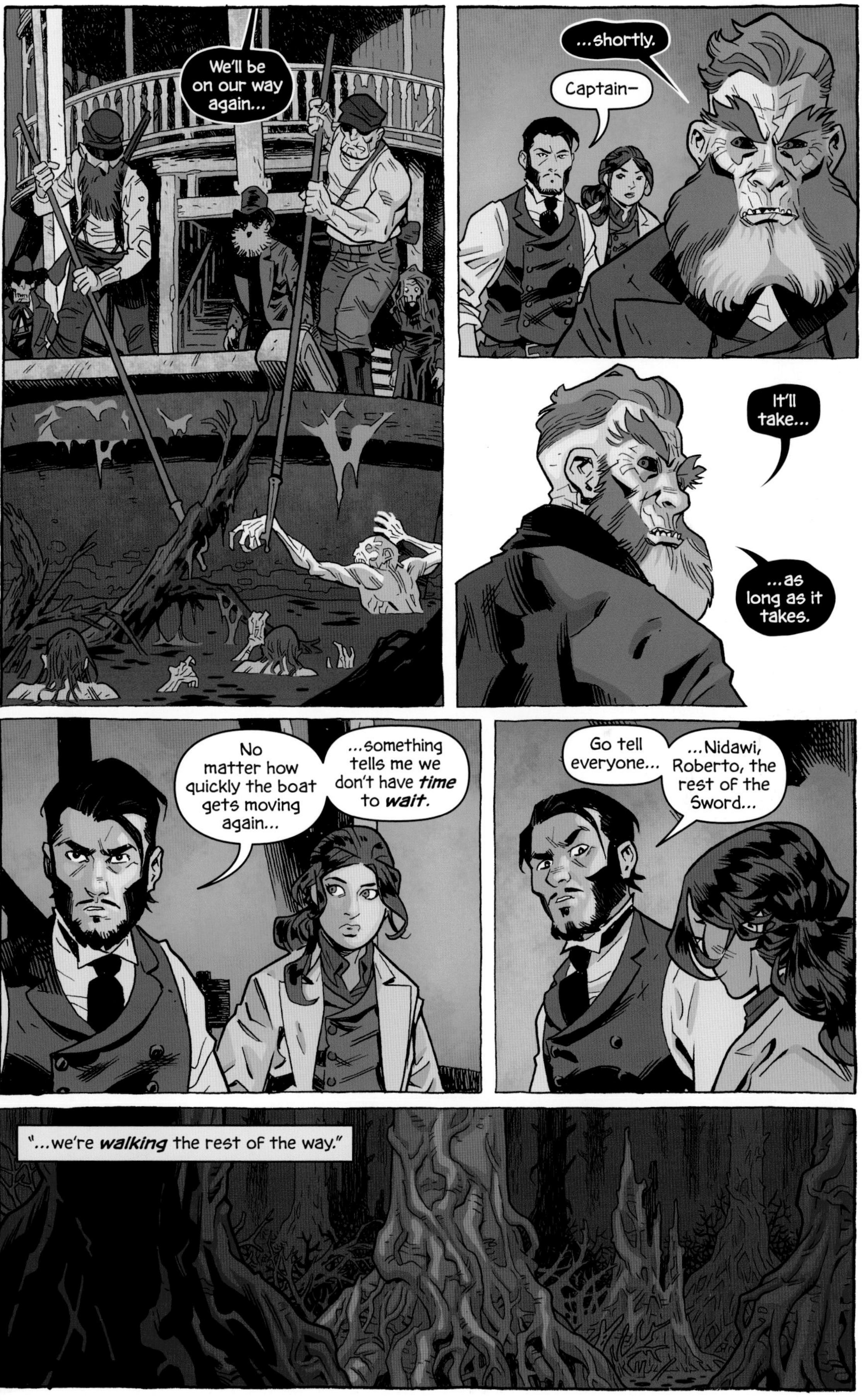
We'll be on our way again...
Captain–
...shortly.
It'll take...
...as long as it takes.
No matter how quickly the boat gets moving again...
...something tells me we don't have *time* to *wait*.
Go tell everyone...
...Nidawi, Roberto, the rest of the Sword...
"...we're *walking* the rest of the way."

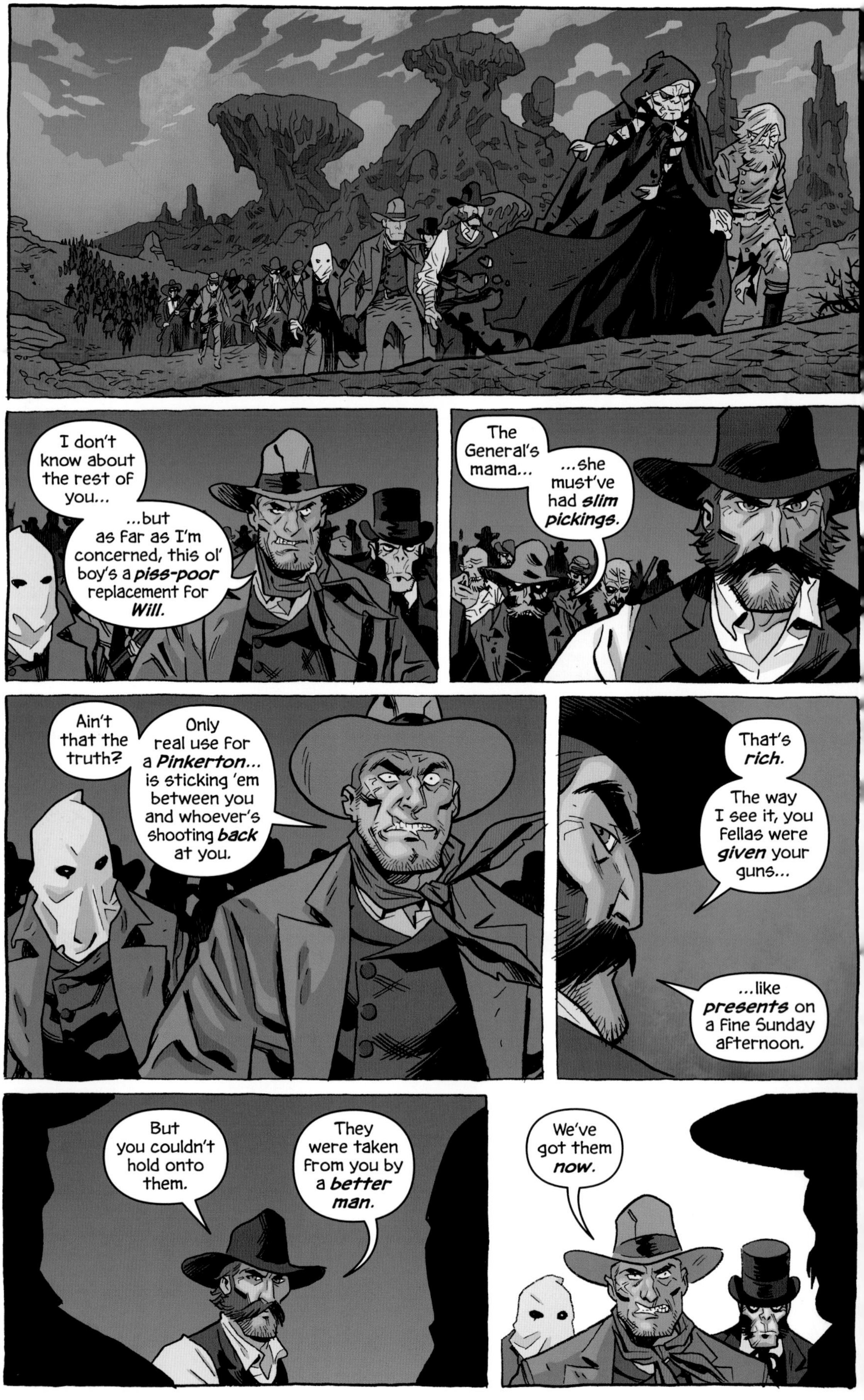
I don't know about the rest of you...
...but as far as I'm concerned, this ol' boy's a *piss-poor* replacement for *Will.*
The General's mama...
...she must've had *slim pickings.*
Ain't that the truth?
Only real use for a *Pinkerton*... is sticking 'em between you and whoever's shooting *back* at you.
That's *rich.*
The way I see it, you fellas were *given* your guns...
...like *presents* on a fine Sunday afternoon.
But you couldn't hold onto them.
They were taken from you by a *better man.*
We've got them *now.*

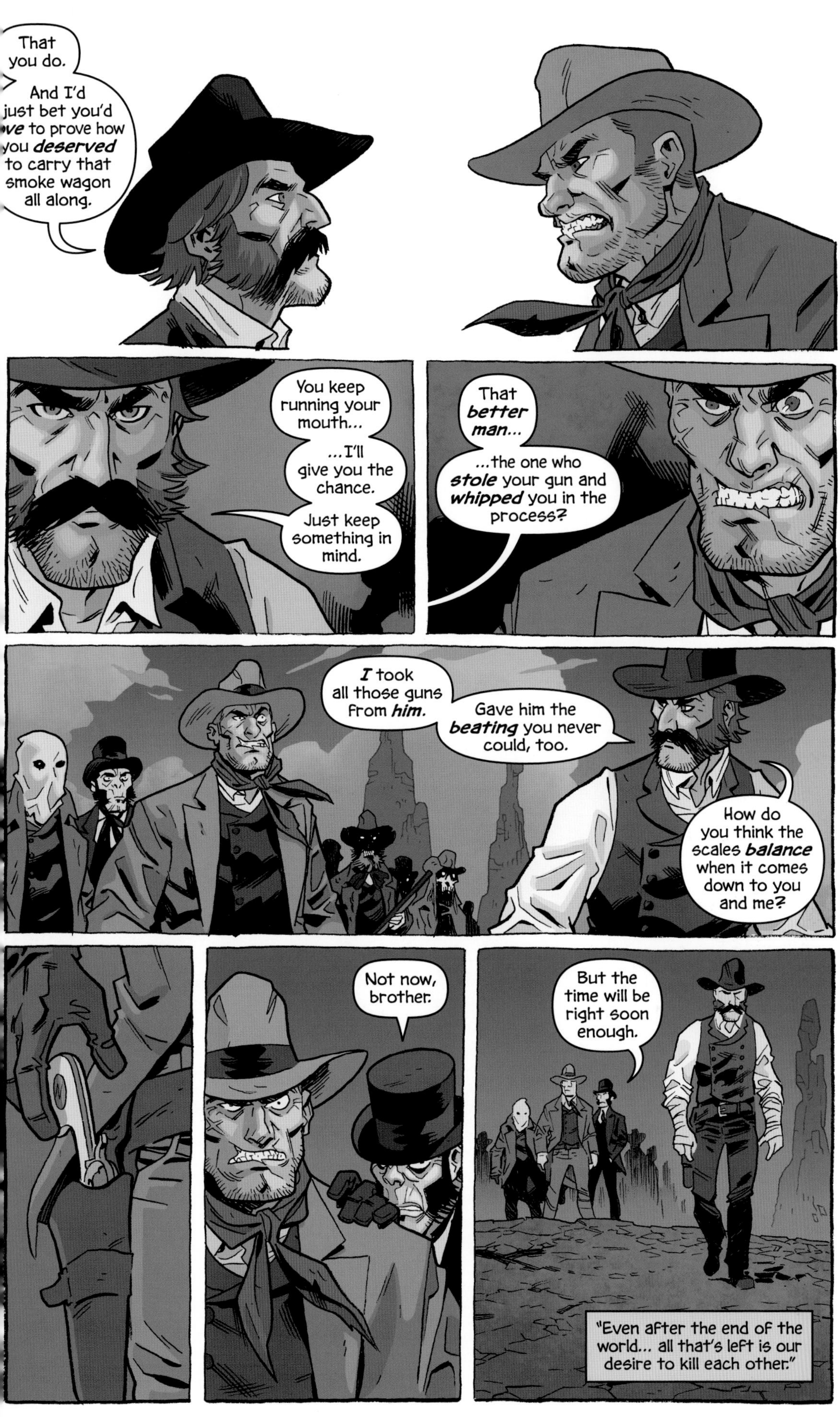
That you do.
And I'd just bet you'd ve to prove how you deserved to carry that smoke wagon all along.
You keep running your mouth...
...I'll give you the chance.
Just keep something in mind.
That better man...
...the one who stole your gun and whipped you in the process?
I took all those guns from him.
Gave him the beating you never could, too.
How do you think the scales balance when it comes down to you and me?
Not now, brother.
But the time will be right soon enough.
"Even after the end of the world... all that's left is our desire to kill each other."

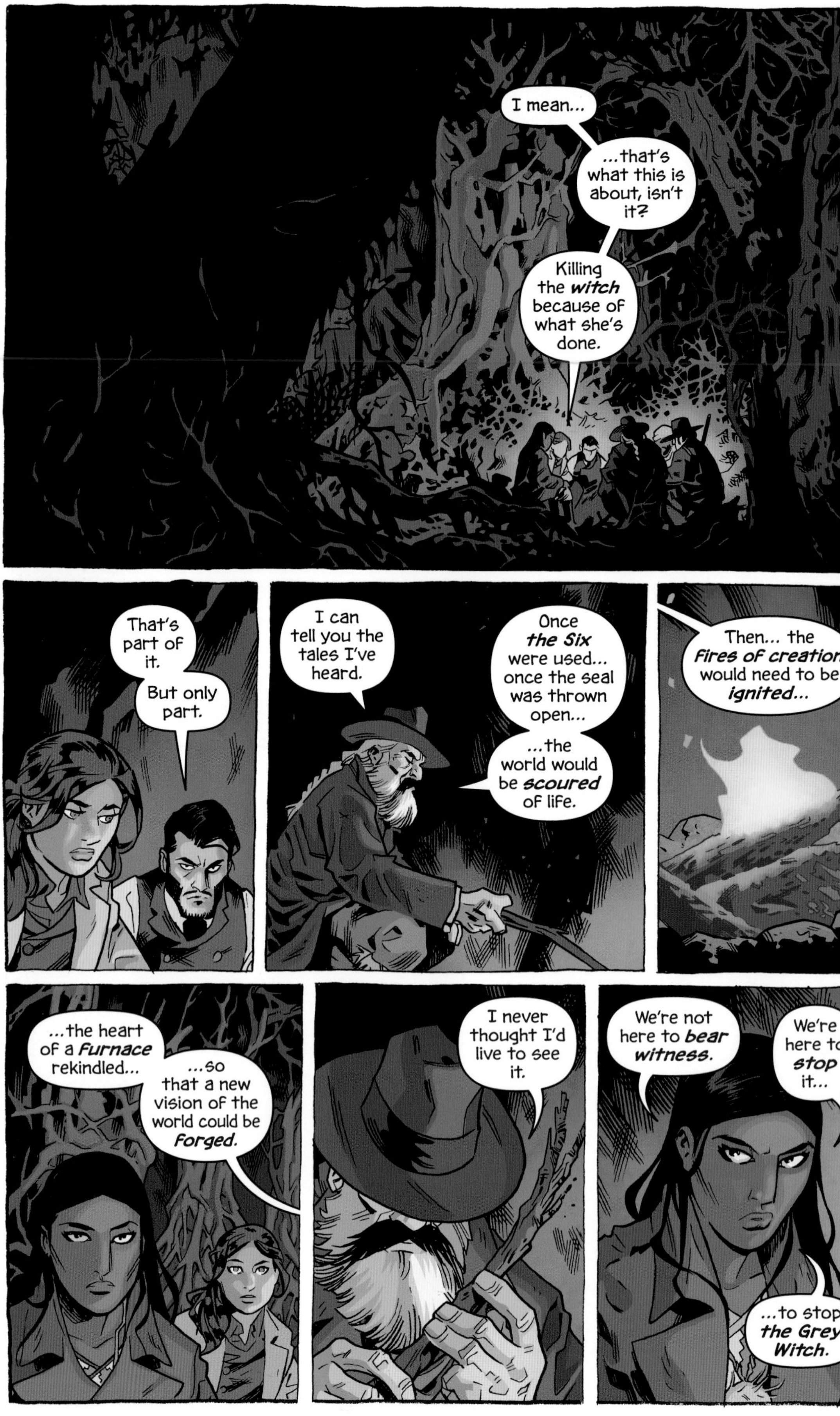
I mean...
...that's what this is about, isn't it?
Killing the *witch* because of what she's done.
That's part of it.
But only part.
I can tell you the tales I've heard.
Once *the Six* were used... once the seal was thrown open...
...the world would be *scoured* of life.
Then... the *Fires of creation* would need to be *ignited...*
...the heart of a *Furnace* rekindled...
...so that a new vision of the world could be *forged.*
I never thought I'd live to see it.
We're not here to *bear witness.*
We're here to *stop* it...
...to stop *the Grey Witch.*

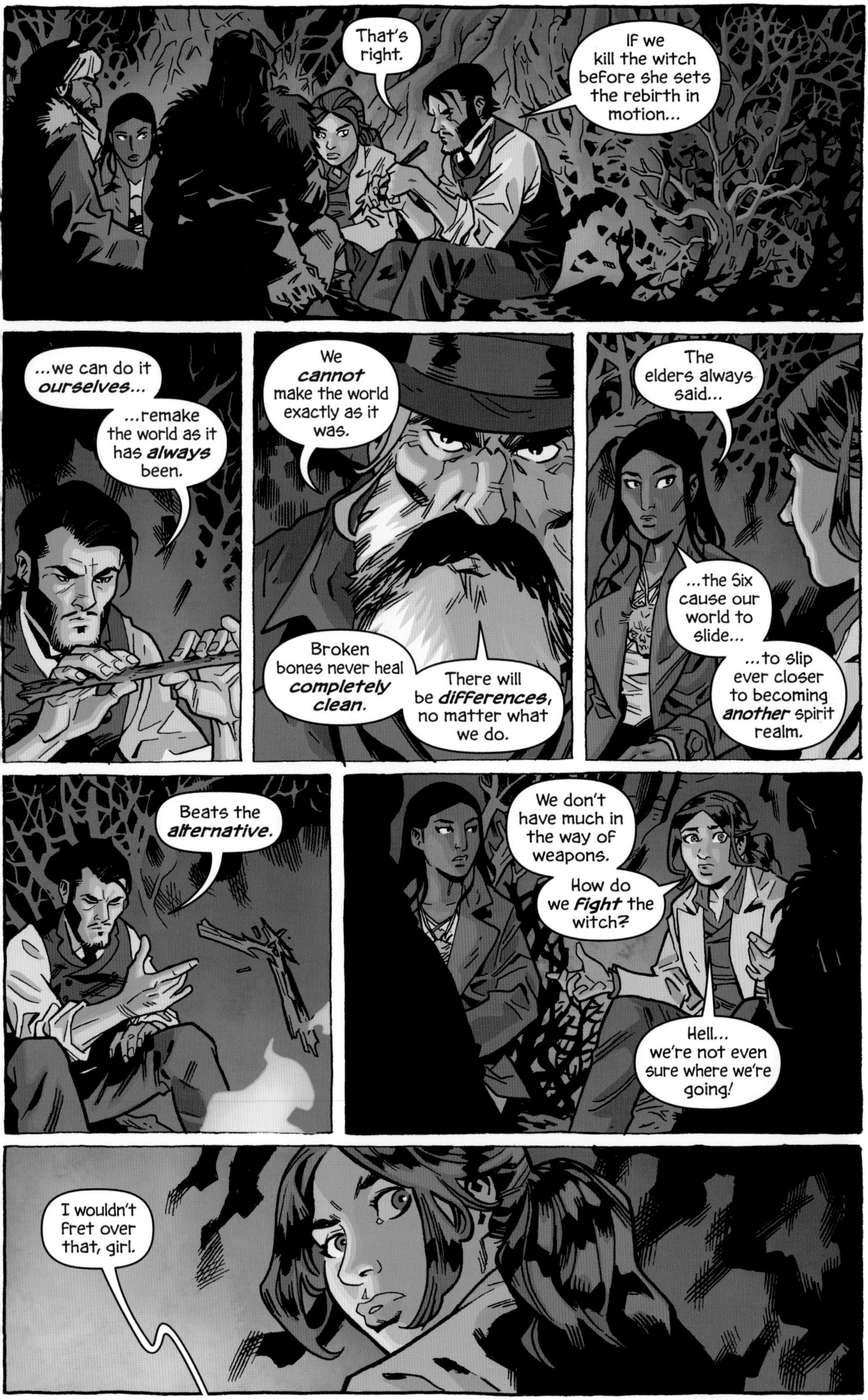
That's right.
If we kill the witch before she sets the rebirth in motion...
...we can do it ourselves...
...remake the world as it has always been.
We cannot make the world exactly as it was.
Broken bones never heal completely clean.
There will be differences, no matter what we do.
The elders always said...
...the Six cause our world to slide...
...to slip ever closer to becoming another spirit realm.
Beats the alternative.
We don't have much in the way of weapons.
How do we fight the witch?
Hell... we're not even sure where we're going!
I wouldn't fret over that, girl.

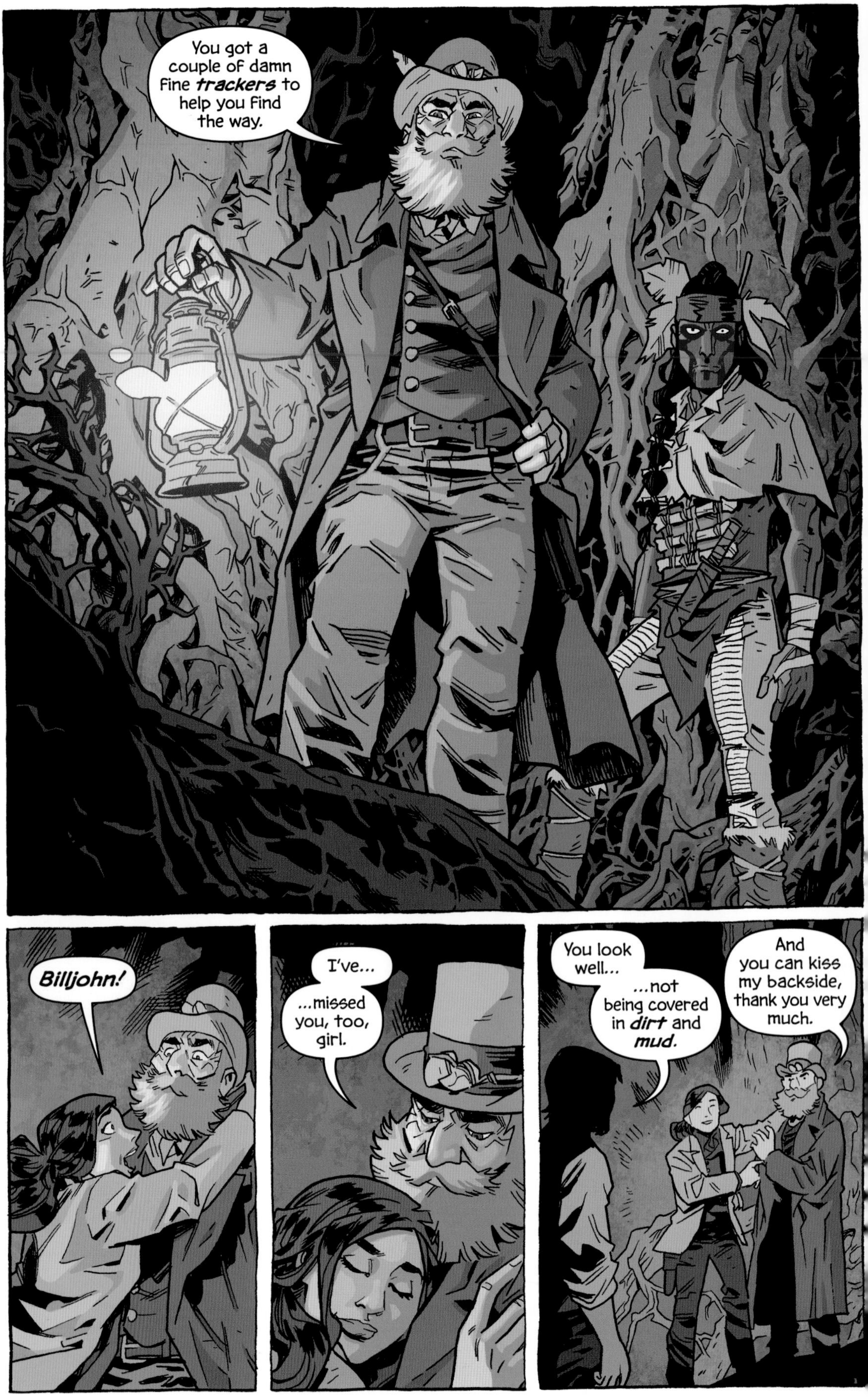
You got a couple of damn fine *trackers* to help you find the way.
Billjohn!
I've...
...missed you, too, girl.
You look well...
...not being covered in *dirt* and *mud.*
And you can kiss my backside, thank you very much.

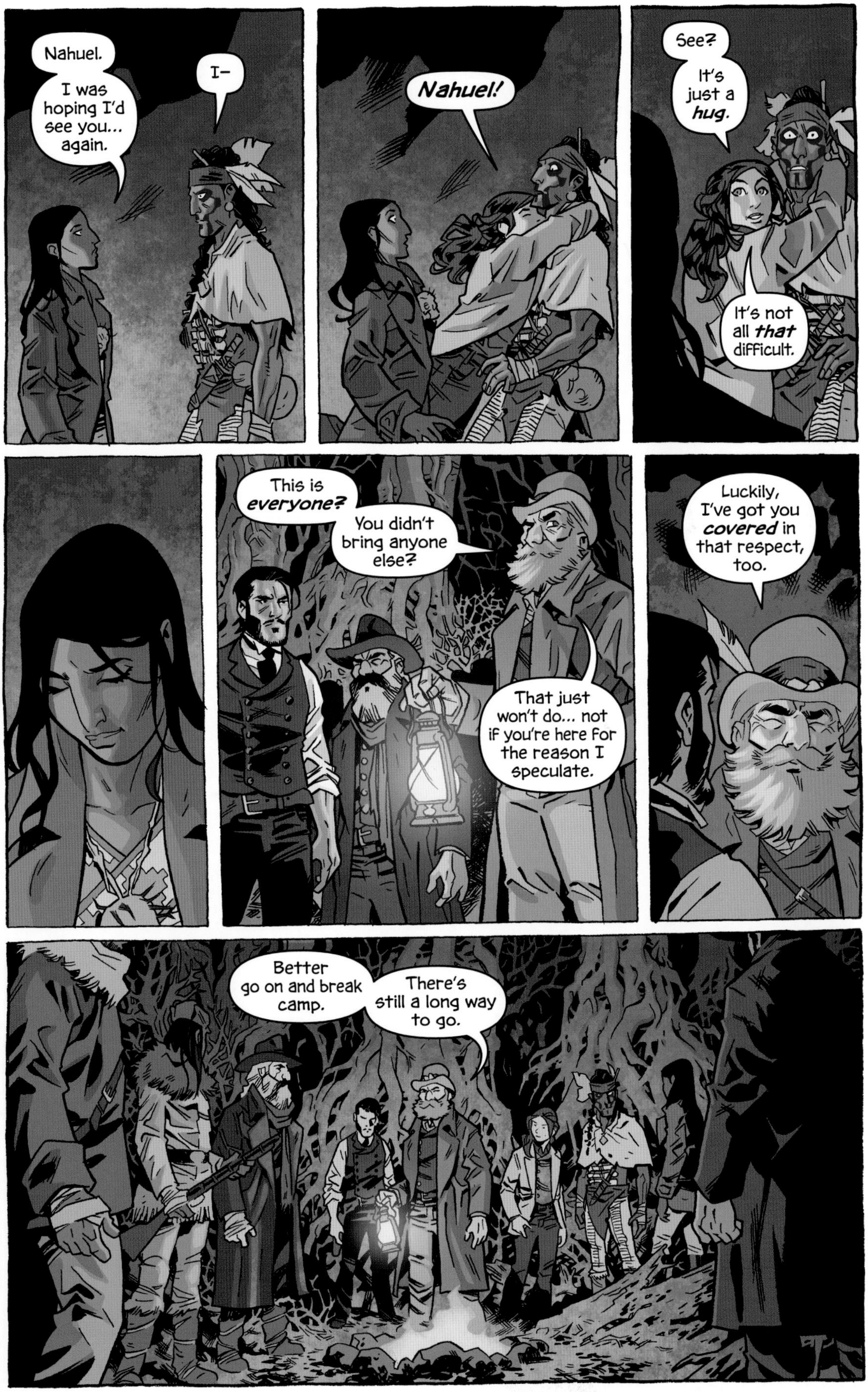
Nahuel.
I was hoping I'd see you... again.
I–
Nahuel!
See?
It's just a *hug*.
It's not all *that* difficult.
This is *everyone?*
You didn't bring anyone else?
That just won't do... not if you're here for the reason I speculate.
Luckily, I've got you *covered* in that respect, too.
Better go on and break camp.
There's still a long way to go.

Where are you taking us, Billjohn?

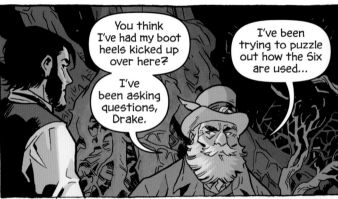

You think I've had my boot heels kicked up over here?

I've been asking questions, Drake.

I've been trying to puzzle out how the Six are used...

...because I knew we'd fail to keep those guns out of the clutches of the General and his ilk.

Time and again, I've heard tell of the Devil's Workshop...

...the spot where all earthly creation can be undone.

Where do we find it?

Hell, Drake...

...you ought to know where we're heading.

Same place we've been heading from the very moment we drew our first breath.

We're going to *Boot Hill!*

CHAPTER THREE

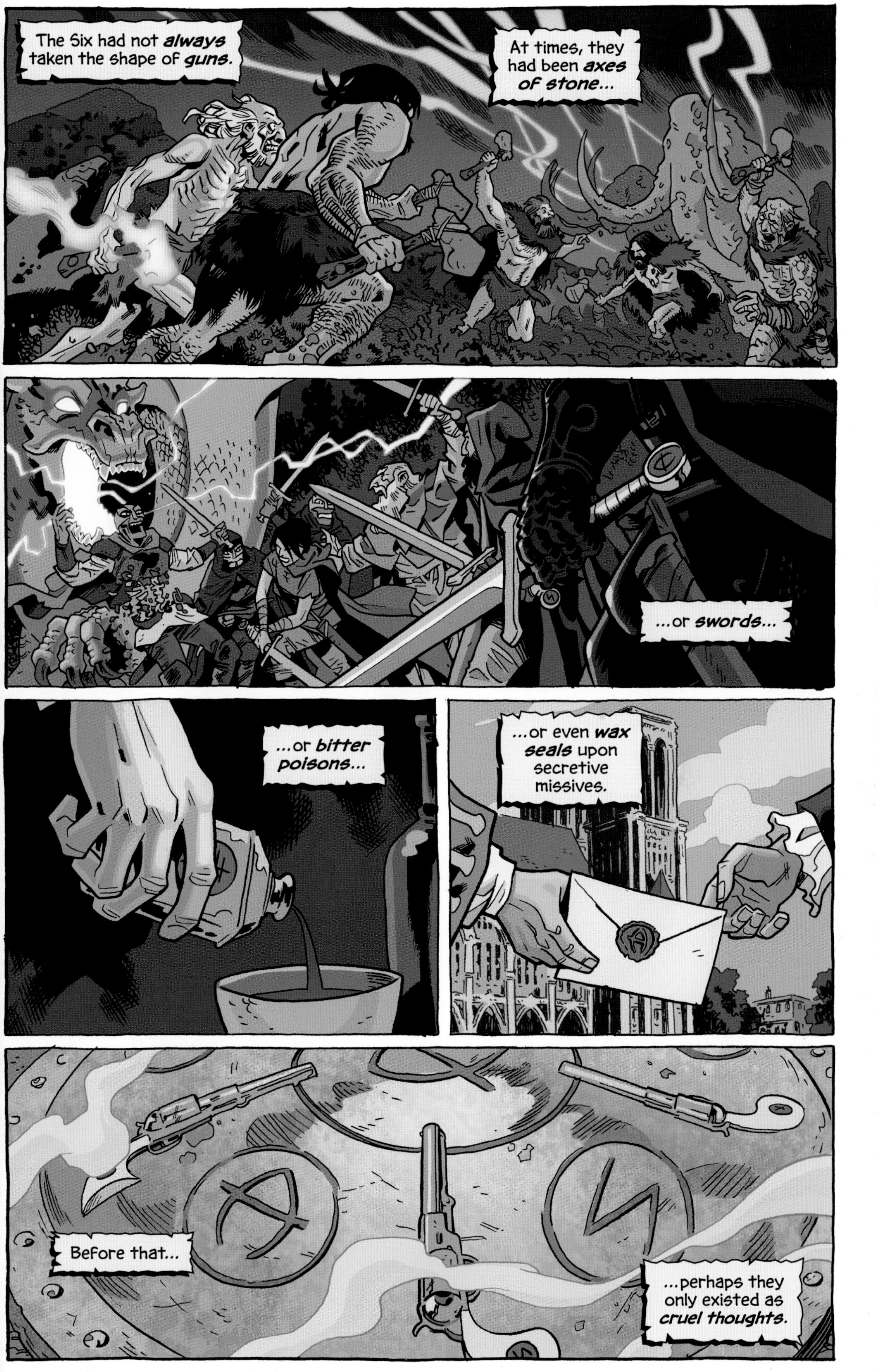
The Six had not *always* taken the shape of *guns*.
At times, they had been *axes of stone*...
...or *swords*...
...or *bitter poisons*...
...or even *wax seals* upon secretive missives.
Before that...
...perhaps they only existed as *cruel thoughts*.

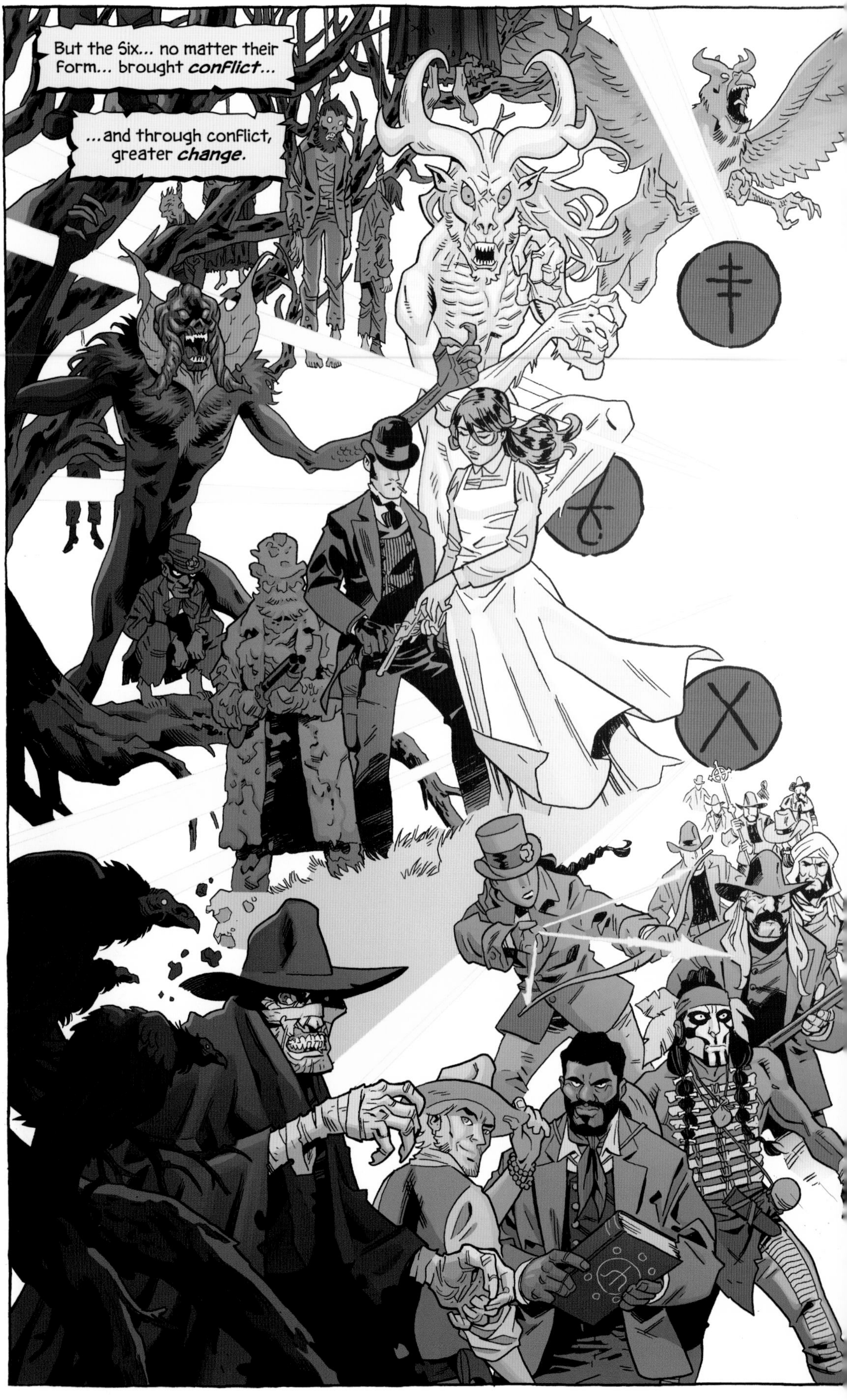
But the Six... no matter their form... brought *conflict*...
...and through conflict, greater *change*.

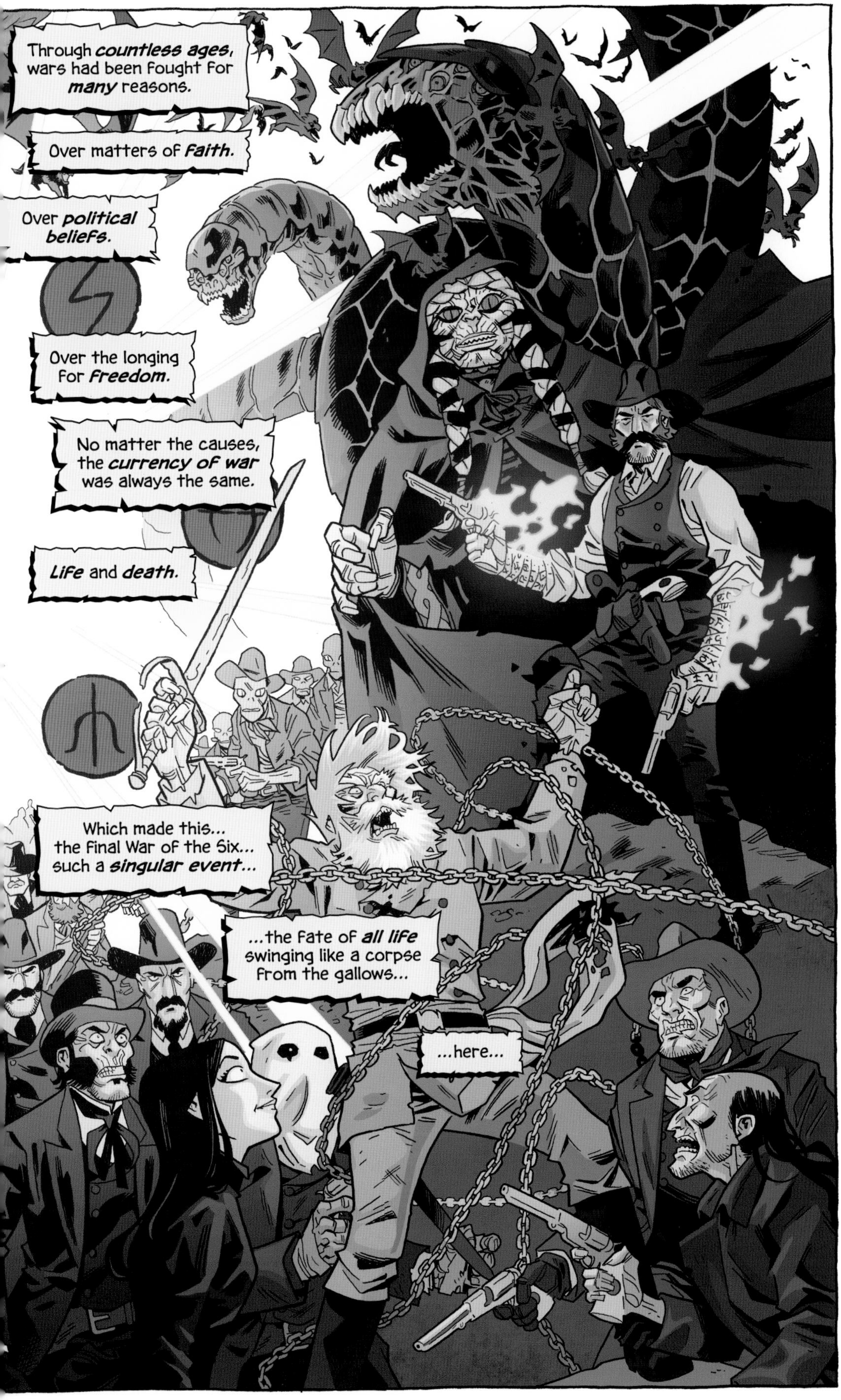

Through *countless ages*, wars had been fought for *many* reasons.
Over matters of *faith*.
Over *political beliefs*.
Over the longing for *freedom*.
No matter the causes, the *currency of war* was always the same.
Life and *death*.
Which made this... the final War of the Six... such a *singular event*...
...the fate of *all life* swinging like a corpse from the gallows...
...here...

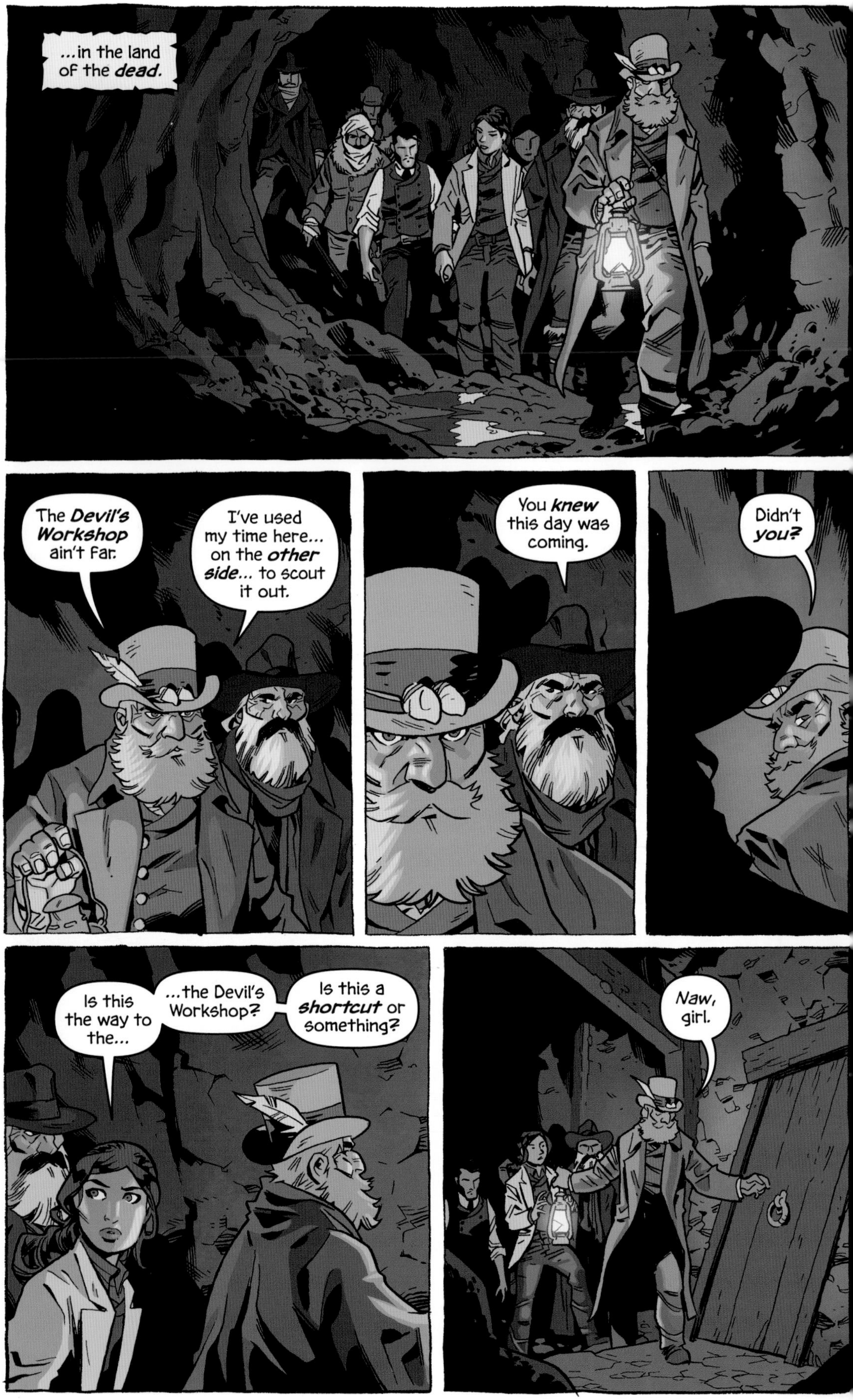
...in the land of the *dead.*
The *Devil's Workshop* ain't far.
I've used my time here... on the *other side*... to scout it out.
You *knew* this day was coming.
Didn't *you?*
Is this the way to the...
...the Devil's Workshop?
Is this a *shortcut* or something?
Naw, girl.

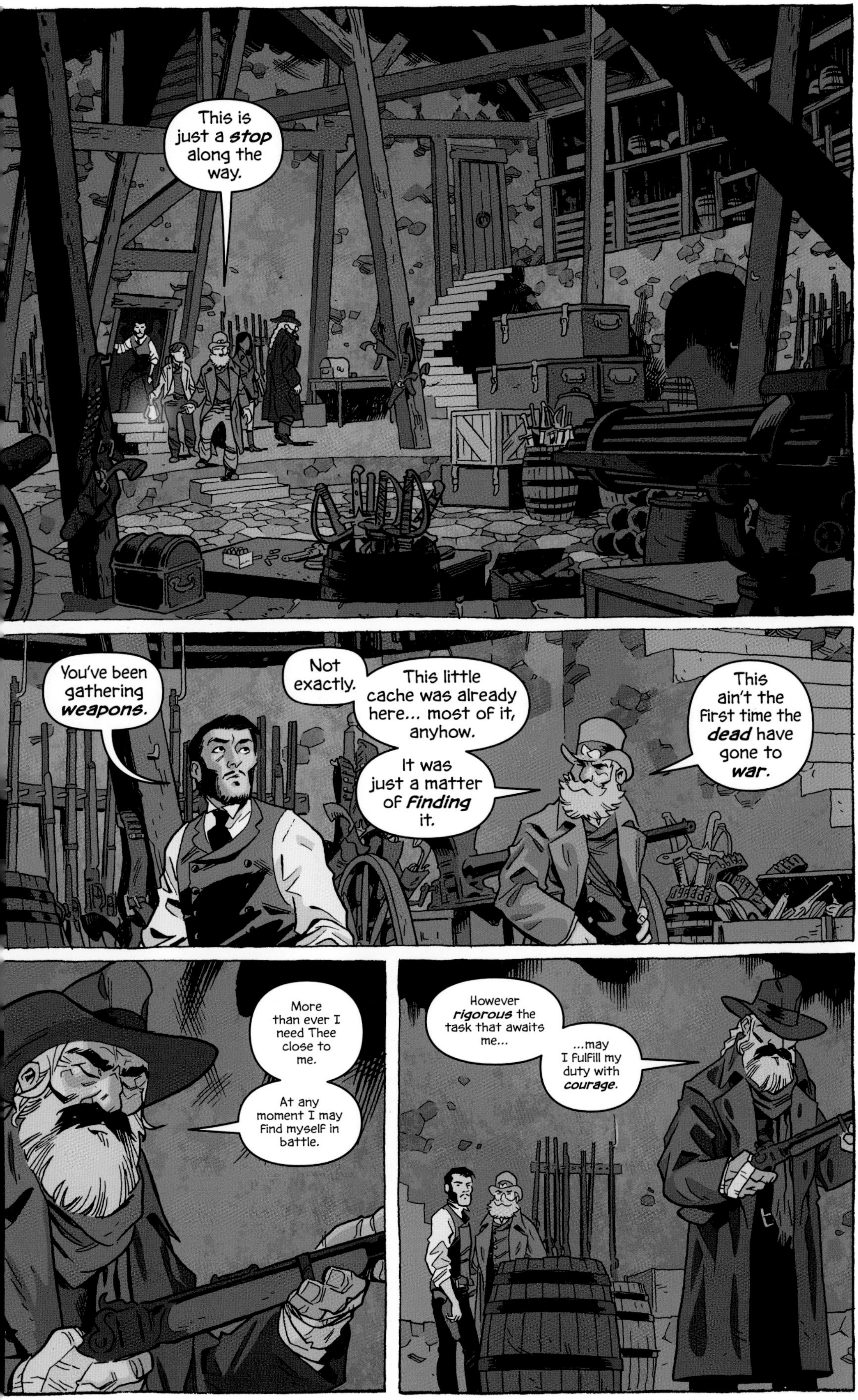
This is just a *stop* along the way.
You've been gathering *weapons.*
Not exactly.
This little cache was already here... most of it, anyhow.
It was just a matter of *finding* it.
This ain't the first time the *dead* have gone to *war.*
More than ever I need Thee close to me.
At any moment I may find myself in battle.
However *rigorous* the task that awaits me...
...may I fulfill my duty with *courage.*

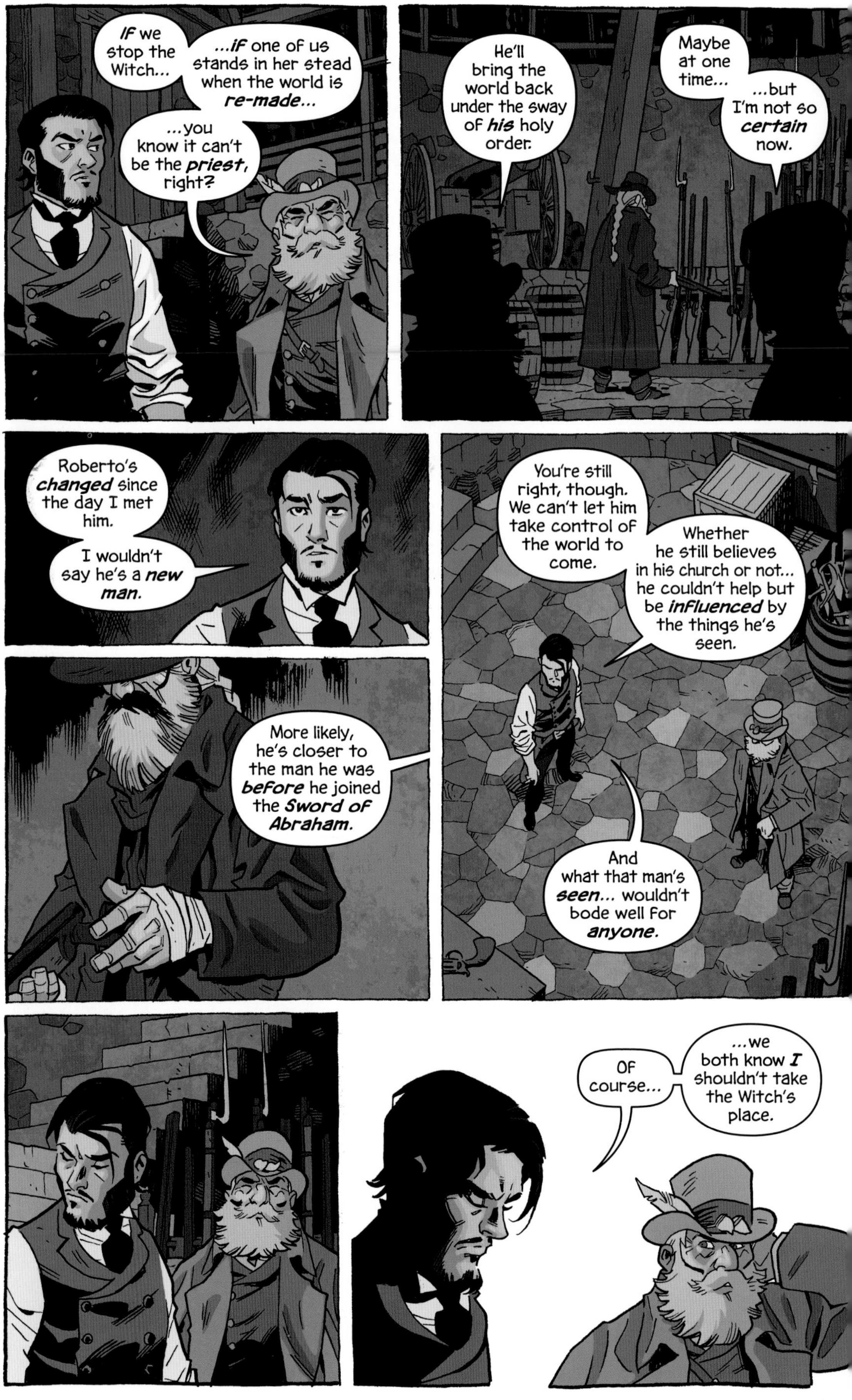

IF we stop the Witch...
...IF one of us stands in her stead when the world is re-made...
...you know it can't be the priest, right?
He'll bring the world back under the sway of his holy order.
Maybe at one time...
...but I'm not so certain now.
Roberto's changed since the day I met him.
I wouldn't say he's a new man.
You're still right, though. We can't let him take control of the world to come.
Whether he still believes in his church or not... he couldn't help but be influenced by the things he's seen.
More likely, he's closer to the man he was before he joined the Sword of Abraham.
And what that man's seen... wouldn't bode well for anyone.
Of course...
...we both know I shouldn't take the Witch's place.

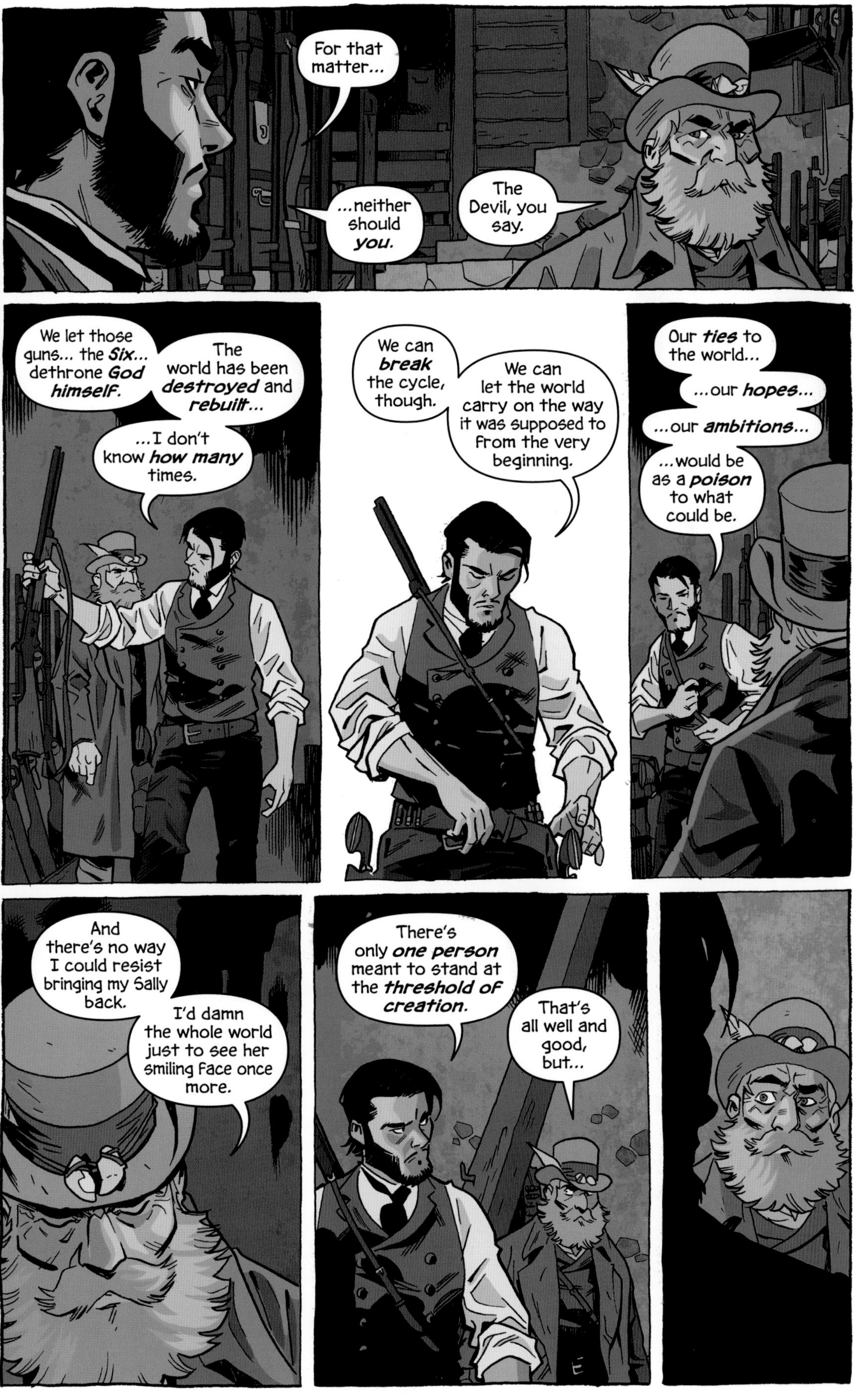

For that matter...
...neither should you.
The Devil, you say.
We let those guns... the Six... dethrone God himself.
The world has been destroyed and rebuilt...
...I don't know how many times.
We can break the cycle, though.
We can let the world carry on the way it was supposed to from the very beginning.
Our ties to the world...
...our hopes...
...our ambitions...
...would be as a poison to what could be.
And there's no way I could resist bringing my Sally back.
I'd damn the whole world just to see her smiling face once more.
There's only one person meant to stand at the threshold of creation.
That's all well and good, but...

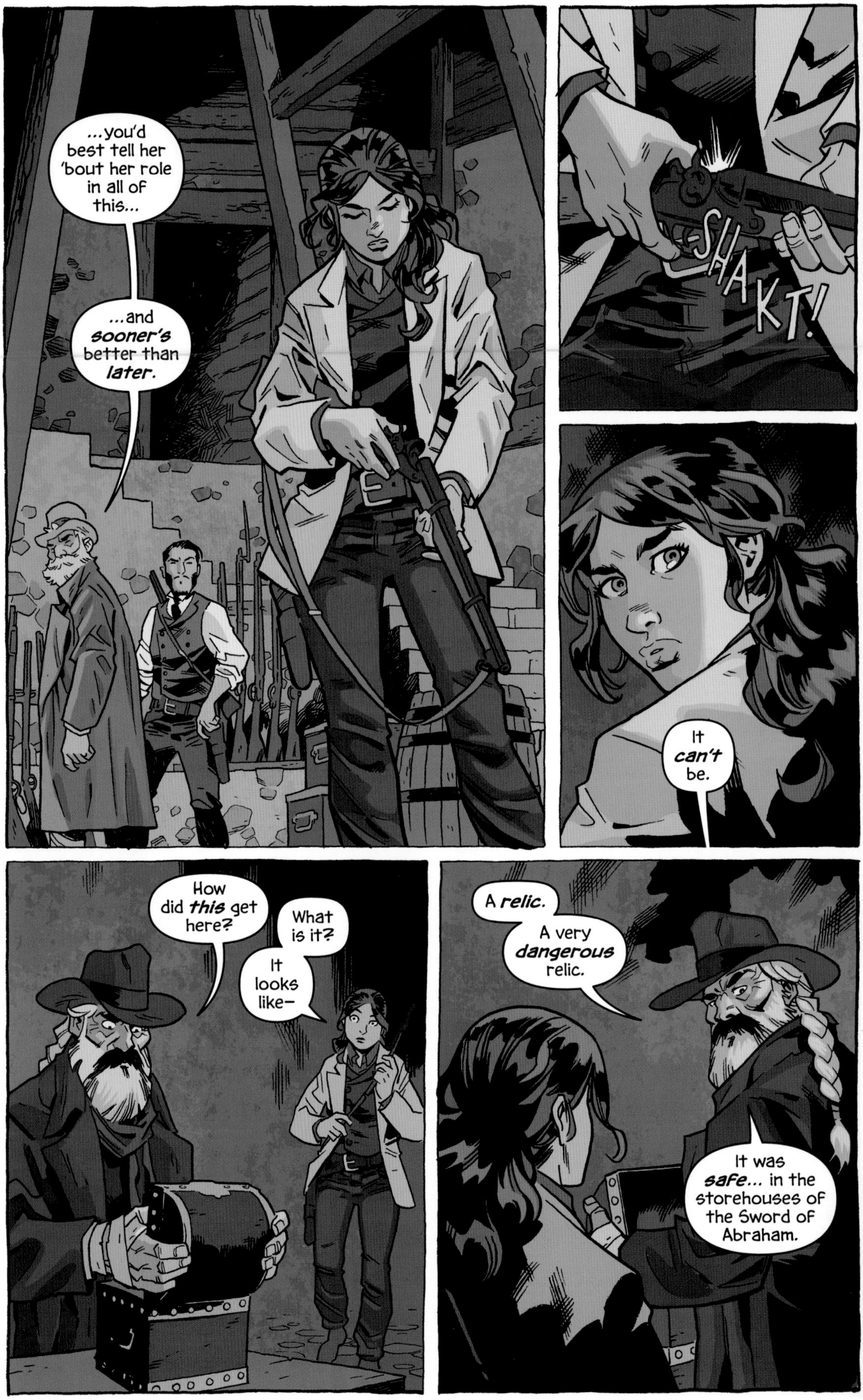
...you'd best tell her 'bout her role in all of this...
...and *sooner's* better than *later*.
-SHAKT!
It *can't* be.
How did *this* get here?
What is it?
It looks like–
A *relic*.
A very *dangerous* relic.
It was *safe*... in the storehouses of the Sword of Abraham.

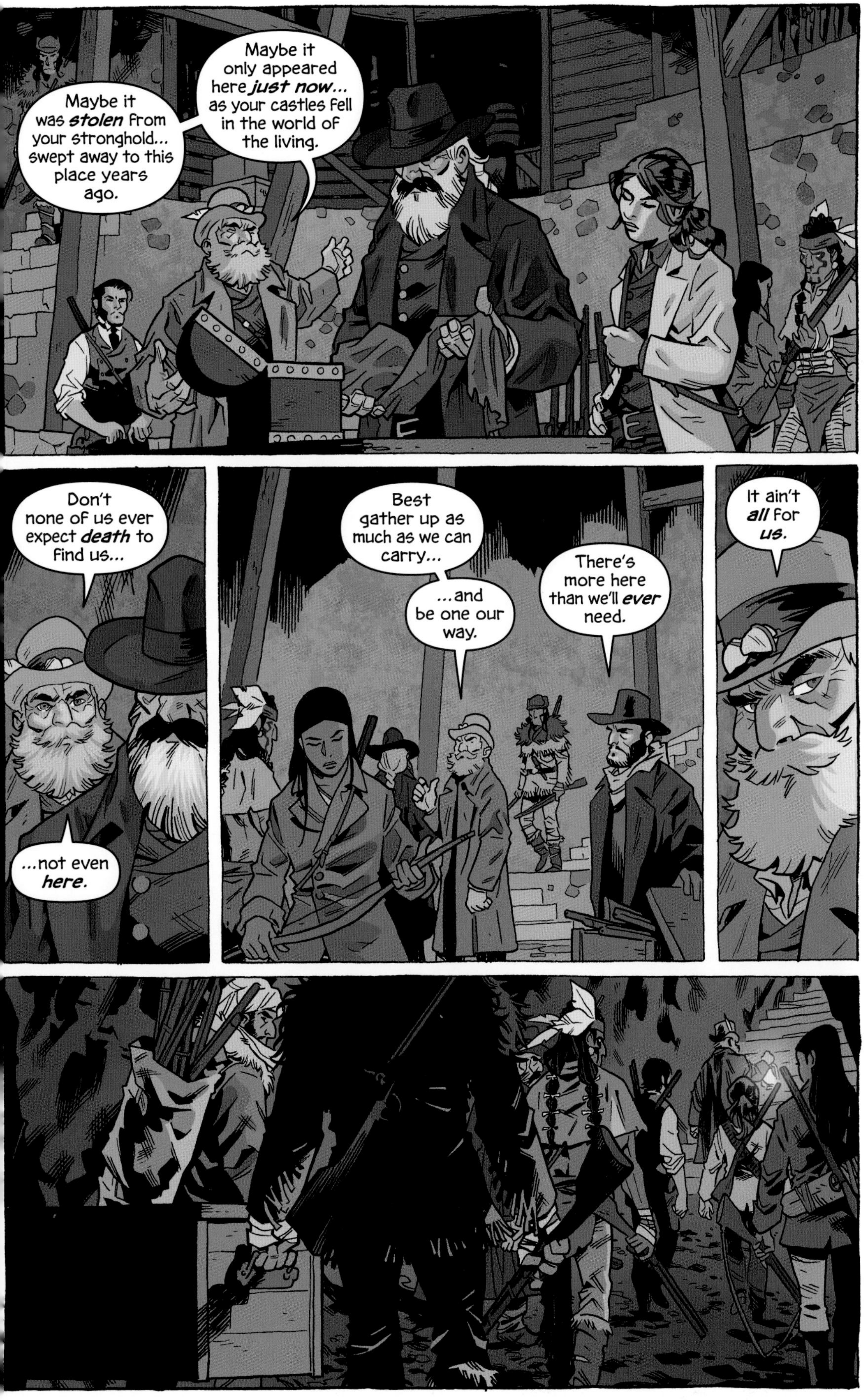
Maybe it was *stolen* from your stronghold... swept away to this place years ago.
Maybe it only appeared here *just now*... as your castles fell in the world of the living.
Don't none of us ever expect *death* to find us...
...not even *here*.
Best gather up as much as we can carry...
...and be one our way.
There's more here than we'll *ever* need.
It ain't *all* for *us*.

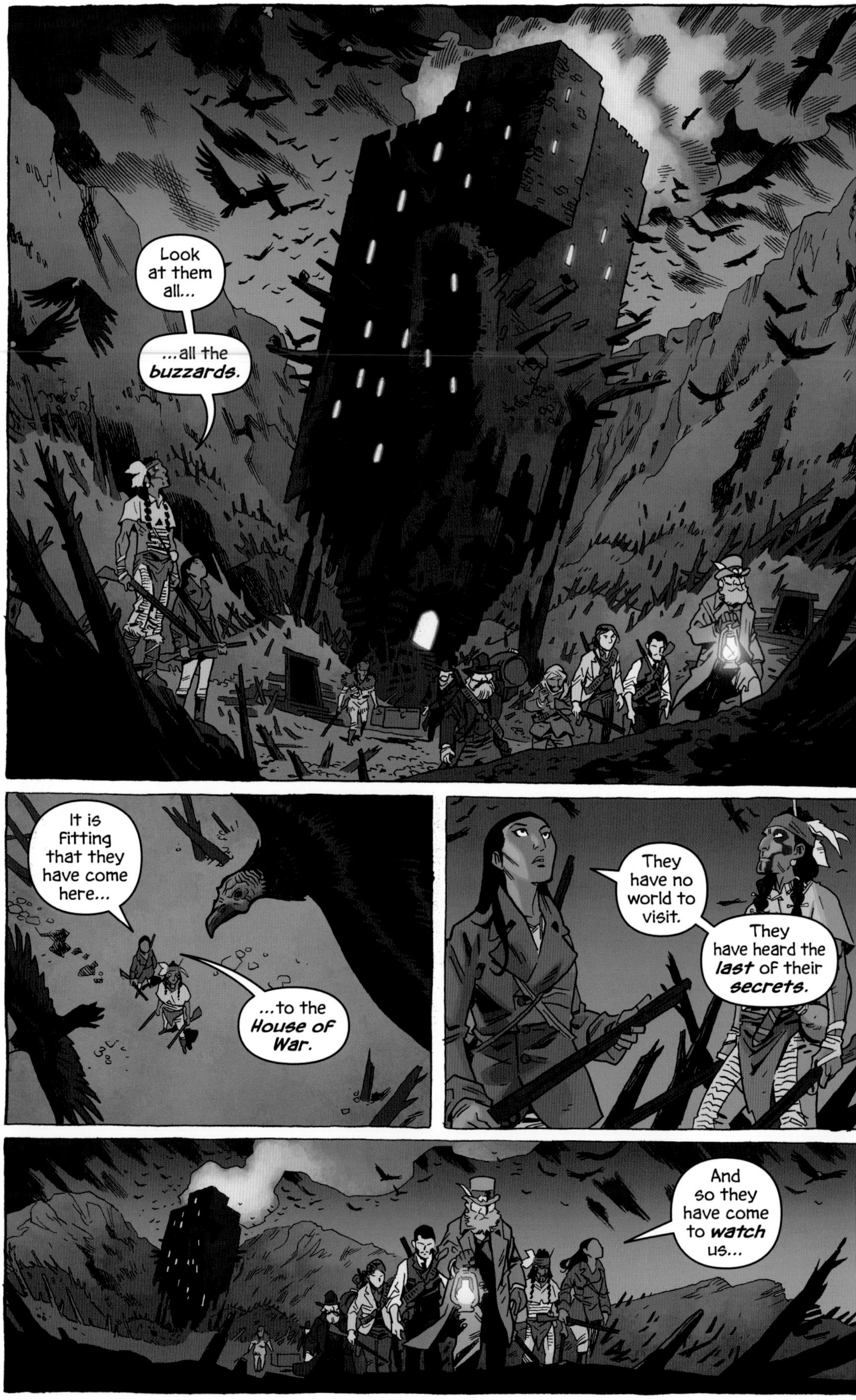
Look at them all...
...all the *buzzards.*
It is fitting that they have come here...
...to the *House of War.*
They have no world to visit.
They have heard the *last* of their *secrets.*
And so they have come to *watch* us...

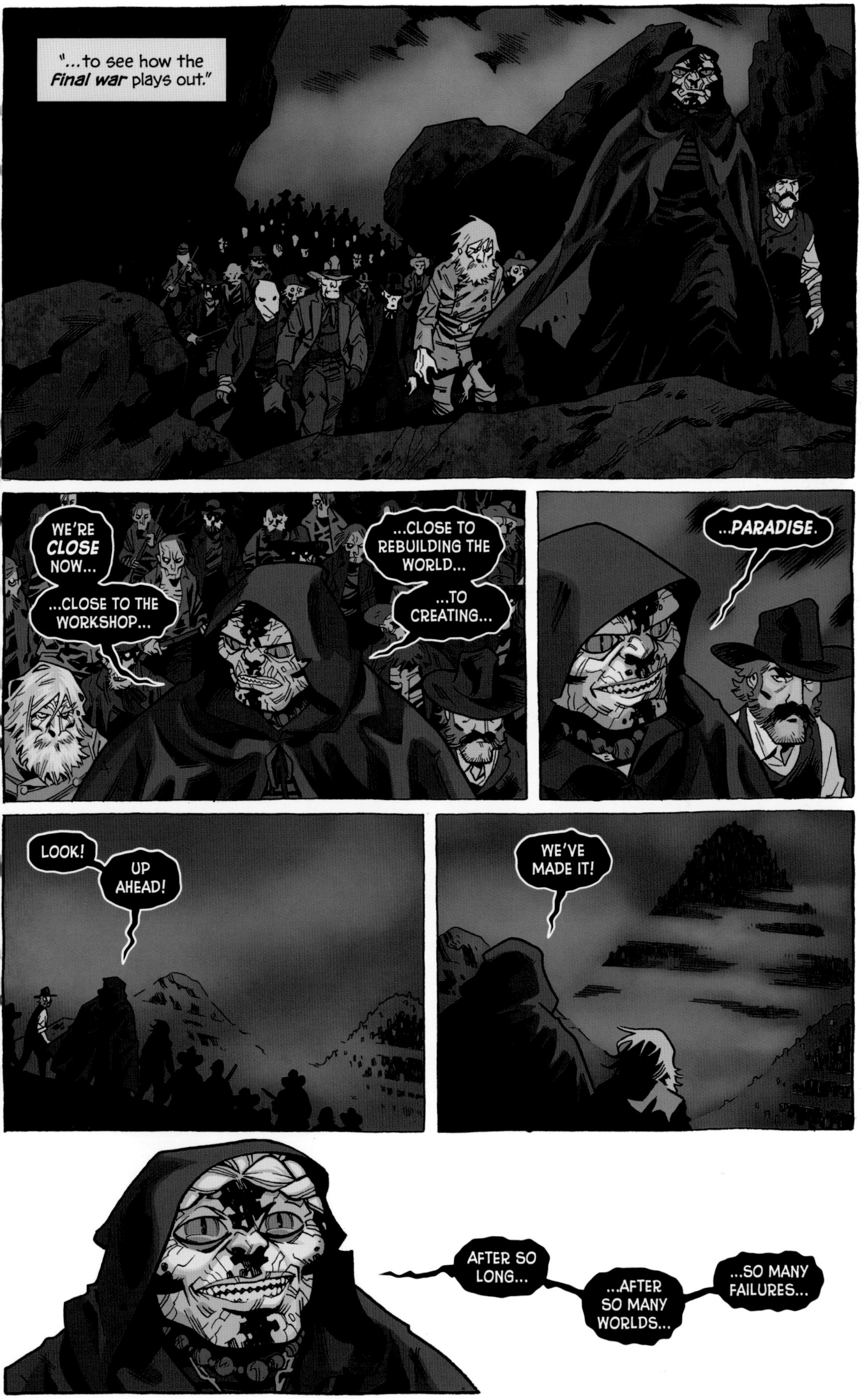
"...to see how the *Final war* plays out."
WE'RE *CLOSE* NOW...
...CLOSE TO THE WORKSHOP...
...CLOSE TO REBUILDING THE WORLD...
...TO CREATING...
...*PARADISE*.
LOOK!
UP AHEAD!
WE'VE MADE IT!
AFTER SO LONG...
...AFTER SO MANY WORLDS...
...SO MANY FAILURES...

...I'M FINALLY HERE.

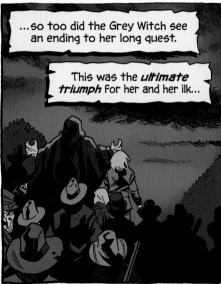

...so too did the Grey Witch see an ending to her long quest.

This was the *ultimate triumph* for her and her ilk...

...whether they wanted *power*...

...or *vengeance*...

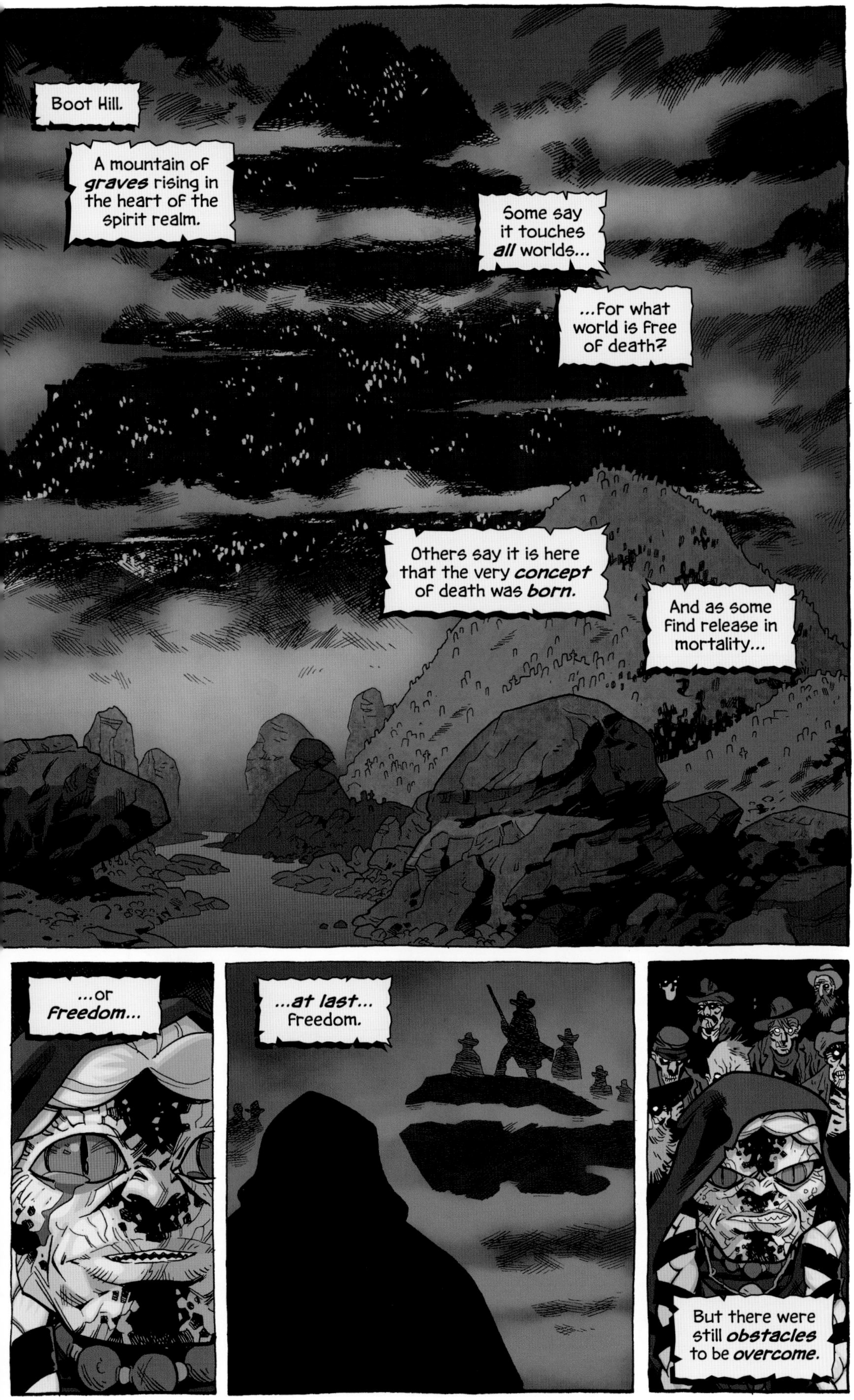
Boot Hill.
A mountain of *graves* rising in the heart of the spirit realm.
Some say it touches *all* worlds...
...for what world is free of death?
Others say it is here that the very *concept* of death was *born.*
And as some find release in mortality...
...or *freedom*...
...*at last*... freedom.
But there were still *obstacles* to be *overcome.*

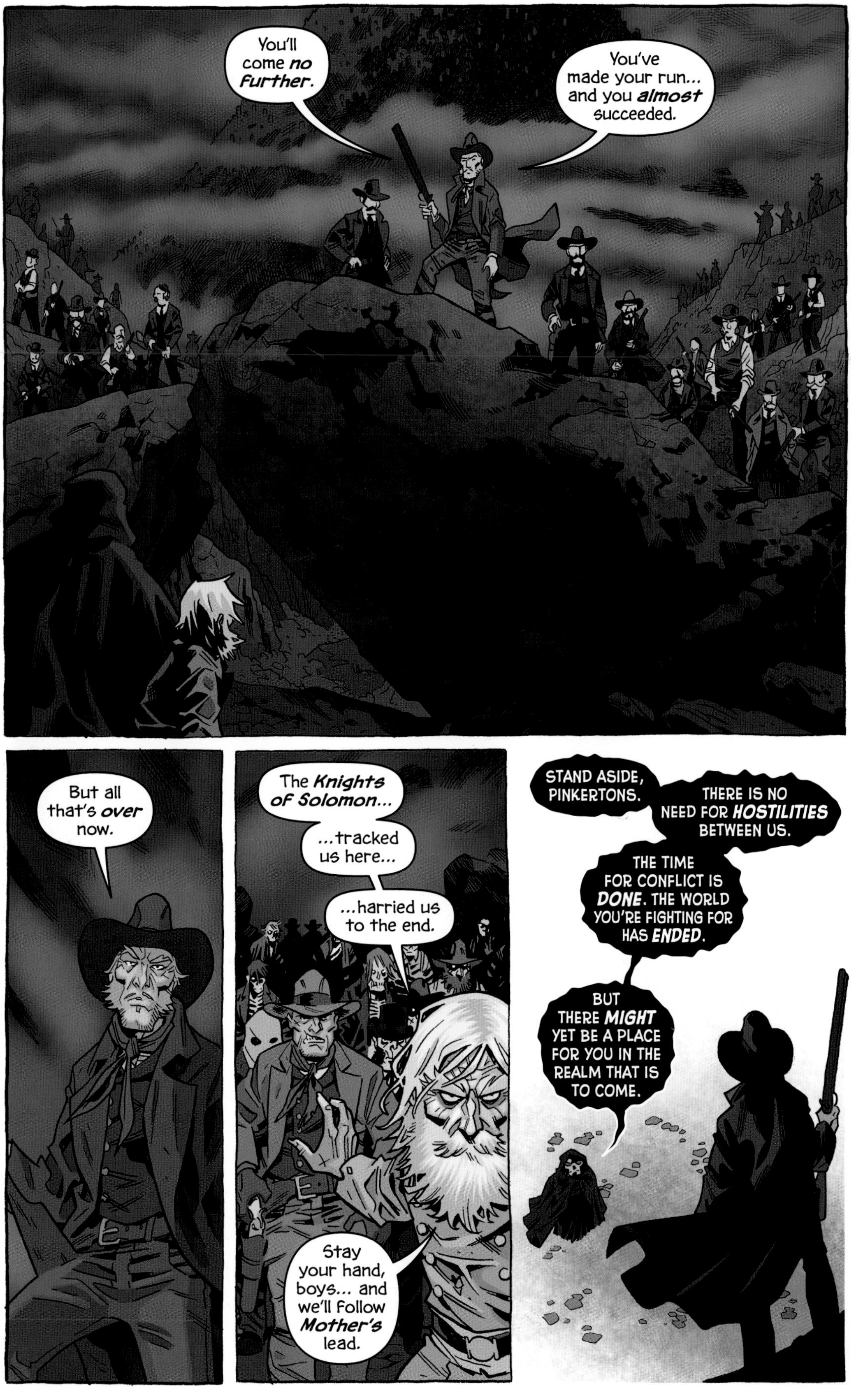

You'll come *no further*.
You've made your run... and you *almost* succeeded.
But all that's *over* now.
The *Knights of Solomon*...
...tracked us here...
...harried us to the end.
Stay your hand, boys... and we'll follow *Mother's* lead.
STAND ASIDE, PINKERTONS.
THERE IS NO NEED FOR *HOSTILITIES* BETWEEN US.
THE TIME FOR CONFLICT IS *DONE*. THE WORLD YOU'RE FIGHTING FOR HAS *ENDED*.
BUT THERE *MIGHT* YET BE A PLACE FOR YOU IN THE REALM THAT IS TO COME.

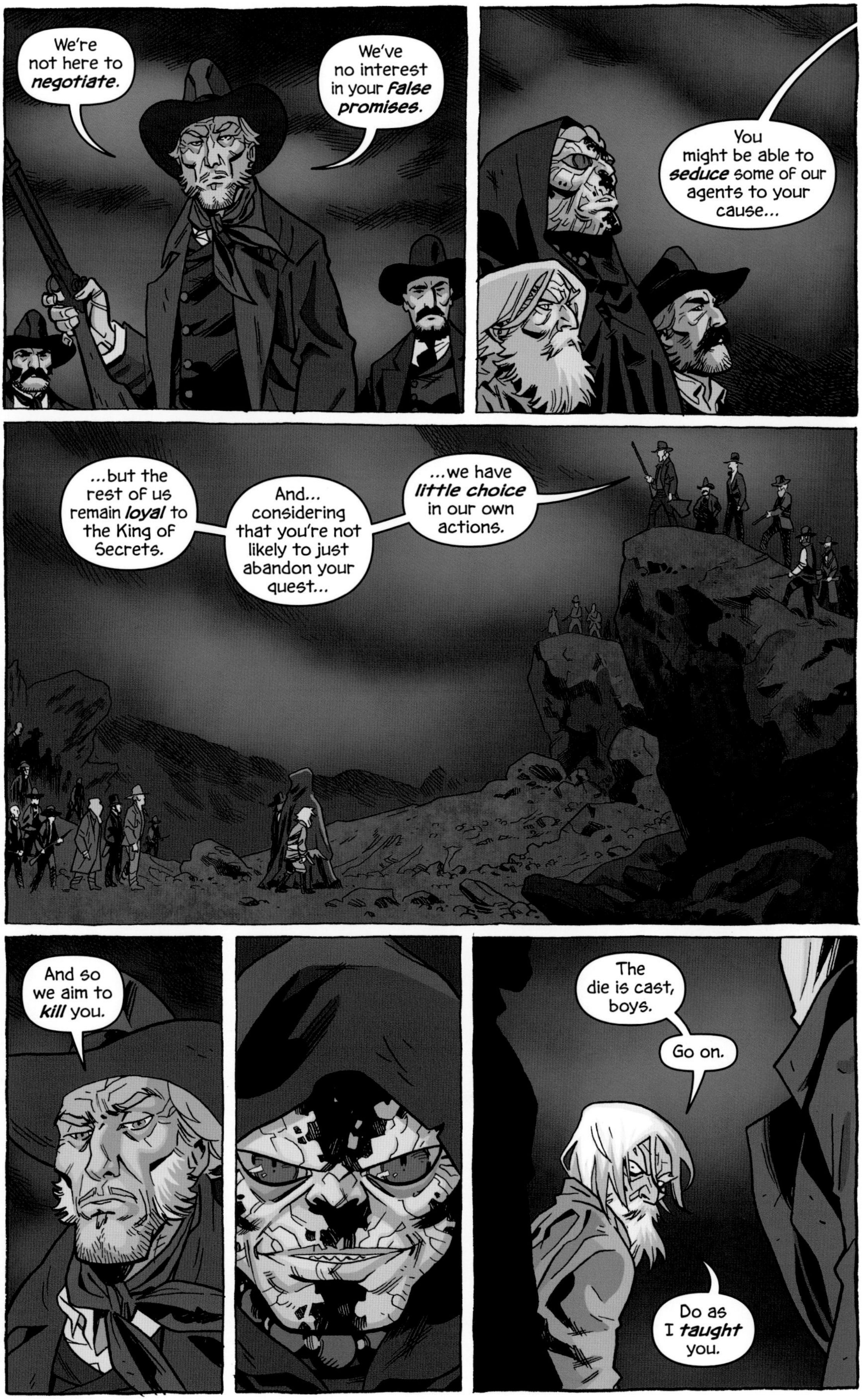
We're not here to negotiate.
We've no interest in your false promises.
You might be able to seduce some of our agents to your cause...
...but the rest of us remain loyal to the King of Secrets.
And... considering that you're not likely to just abandon your quest...
...we have little choice in our own actions.
And so we aim to kill you.
The die is cast, boys.
Go on.
Do as I taught you.

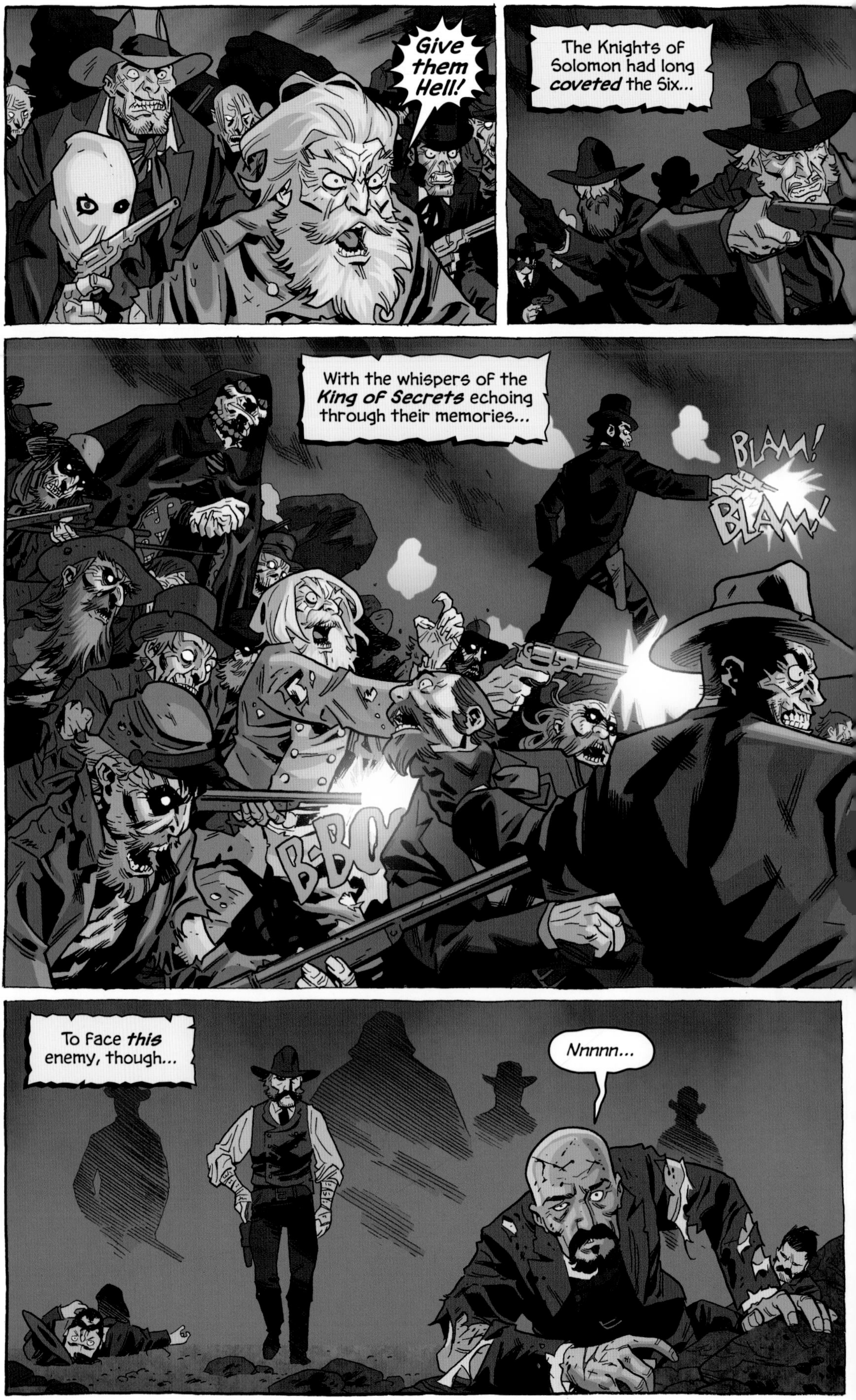

Give them Hell!
The Knights of Solomon had long *coveted* the Six...
With the whispers of the *King of Secrets* echoing through their memories...
BLAM!
BLAM!
To face *this* enemy, though...
Nnnnn...

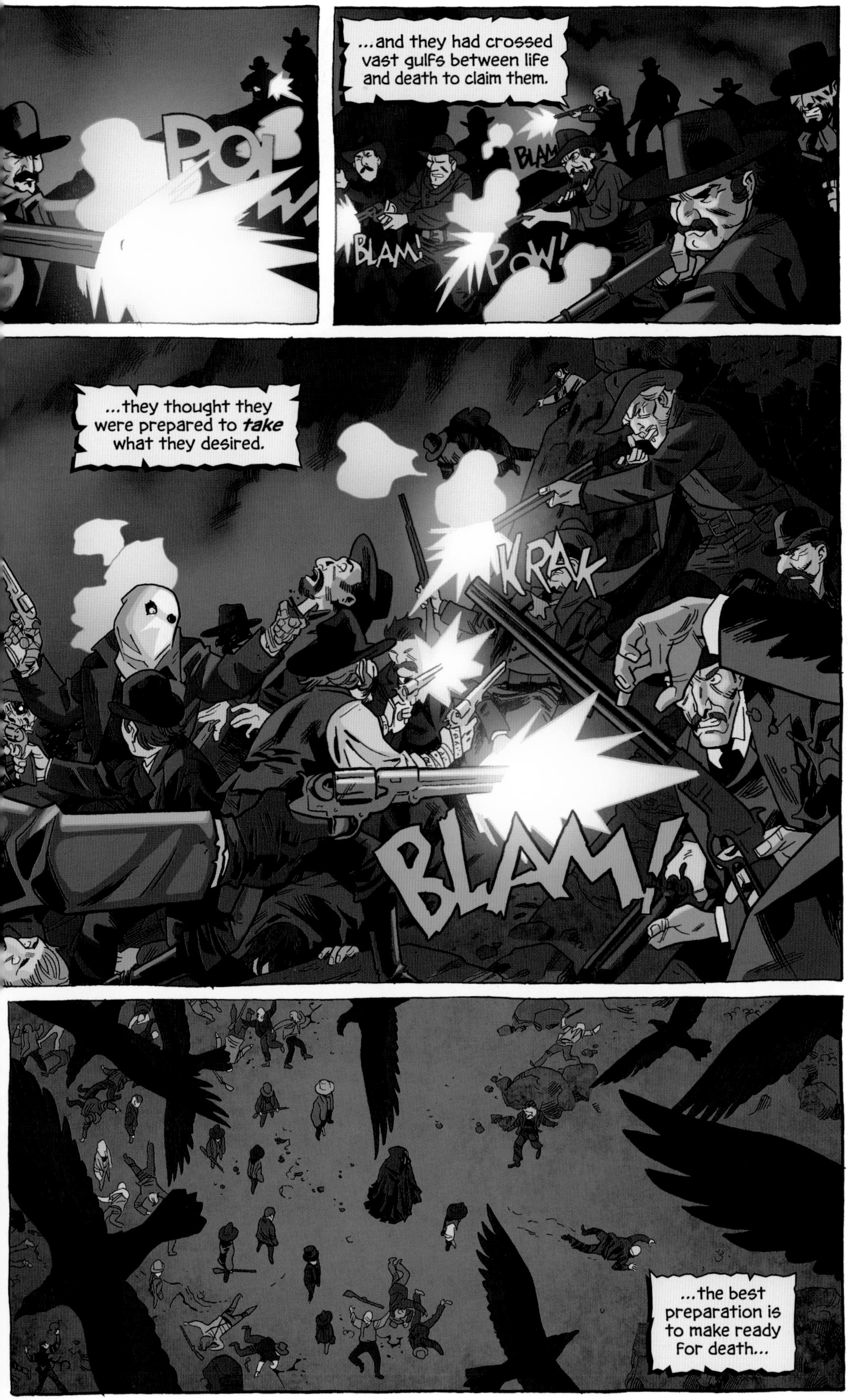

POW!
...and they had crossed vast gulfs between life and death to claim them.
BLAM
BLAM!
POW!
...they thought they were prepared to *take* what they desired.
KRAK
BLAM!
...the best preparation is to make ready for death...

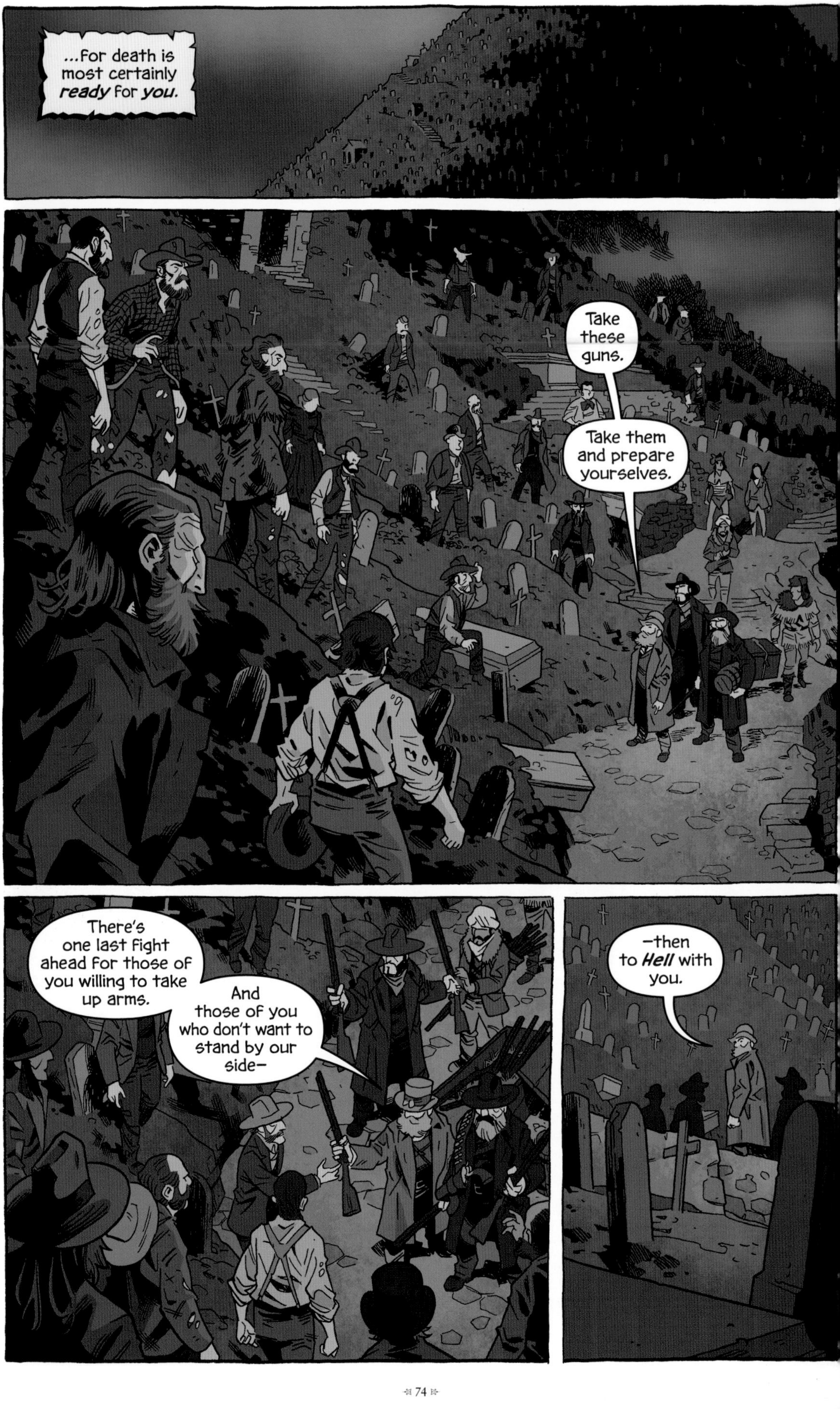
...for death is most certainly *ready* for *you.*
Take these guns.
Take them and prepare yourselves.
There's one last fight ahead for those of you willing to take up arms.
And those of you who don't want to stand by our side–
–then to *Hell* with you.

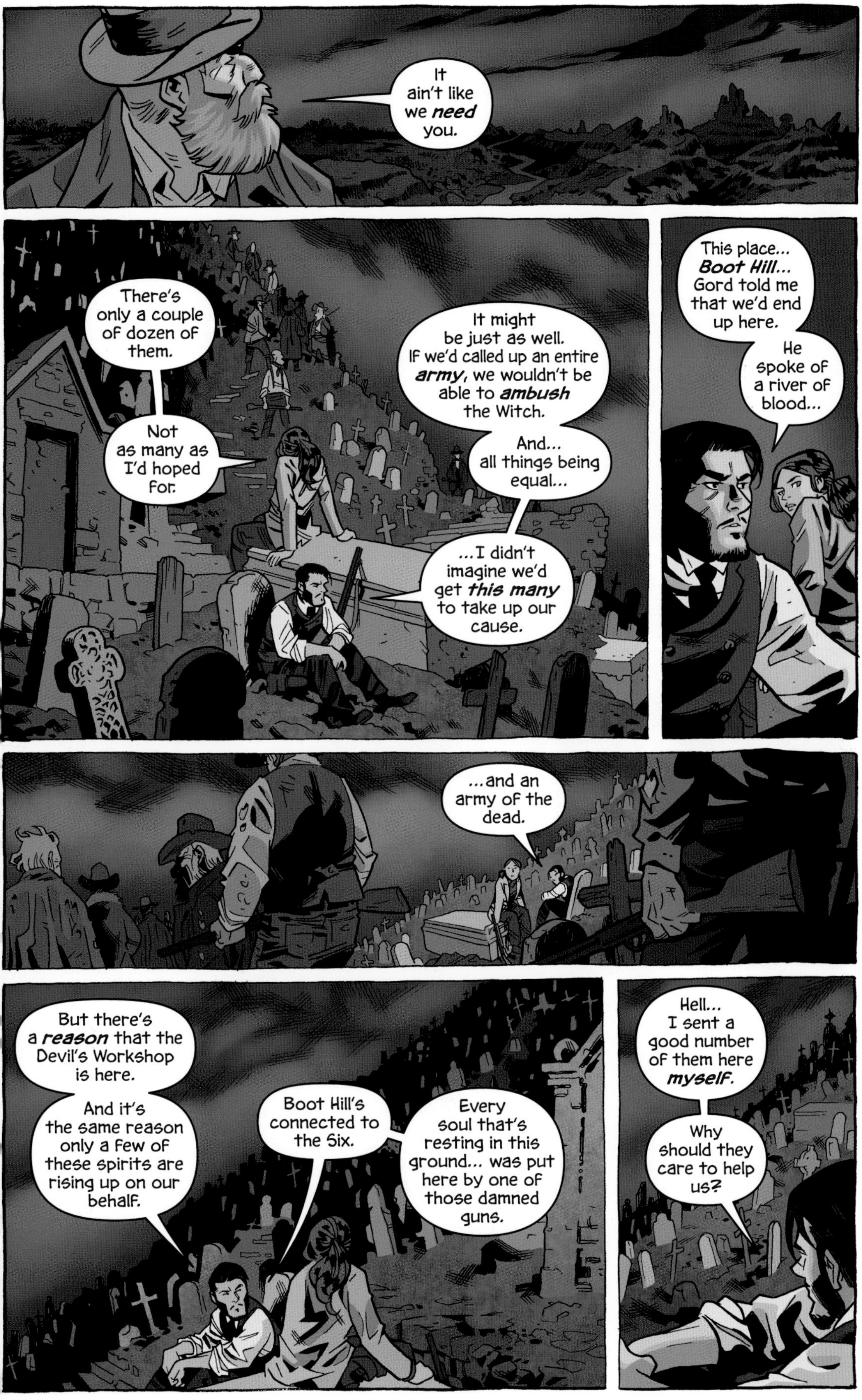

It ain't like we *need* you.
There's only a couple of dozen of them.
Not as many as I'd hoped for.
It might be just as well. If we'd called up an entire *army*, we wouldn't be able to *ambush* the Witch.
And... all things being equal...
...I didn't imagine we'd get *this many* to take up our cause.
This place... *Boot Hill*... Gord told me that we'd end up here.
He spoke of a river of blood...
...and an army of the dead.
But there's a *reason* that the Devil's Workshop is here.
And it's the same reason only a few of these spirits are rising up on our behalf.
Boot Hill's connected to the Six.
Every soul that's resting in this ground... was put here by one of those damned guns.
Hell... I sent a good number of them here *myself*.
Why should they care to help us?

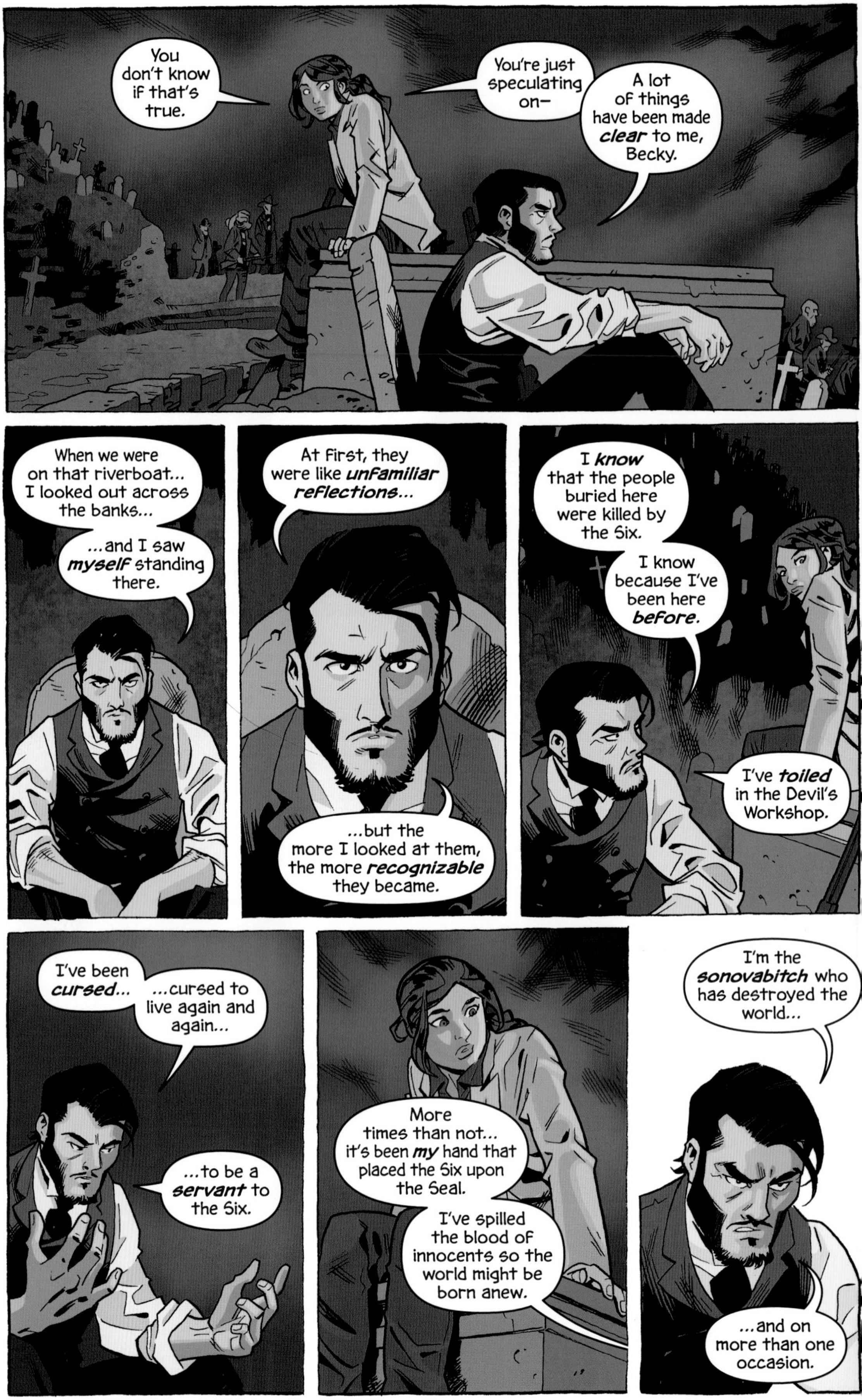

You don't know if that's true.
You're just speculating on–
A lot of things have been made clear to me, Becky.
When we were on that riverboat... I looked out across the banks...
...and I saw myself standing there.
At first, they were like unfamiliar reflections...
...but the more I looked at them, the more recognizable they became.
I know that the people buried here were killed by the Six.
I know because I've been here before.
I've toiled in the Devil's Workshop.
I've been cursed...
...cursed to live again and again...
...to be a servant to the Six.
More times than not... it's been my hand that placed the Six upon the Seal.
I've spilled the blood of innocents so the world might be born anew.
I'm the sonovabitch who has destroyed the world...
...and on more than one occasion.

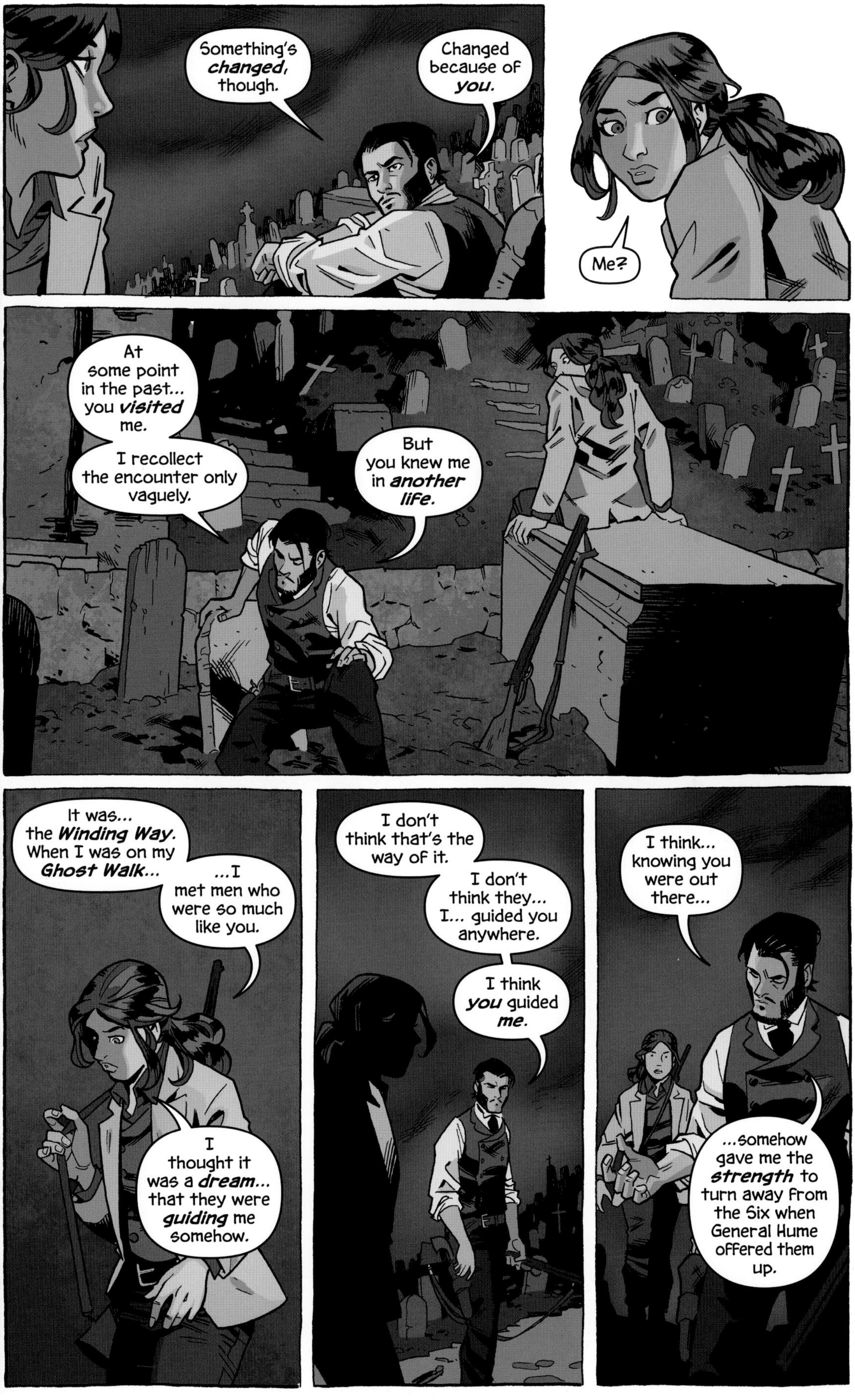
Something's changed, though.
Changed because of you.
Me?
At some point in the past... you visited me.
I recollect the encounter only vaguely.
But you knew me in another life.
It was... the Winding Way. When I was on my Ghost Walk...
...I met men who were so much like you.
I thought it was a dream... that they were guiding me somehow.
I don't think that's the way of it.
I don't think they... I... guided you anywhere.
I think you guided me.
I think... knowing you were out there...
...somehow gave me the strength to turn away from the Six when General Hume offered them up.

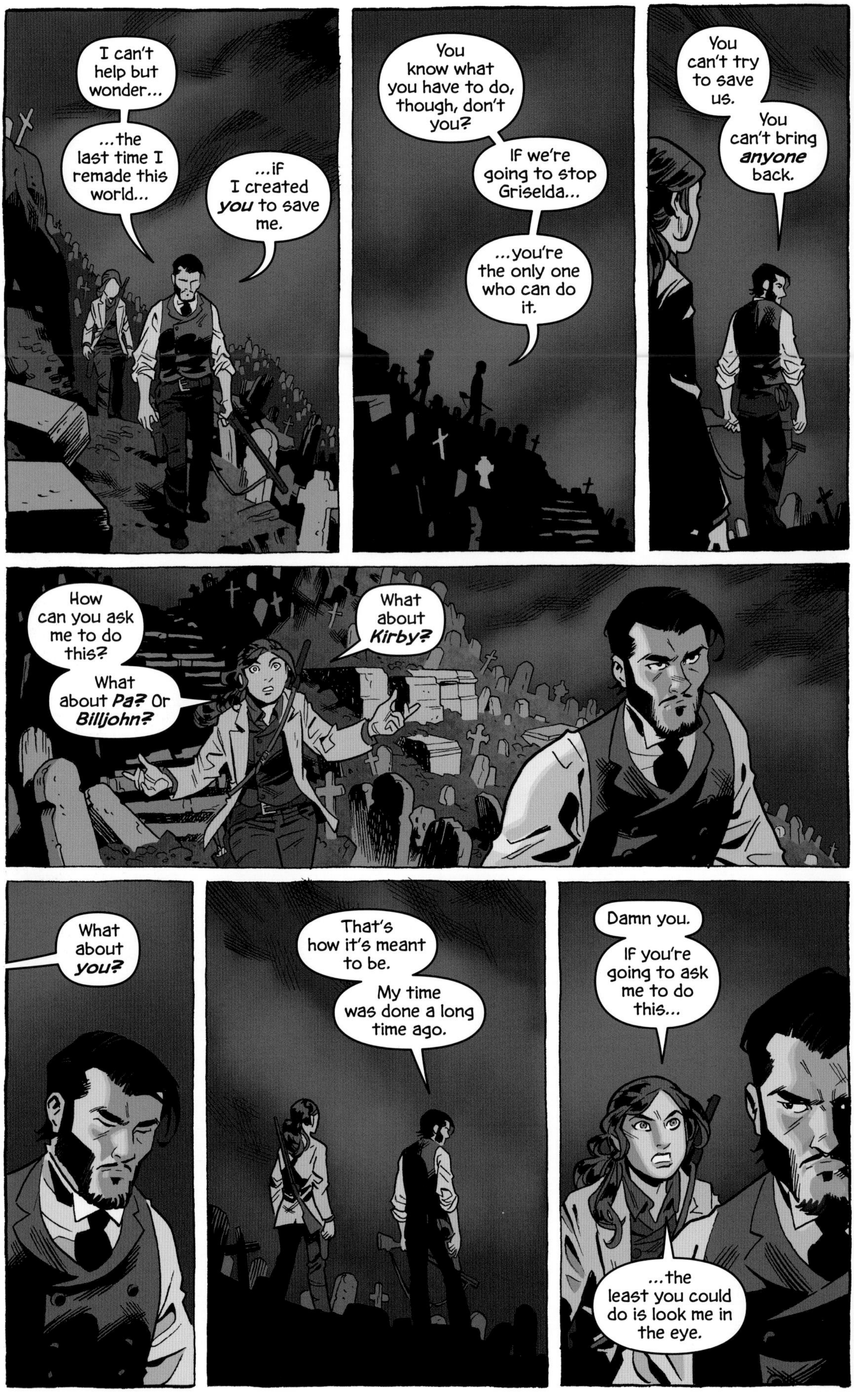
I can't help but wonder...
...the last time I remade this world...
...if I created *you* to save me.
You know what you have to do, though, don't you?
If we're going to stop Griselda...
...you're the only one who can do it.
You can't try to save us.
You can't bring *anyone* back.
How can you ask me to do this?
What about *Pa?* Or *Billjohn?*
What about *Kirby?*
What about *you?*
That's how it's meant to be.
My time was done a long time ago.
Damn you.
If you're going to ask me to do this...
...the least you could do is look me in the eye.

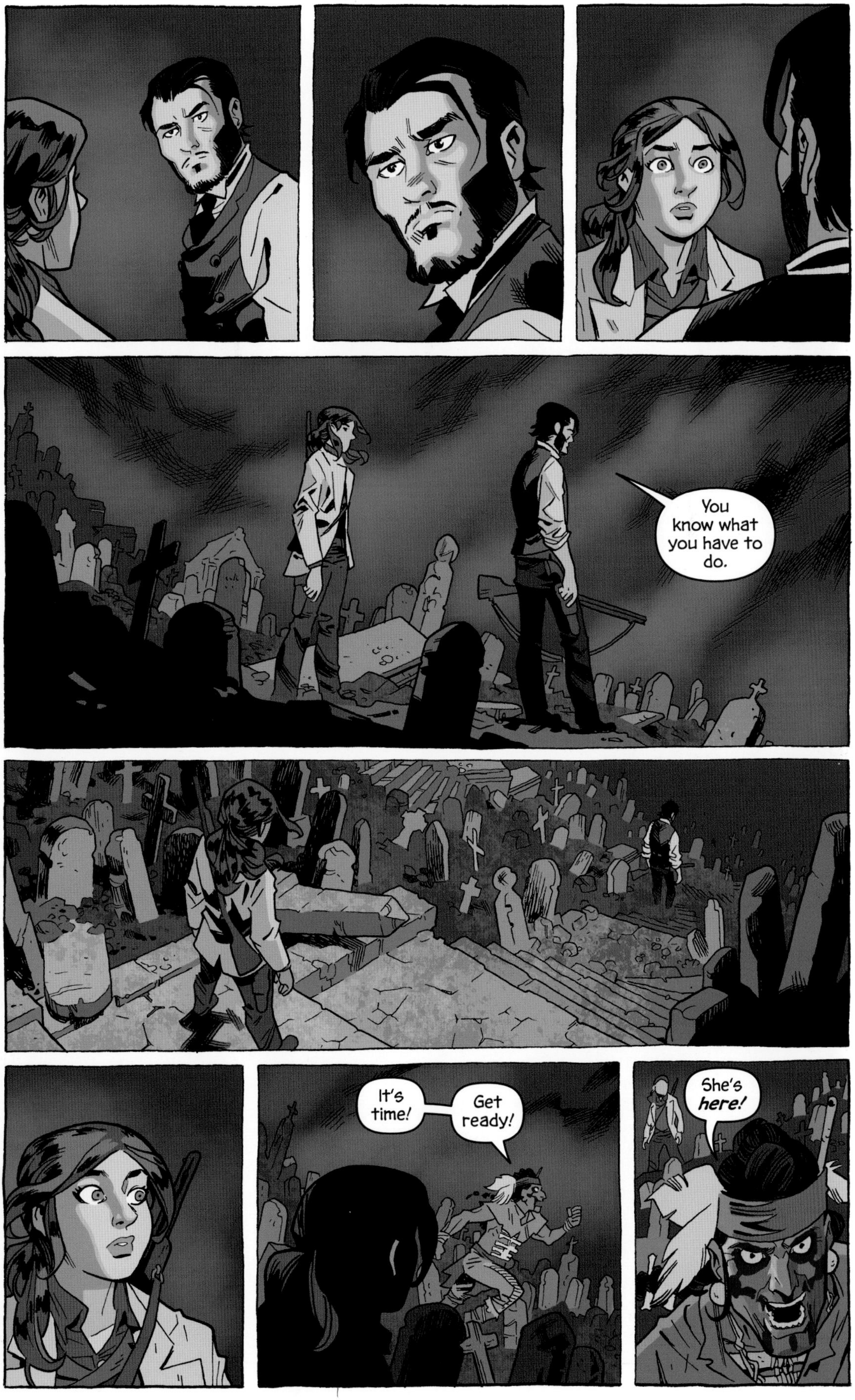
You know what you have to do.
It's time!
Get ready!
She's *here!*

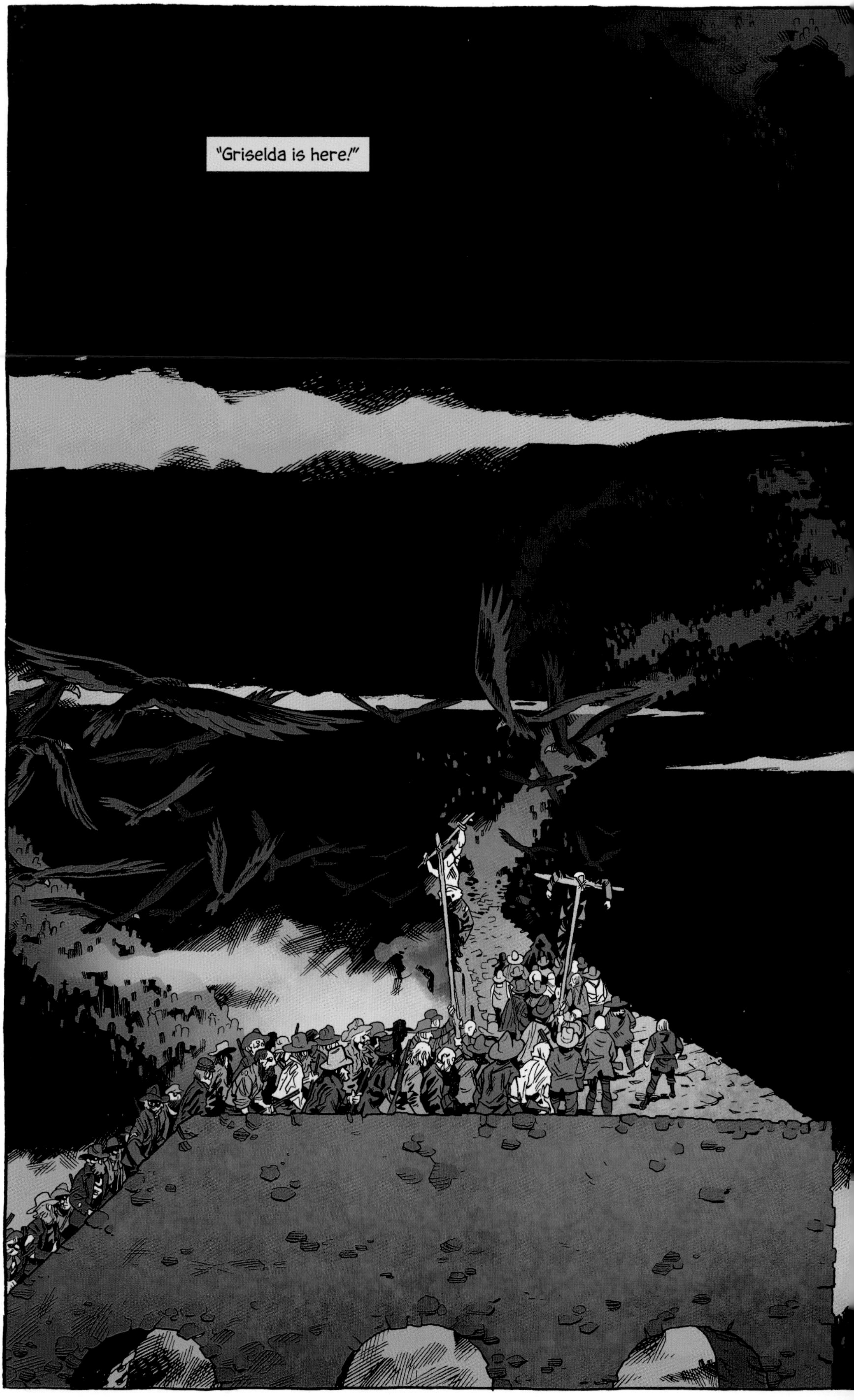
"Griselda is here!"

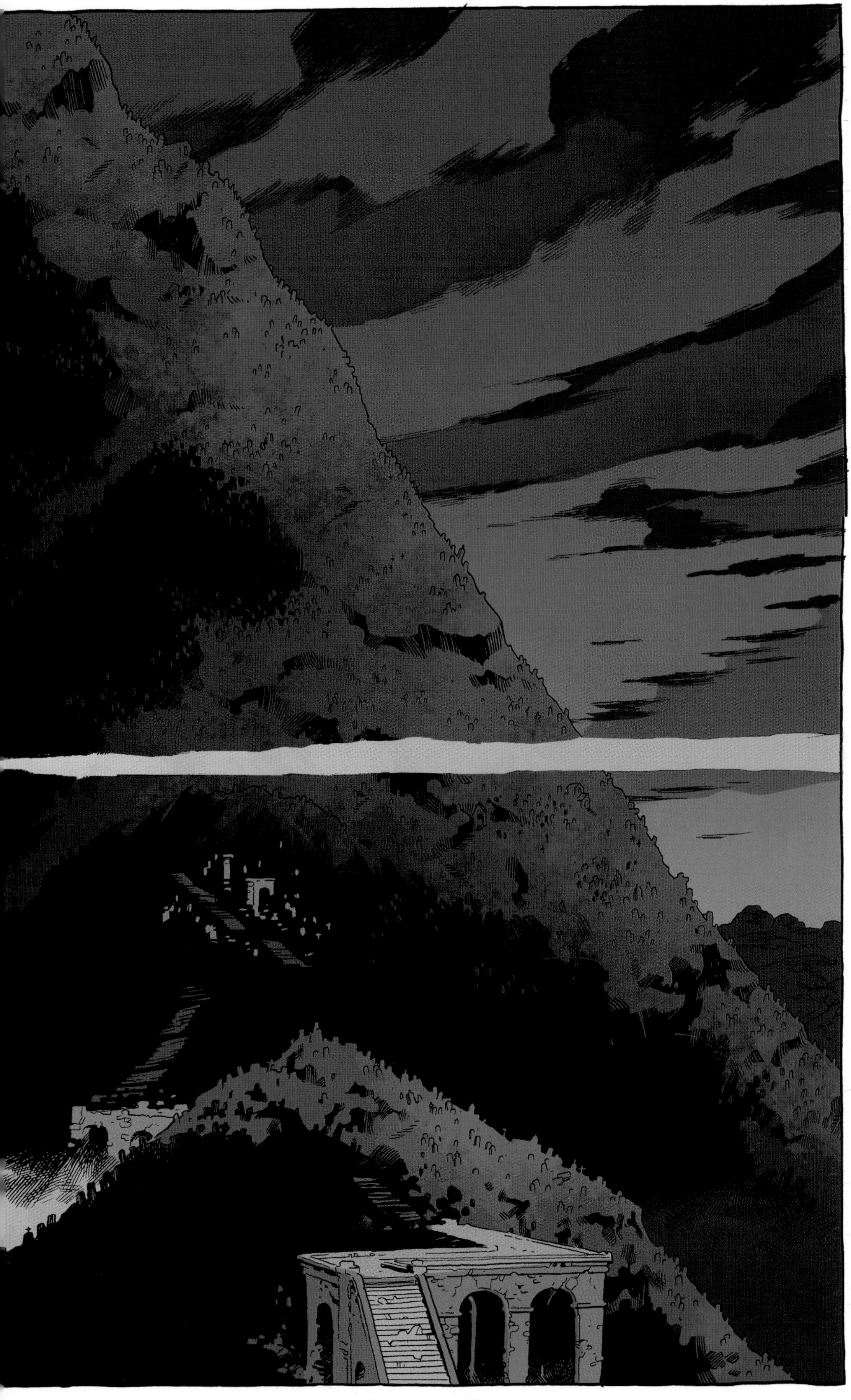

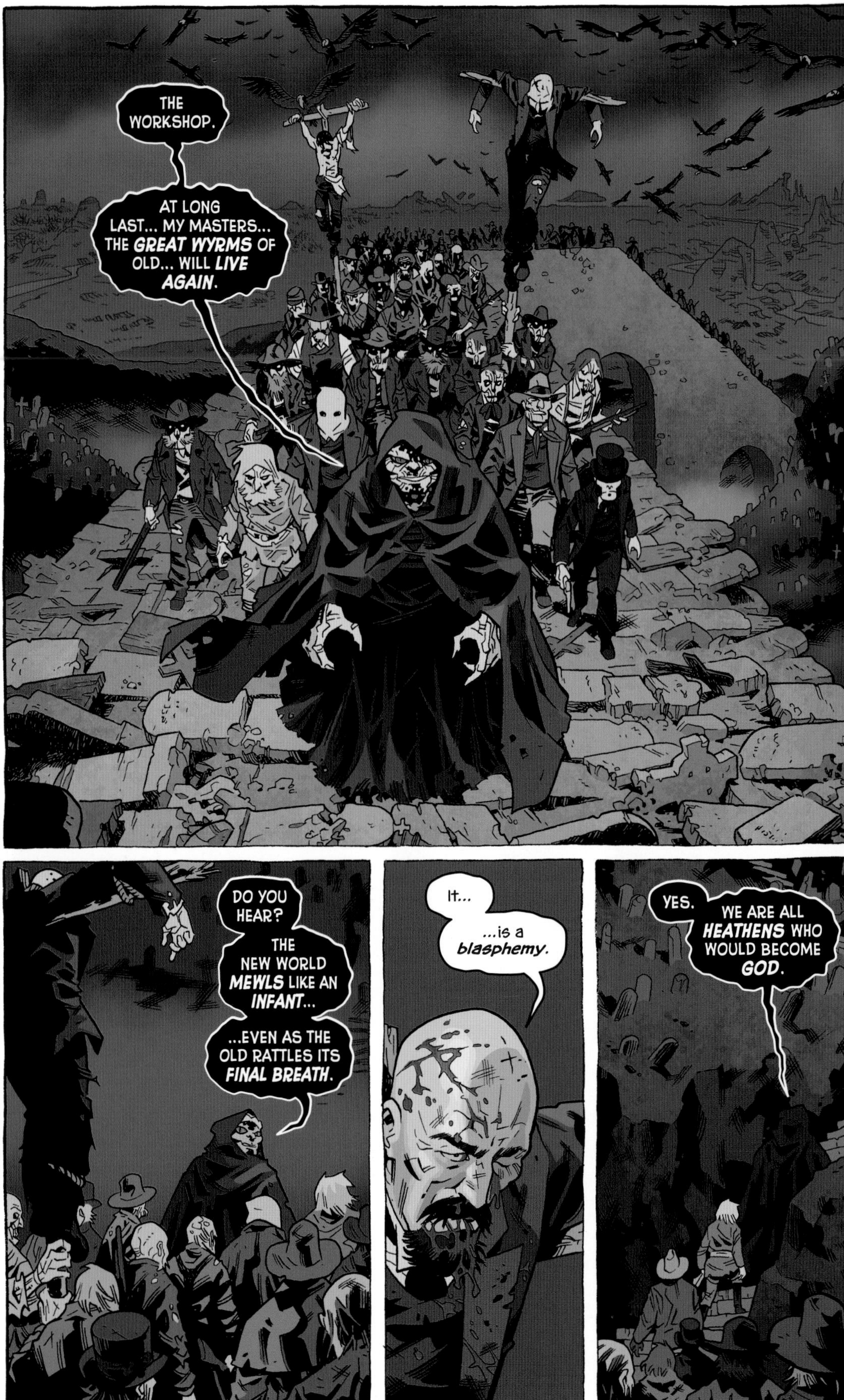
THE WORKSHOP.
AT LONG LAST... MY MASTERS... THE GREAT WYRMS OF OLD... WILL LIVE AGAIN.
DO YOU HEAR?
THE NEW WORLD MEWLS LIKE AN INFANT...
...EVEN AS THE OLD RATTLES ITS FINAL BREATH.
It...
...is a blasphemy.
YES.
WE ARE ALL HEATHENS WHO WOULD BECOME GOD.

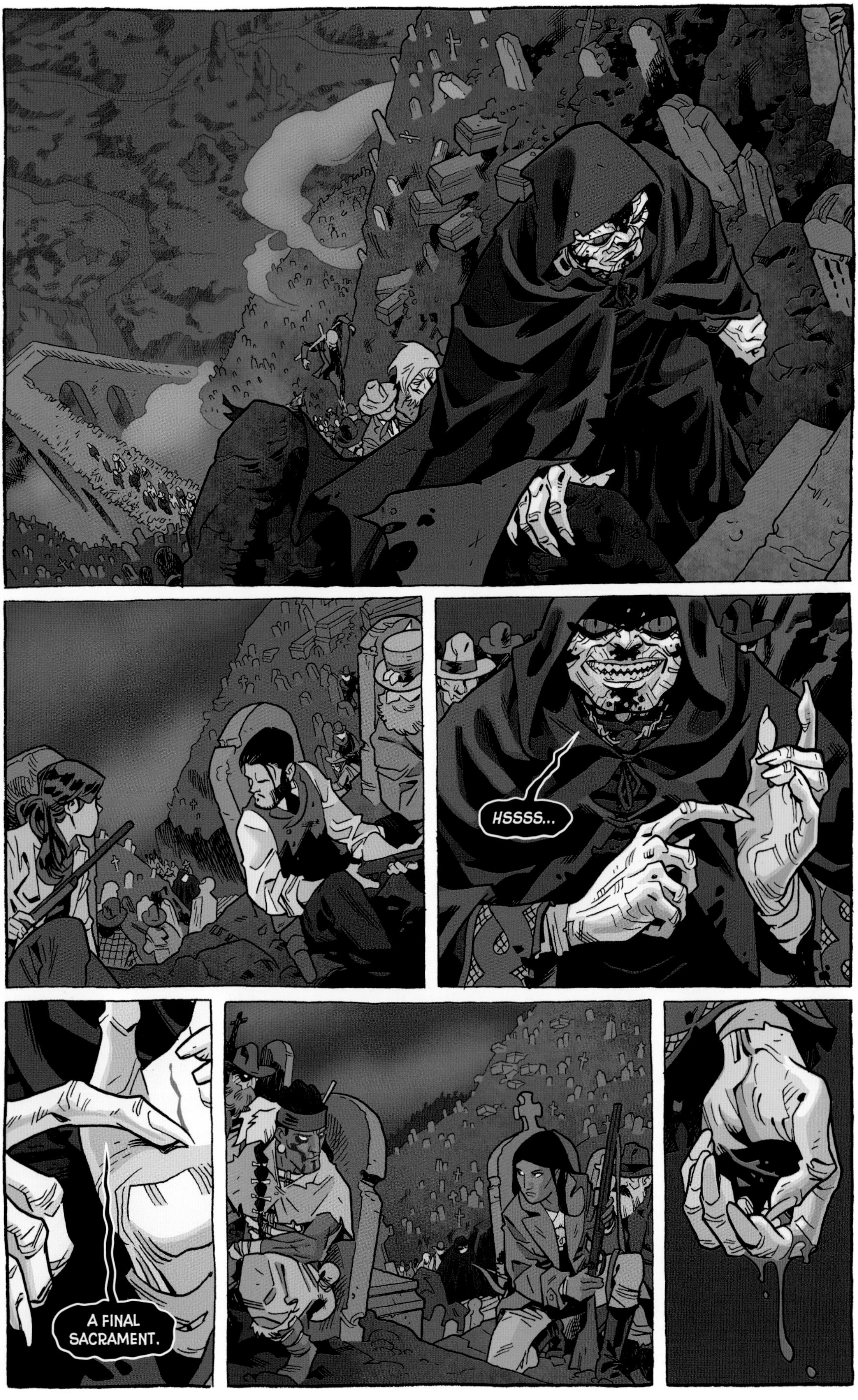
HSSSS...
A FINAL SACRAMENT.

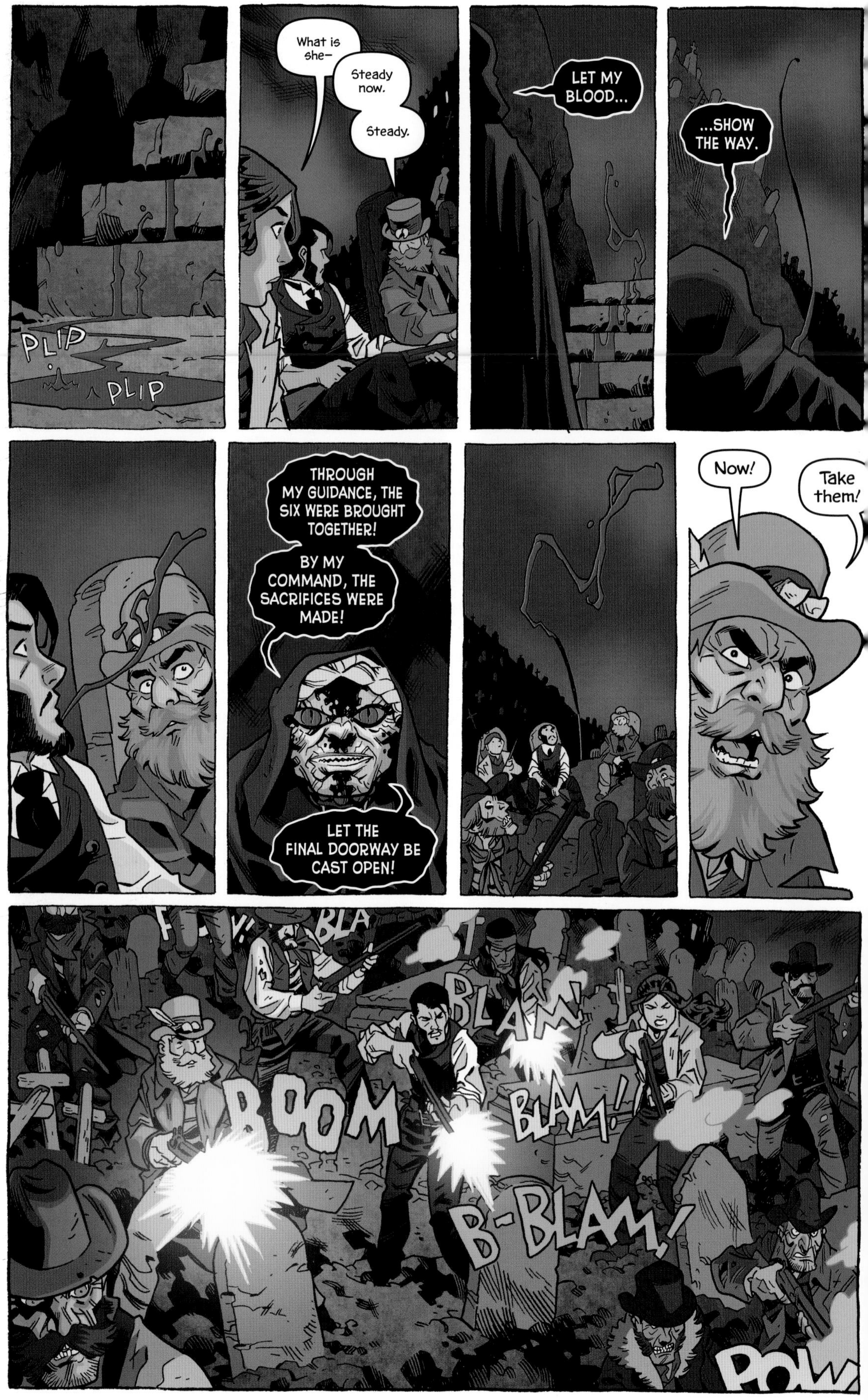
PLIP
PLIP
What is she—
Steady now.
Steady.
LET MY BLOOD...
...SHOW THE WAY.
THROUGH MY GUIDANCE, THE SIX WERE BROUGHT TOGETHER!
BY MY COMMAND, THE SACRIFICES WERE MADE!
LET THE FINAL DOORWAY BE CAST OPEN!
Now!
Take them!
BLA
BLAM!
BOOM
BLAM!
B-BLAM!
POW

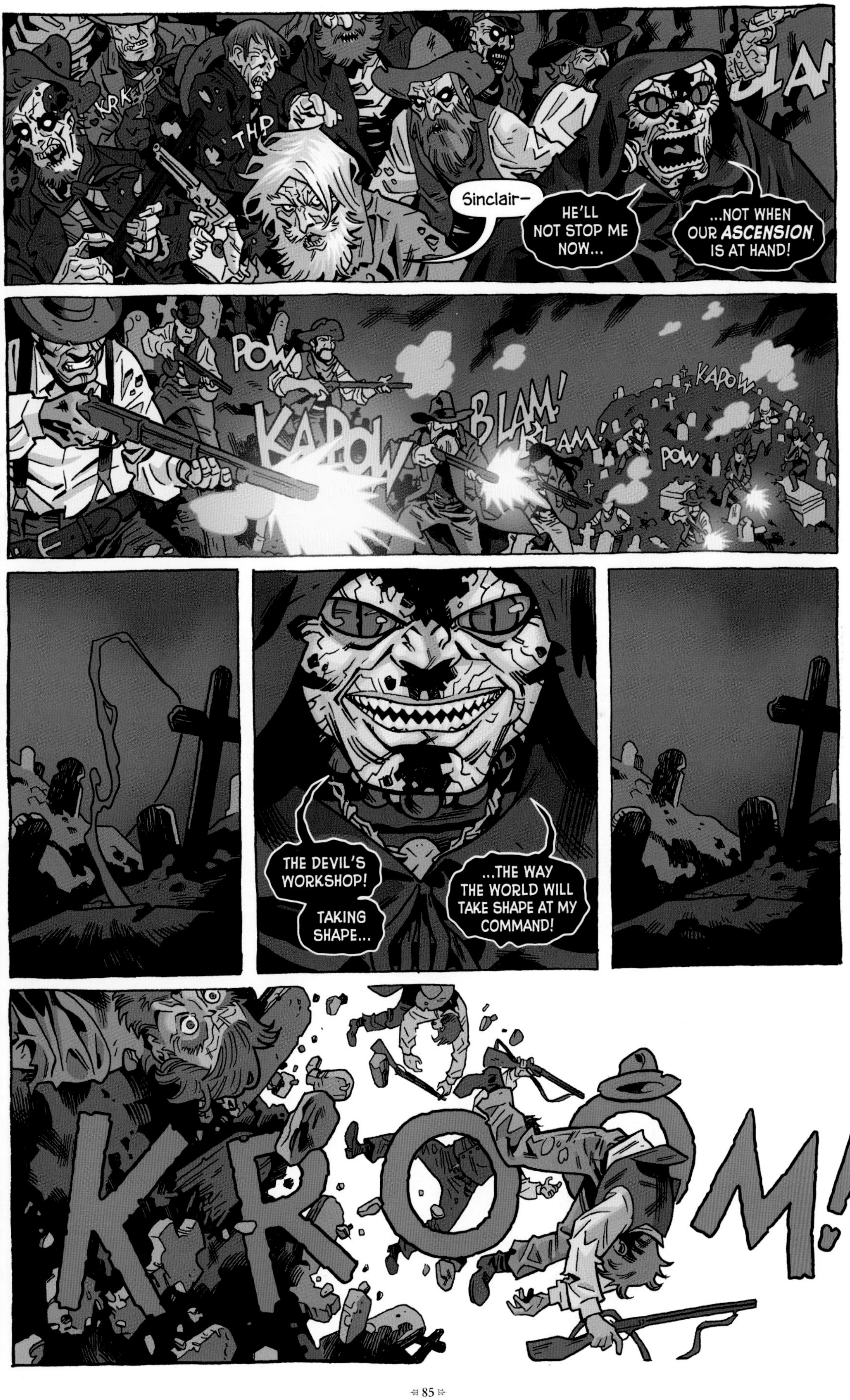
KRK
THP
Sinclair–
HE'LL NOT STOP ME NOW...
...NOT WHEN OUR ASCENSION IS AT HAND!
POW
KAPOW
BLAM!
BLAM!
KAPOW
POW
THE DEVIL'S WORKSHOP!
TAKING SHAPE...
...THE WAY THE WORLD WILL TAKE SHAPE AT MY COMMAND!
KROOM!

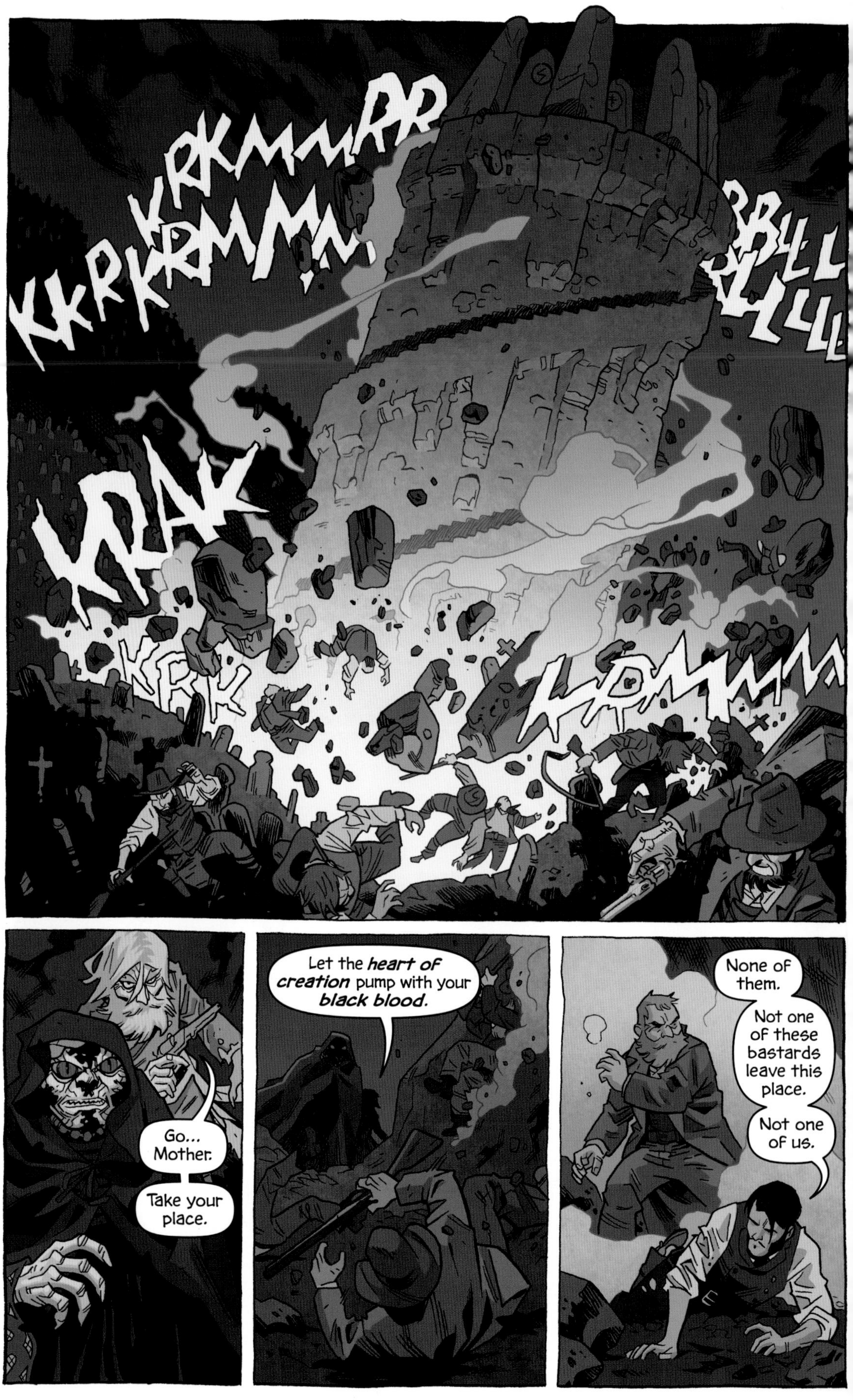
KRKRKRKMMM!!!
KRAK
KRK
Go... Mother.
Take your place.
Let the ***heart of creation*** pump with your ***black blood.***
None of them.
Not one of these bastards leave this place.
Not one of us.

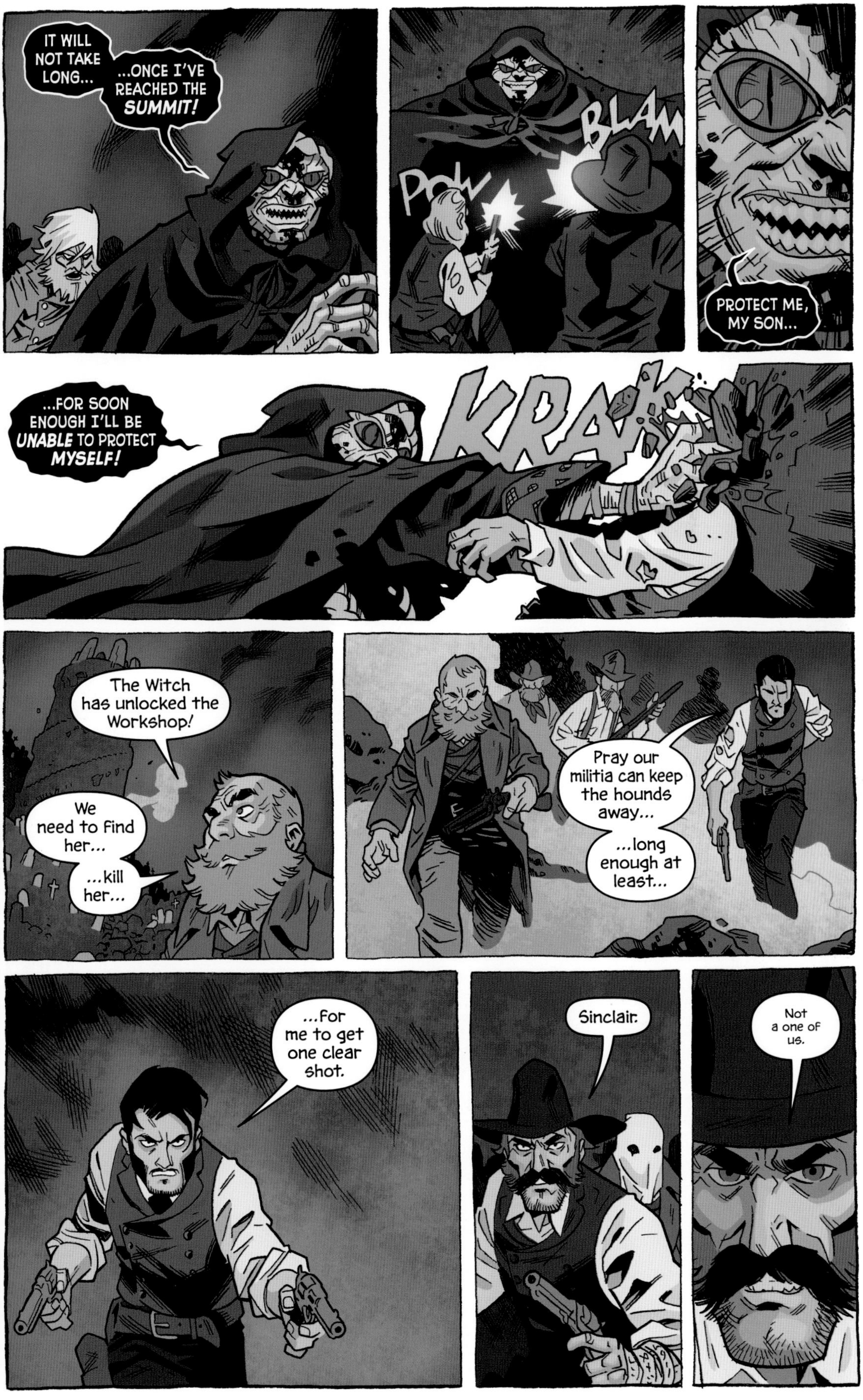

IT WILL NOT TAKE LONG...
...ONCE I'VE REACHED THE SUMMIT!
BLAM
POW
PROTECT ME, MY SON...
...FOR SOON ENOUGH I'LL BE UNABLE TO PROTECT MYSELF!
KRAK
The Witch has unlocked the Workshop!
We need to find her...
...kill her...
Pray our militia can keep the hounds away...
...long enough at least...
...For me to get one clear shot.
Sinclair.
Not a one of us.

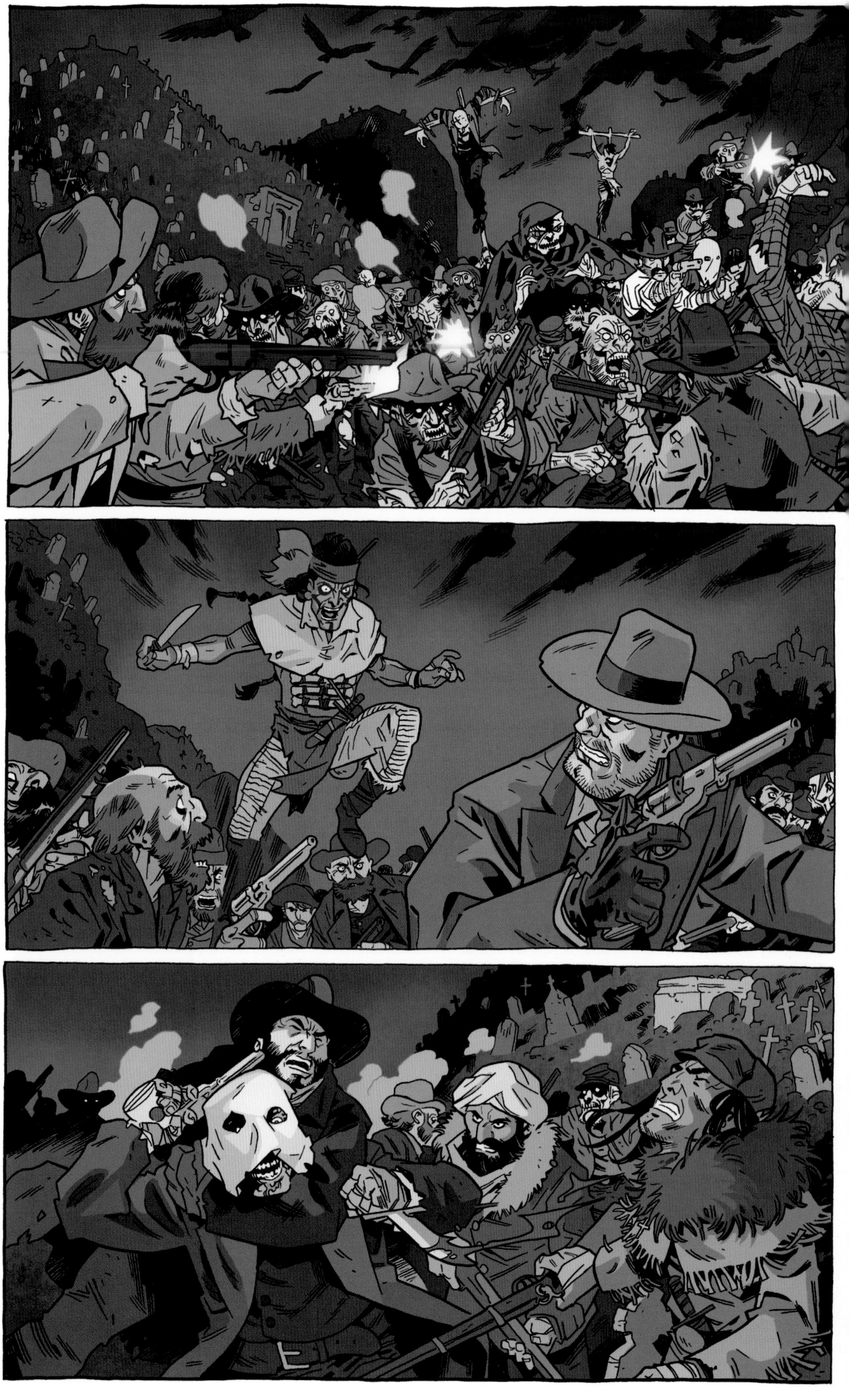

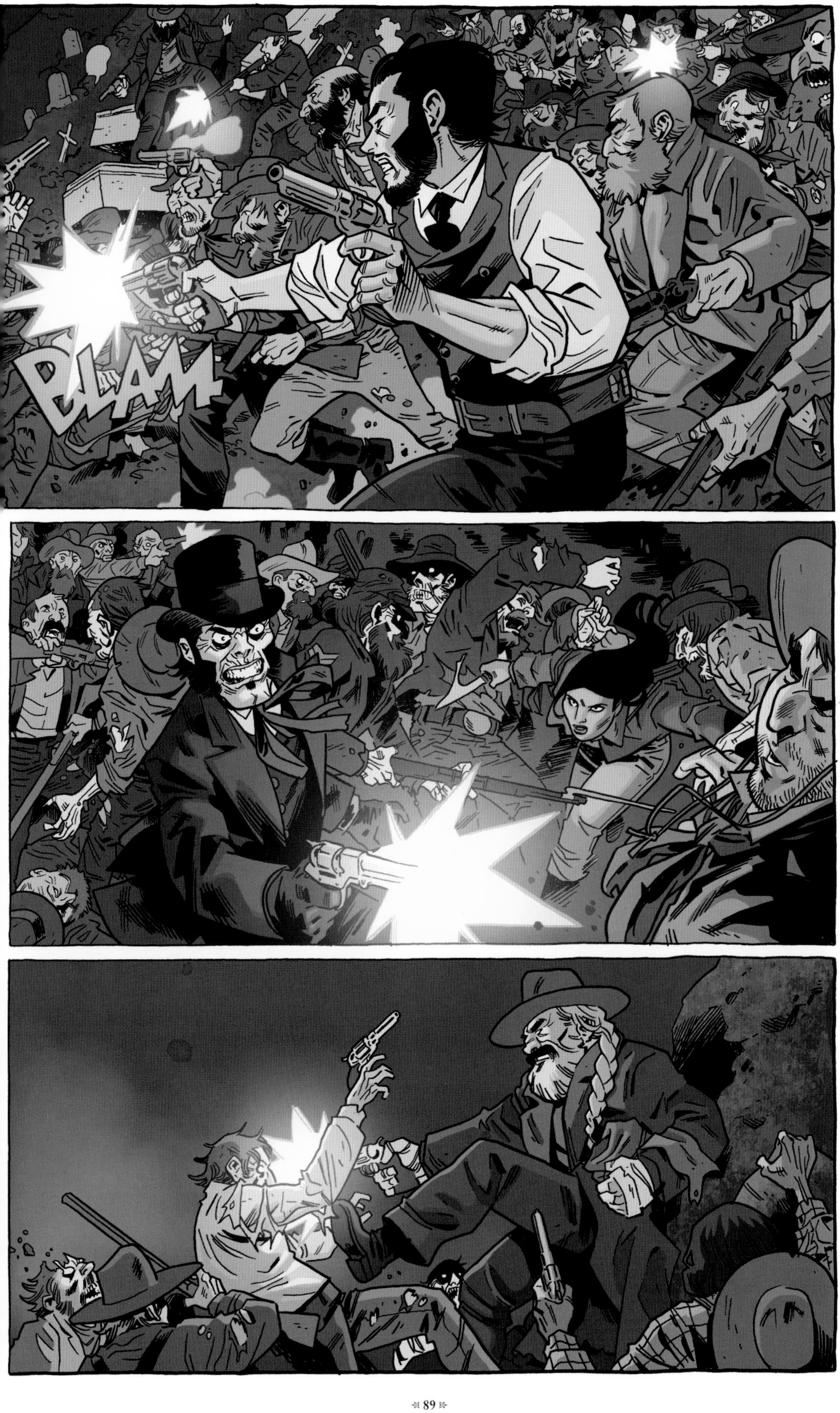
BLAM

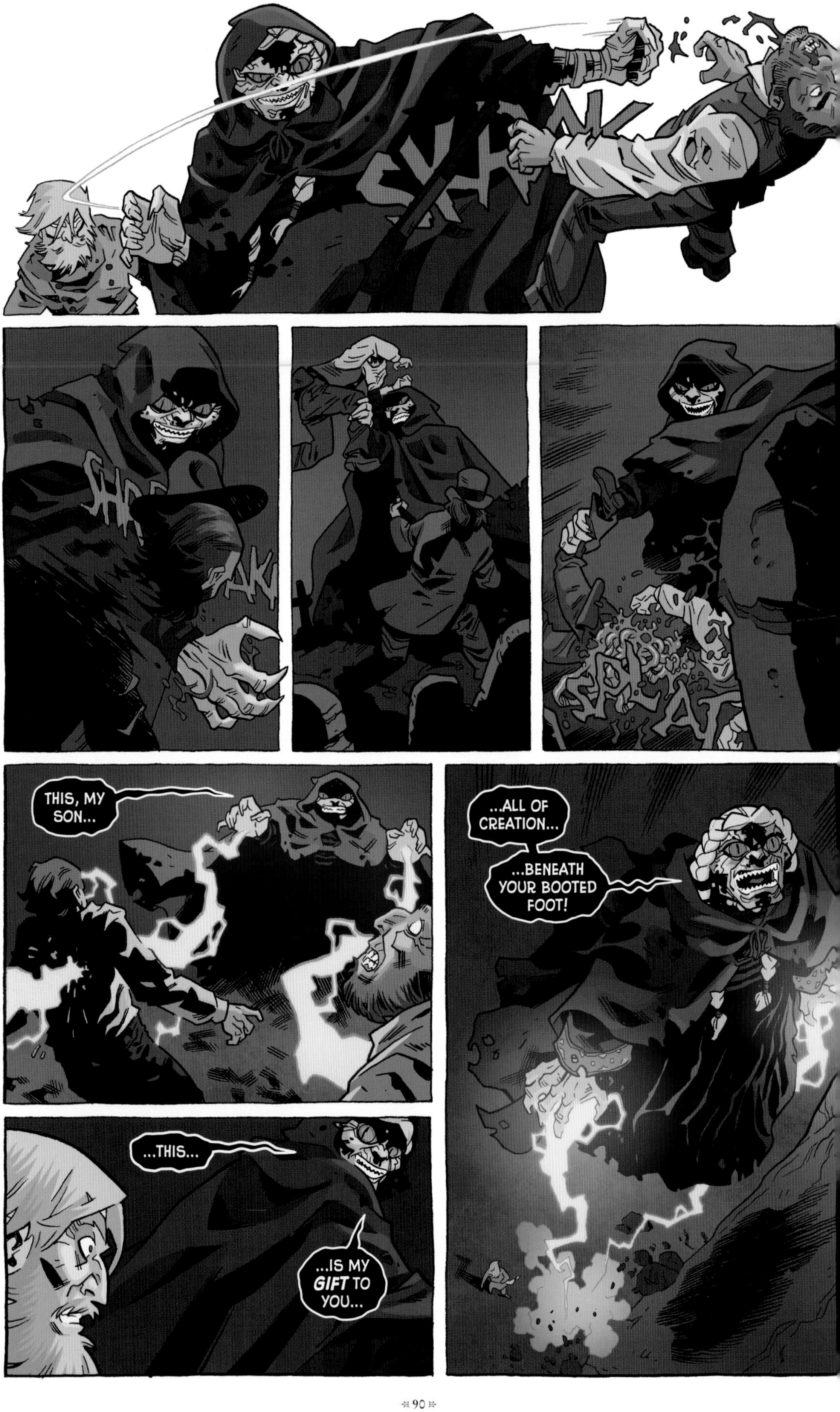
THIS, MY SON...
...THIS...
...IS MY *GIFT* TO YOU...
...ALL OF CREATION...
...BENEATH YOUR BOOTED FOOT!

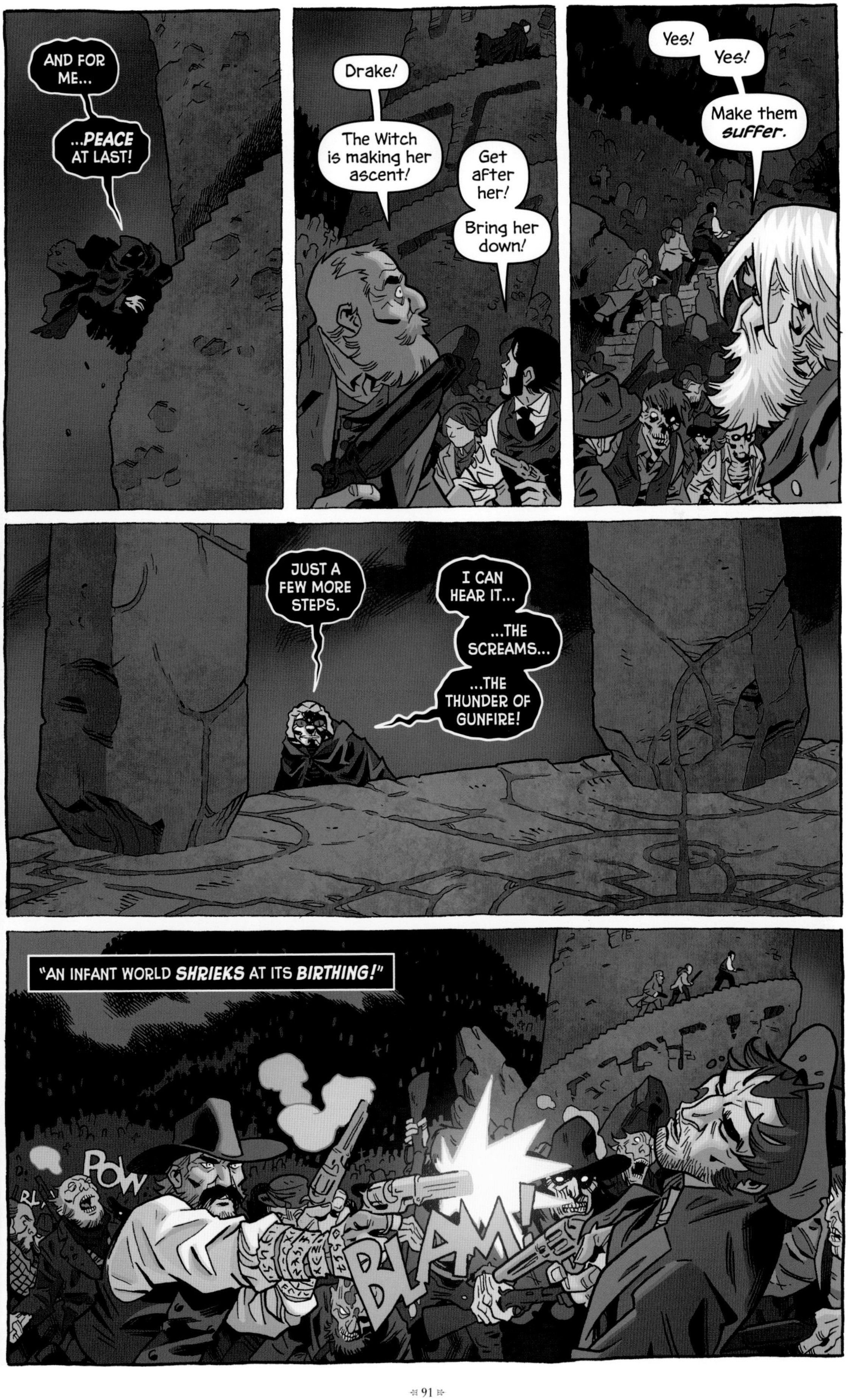

AND FOR ME...
...PEACE AT LAST!
Drake!
The Witch is making her ascent!
Get after her!
Bring her down!
Yes!
Yes!
Make them suffer.
JUST A FEW MORE STEPS.
I CAN HEAR IT...
...THE SCREAMS...
...THE THUNDER OF GUNFIRE!
"AN INFANT WORLD SHRIEKS AT ITS BIRTHING!"
POW
BLAM!

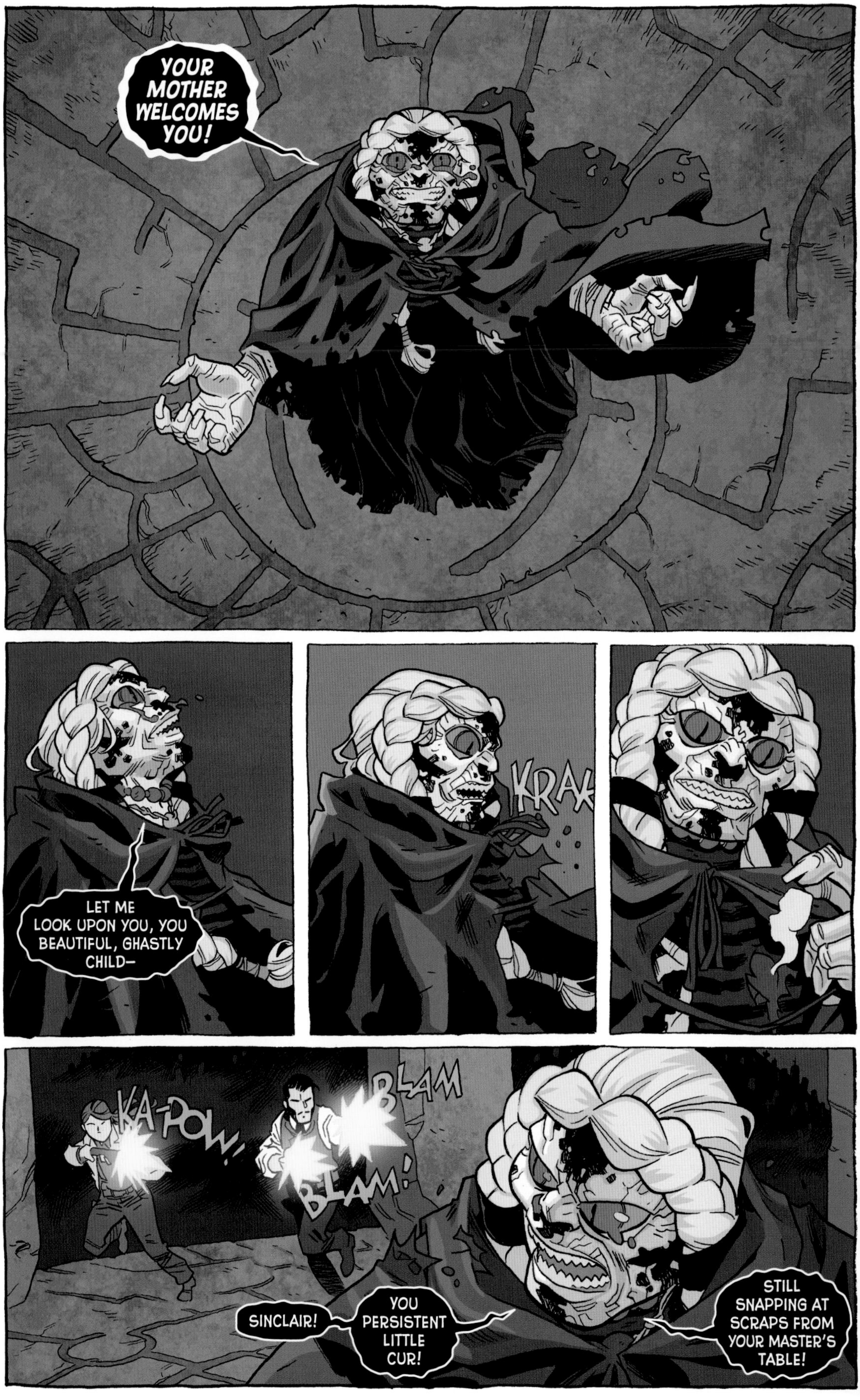
YOUR MOTHER WELCOMES YOU!
LET ME LOOK UPON YOU, YOU BEAUTIFUL, GHASTLY CHILD—
KRAK
KA-POW!
BLAM
BLAM!
SINCLAIR!
YOU PERSISTENT LITTLE CUR!
STILL SNAPPING AT SCRAPS FROM YOUR MASTER'S TABLE!

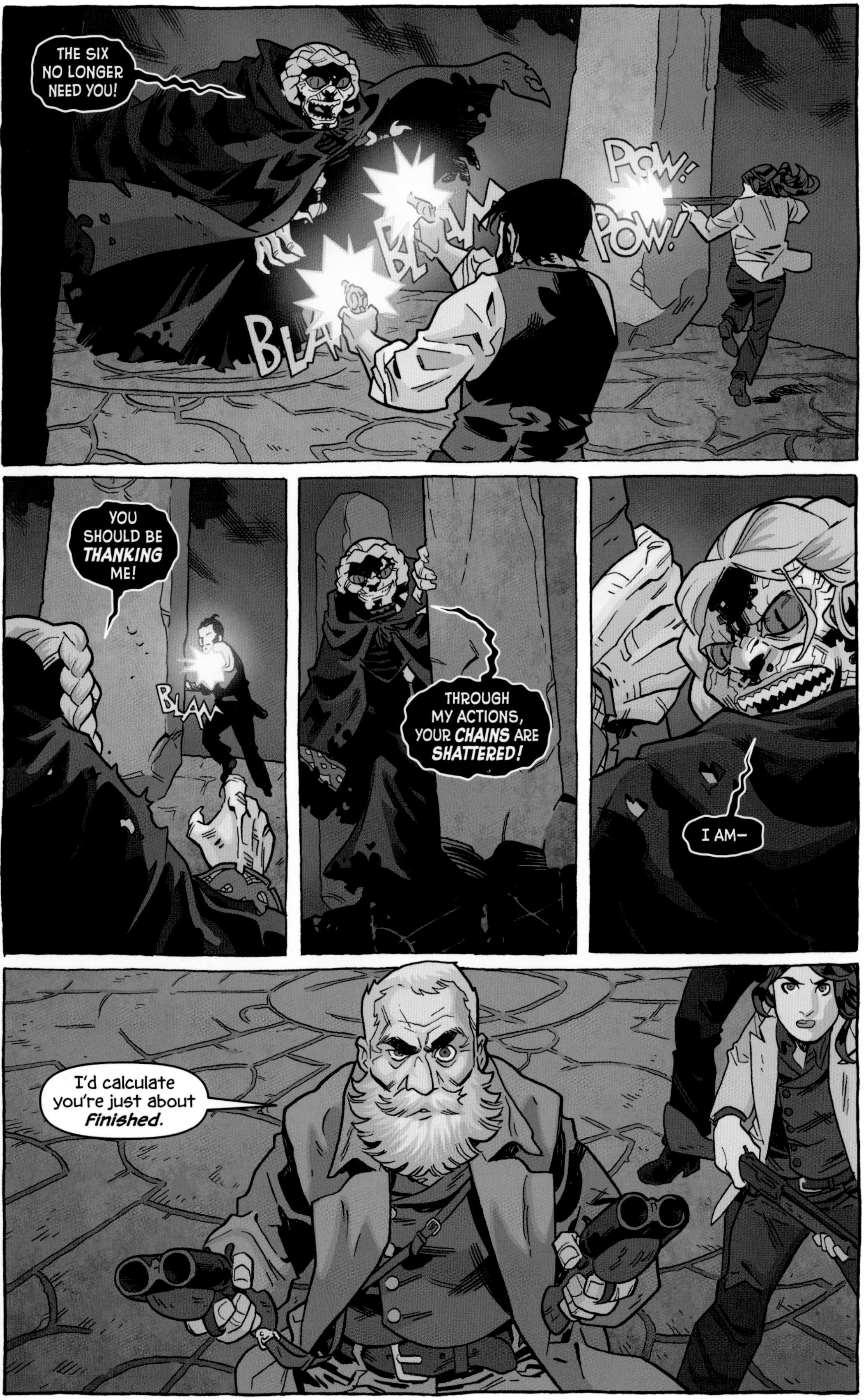
THE SIX NO LONGER NEED YOU!
POW!
POW!
BLAM
BLAM
YOU SHOULD BE THANKING ME!
BLAM
THROUGH MY ACTIONS, YOUR CHAINS ARE SHATTERED!
I AM—
I'd calculate you're just about Finished.

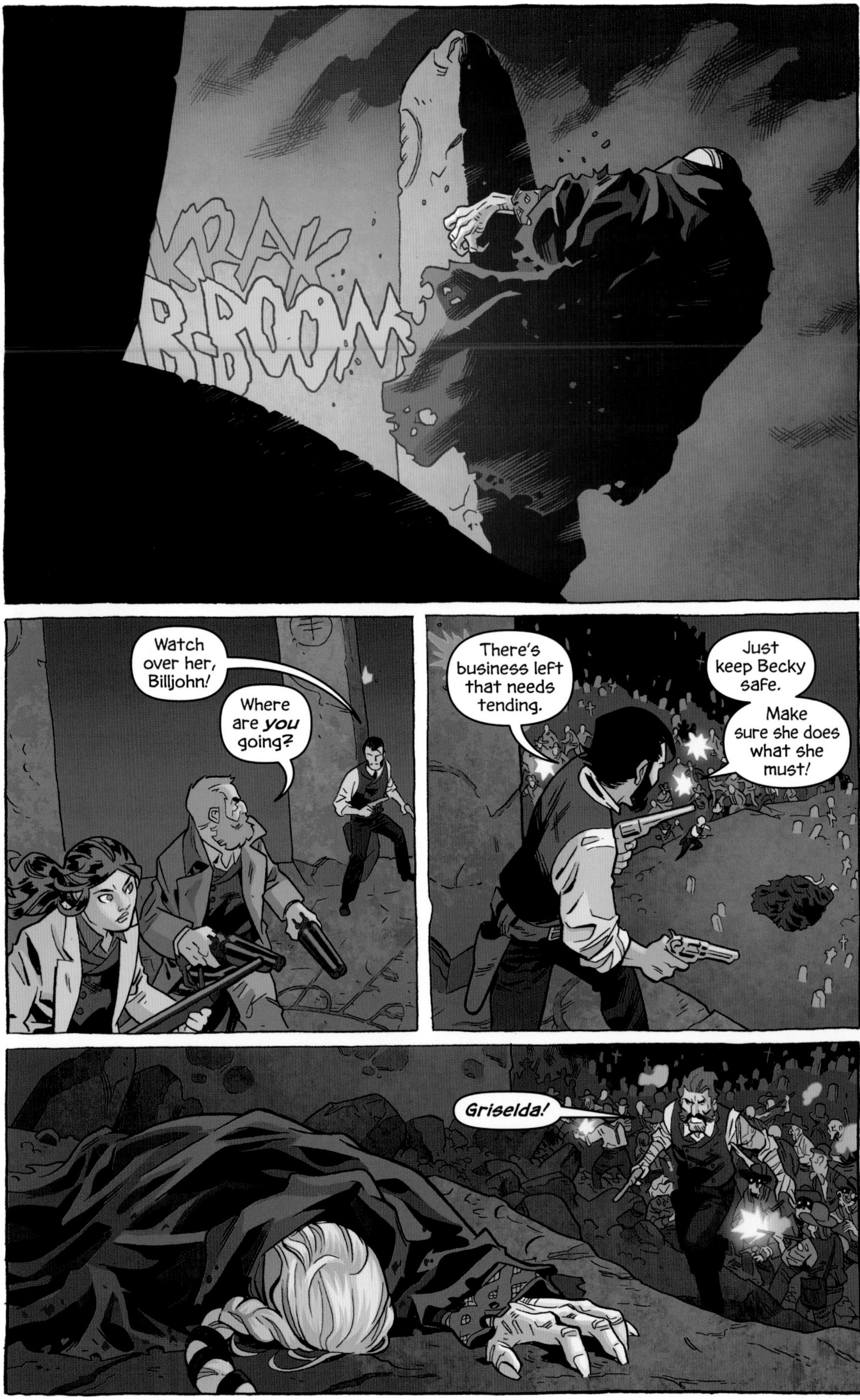
KRAK
B-BOOM
Watch over her, Billjohn!
Where are *you* going?
There's business left that needs tending.
Just keep Becky safe.
Make sure she does what she must!
Griselda!

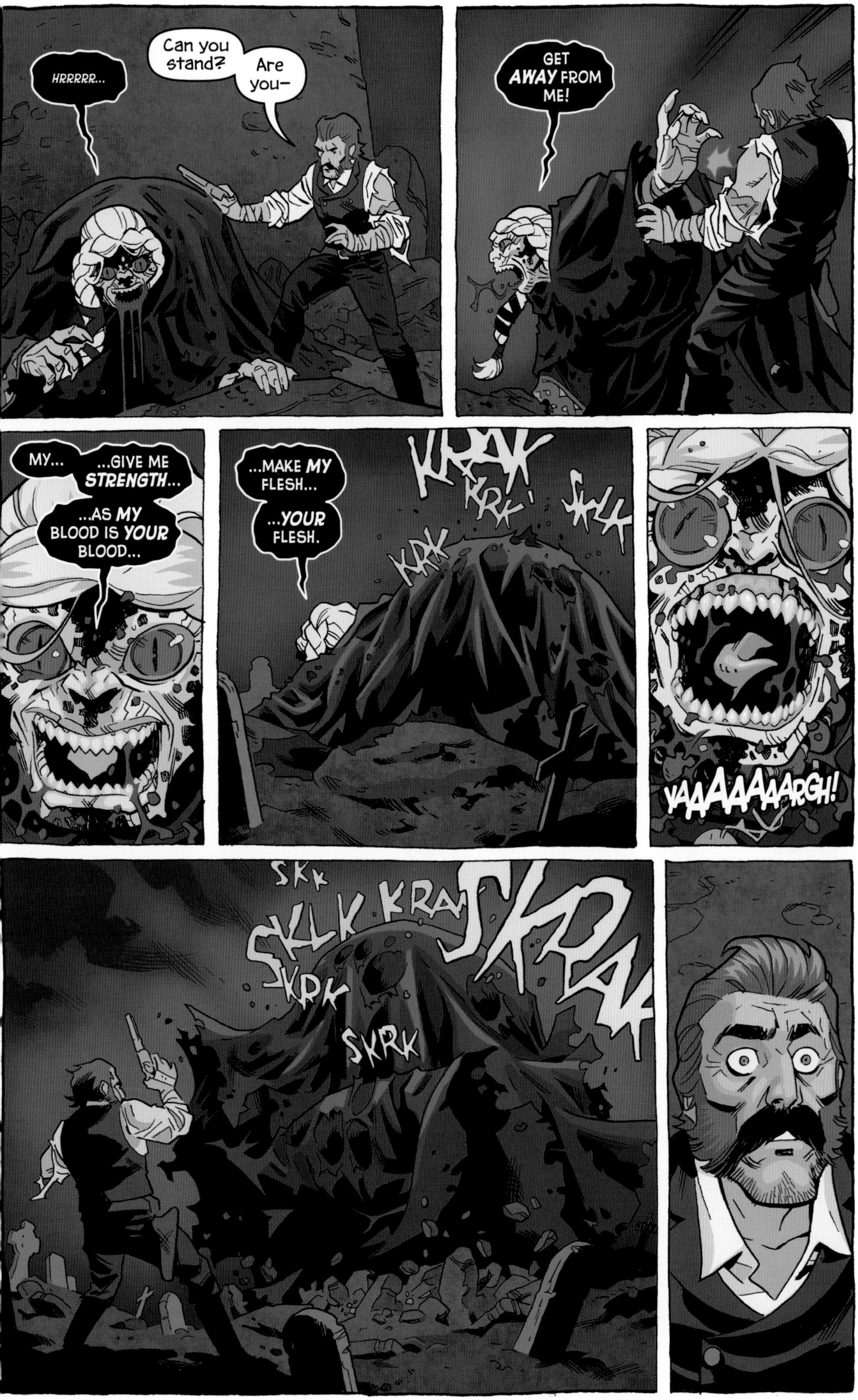
HRRRRR...
Can you stand?
Are you–
GET AWAY FROM ME!
MY...
...GIVE ME STRENGTH...
...AS MY BLOOD IS YOUR BLOOD...
...MAKE MY FLESH...
...YOUR FLESH.
KRAK
KRK!
SKLK
KRK
YAAAAAAARGH!
SKK
SKLK
KRA
SKRAK
SKRK
SKRK

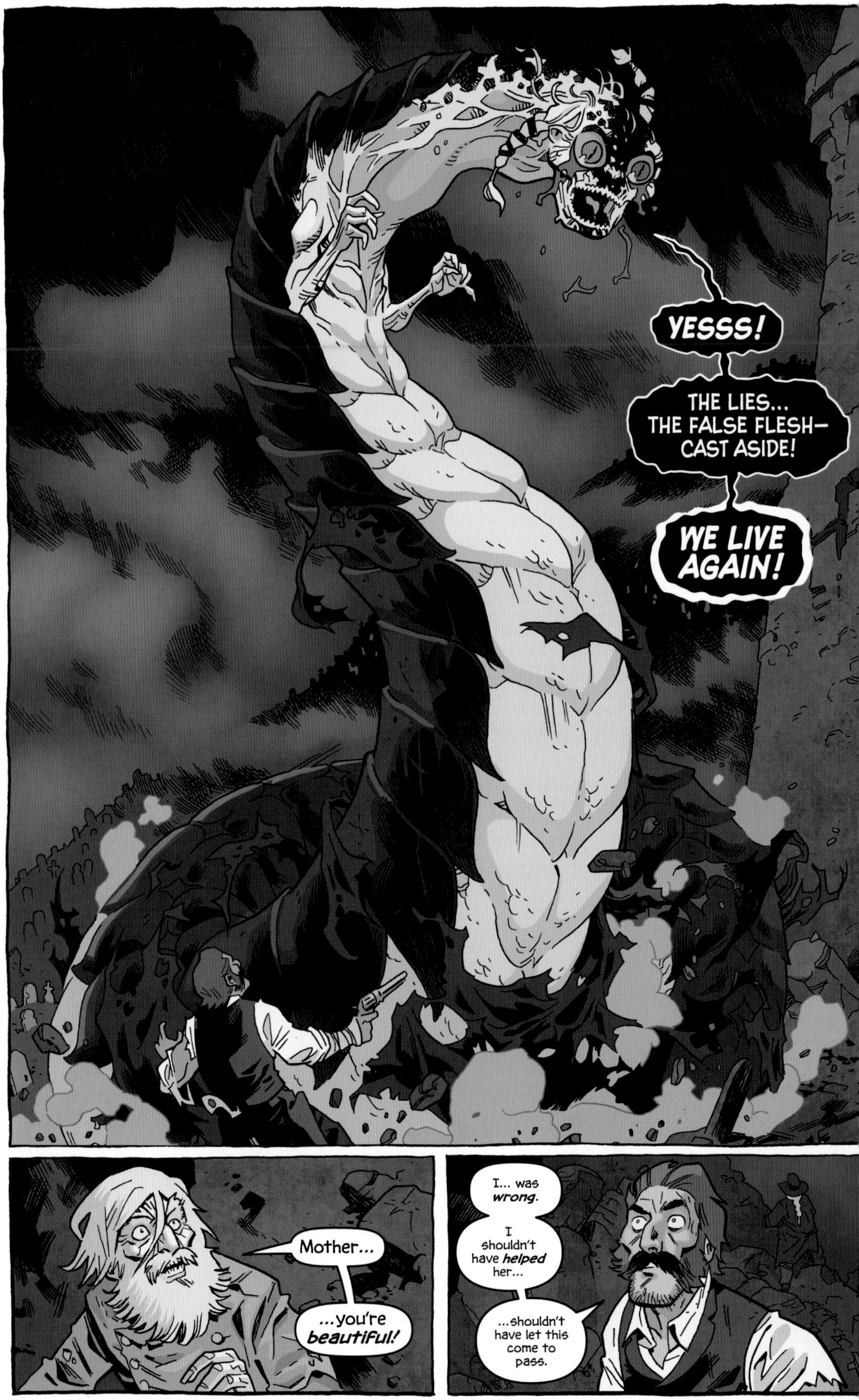
YESSS!
THE LIES... THE FALSE FLESH— CAST ASIDE!
WE LIVE AGAIN!
Mother...
...you're *beautiful!*
I... was *wrong*.
I shouldn't have *helped* her...
...shouldn't have let this come to pass.

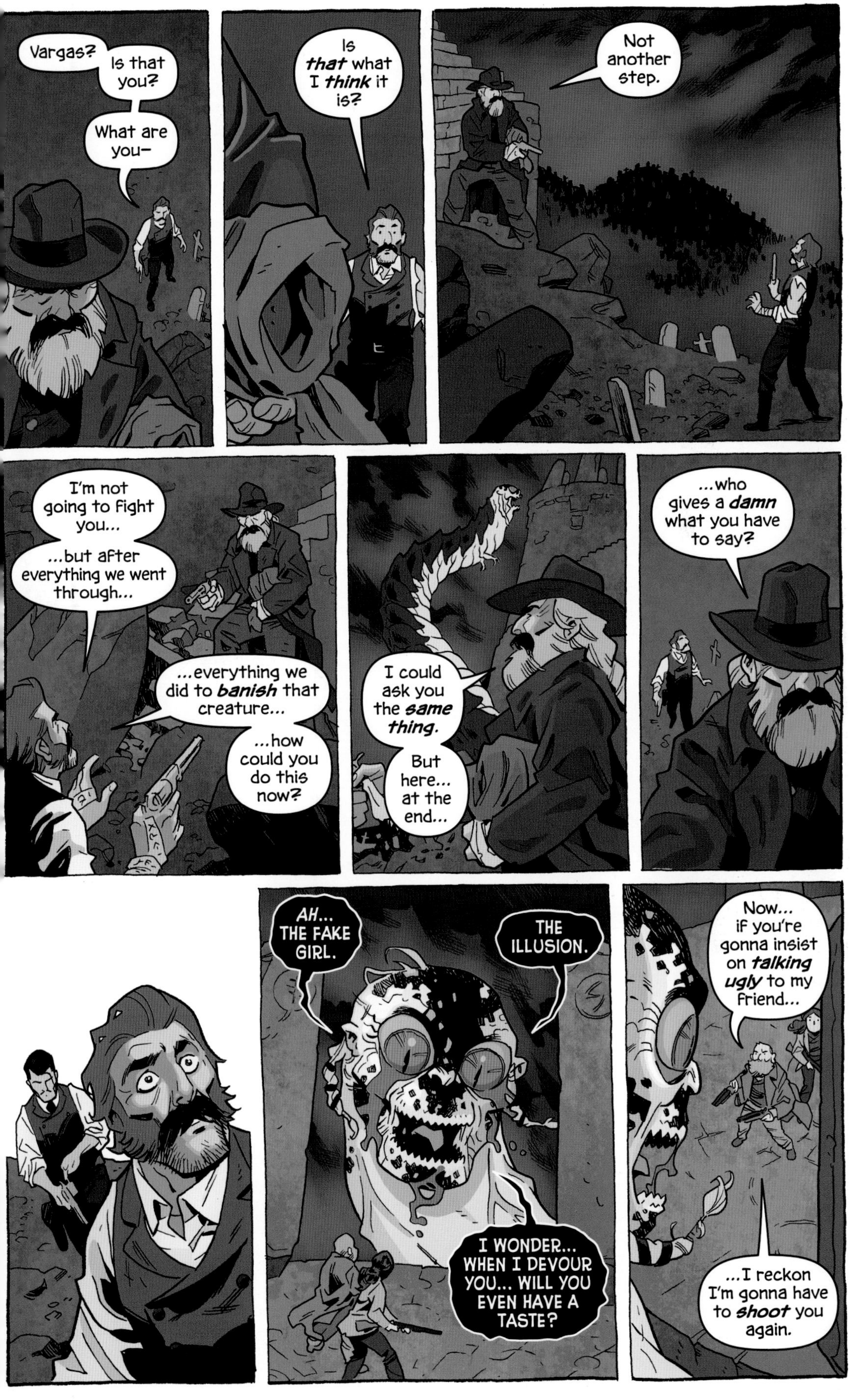
Vargas?
Is that you?
What are you–
Is *that* what I *think* it is?
Not another step.
I'm not going to fight you...
...but after everything we went through...
...everything we did to *banish* that creature...
...how could you do this now?
I could ask you the *same thing*.
But here... at the end...
...who gives a *damn* what you have to say?
AH... THE FAKE GIRL.
THE ILLUSION.
I WONDER... WHEN I DEVOUR YOU... WILL YOU EVEN HAVE A TASTE?
Now... if you're gonna insist on *talking ugly* to my friend...
...I reckon I'm gonna have to *shoot* you again.

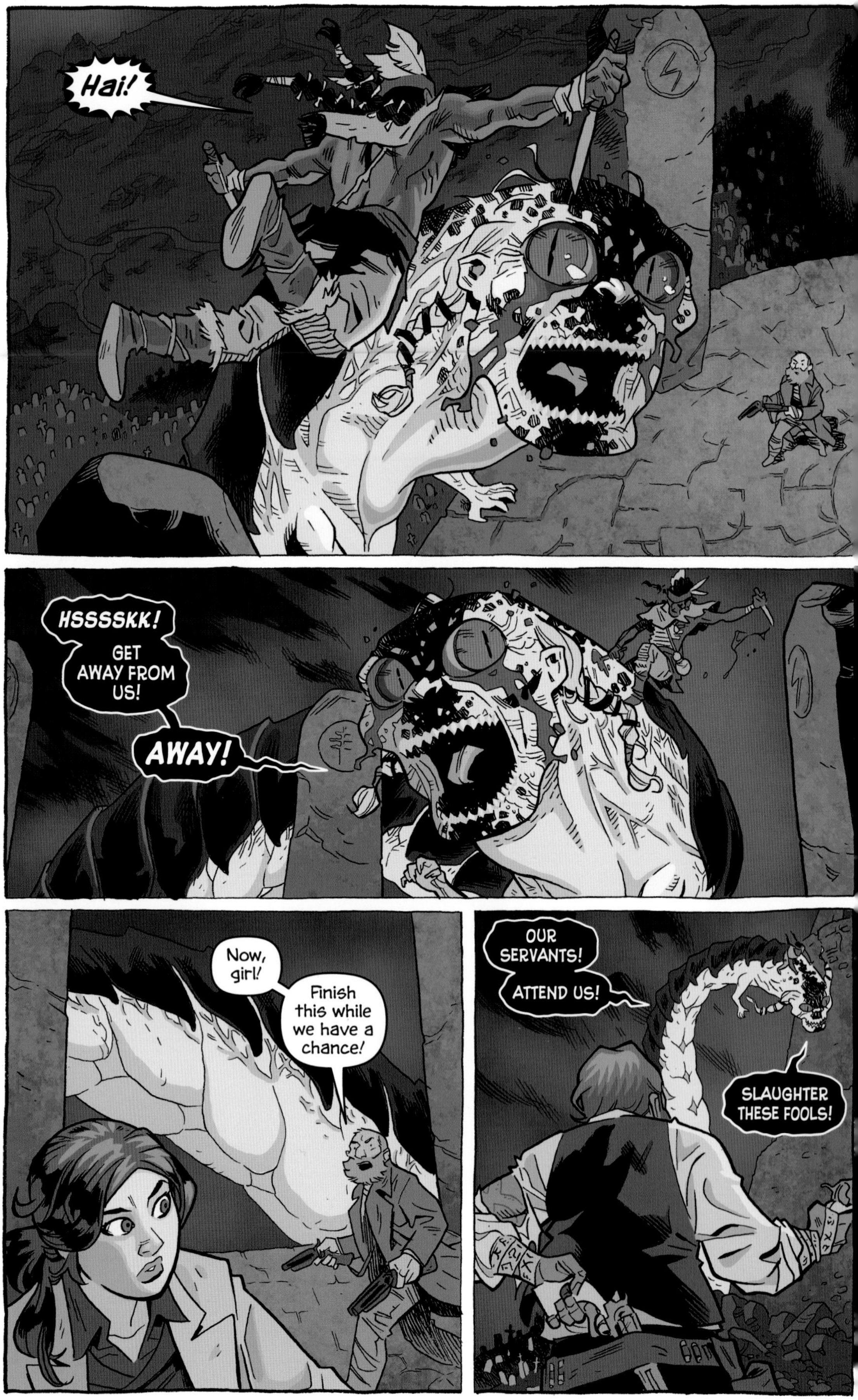
Hai!
HSSSSKK! GET AWAY FROM US!
AWAY!
Now, girl!
Finish this while we have a chance!
OUR SERVANTS!
ATTEND US!
SLAUGHTER THESE FOOLS!

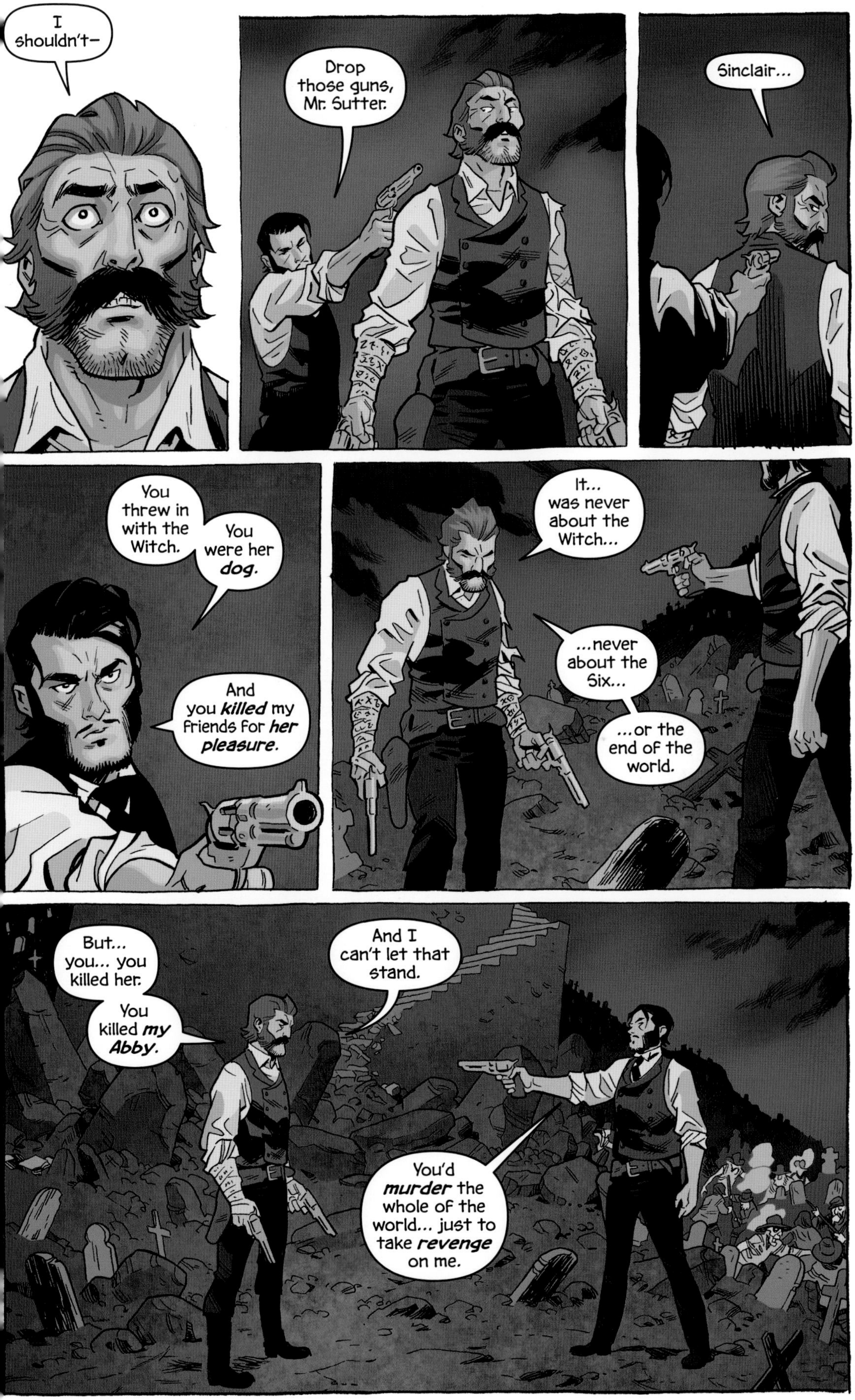
I shouldn't–
Drop those guns, Mr. Sutter.
Sinclair...
You threw in with the Witch.
You were her **dog**.
And you **killed** my friends for **her pleasure**.
It... was never about the Witch...
...never about the Six...
...or the end of the world.
But... you... you killed her.
You killed **my Abby**.
And I can't let that stand.
You'd **murder** the whole of the world... just to take **revenge** on me.

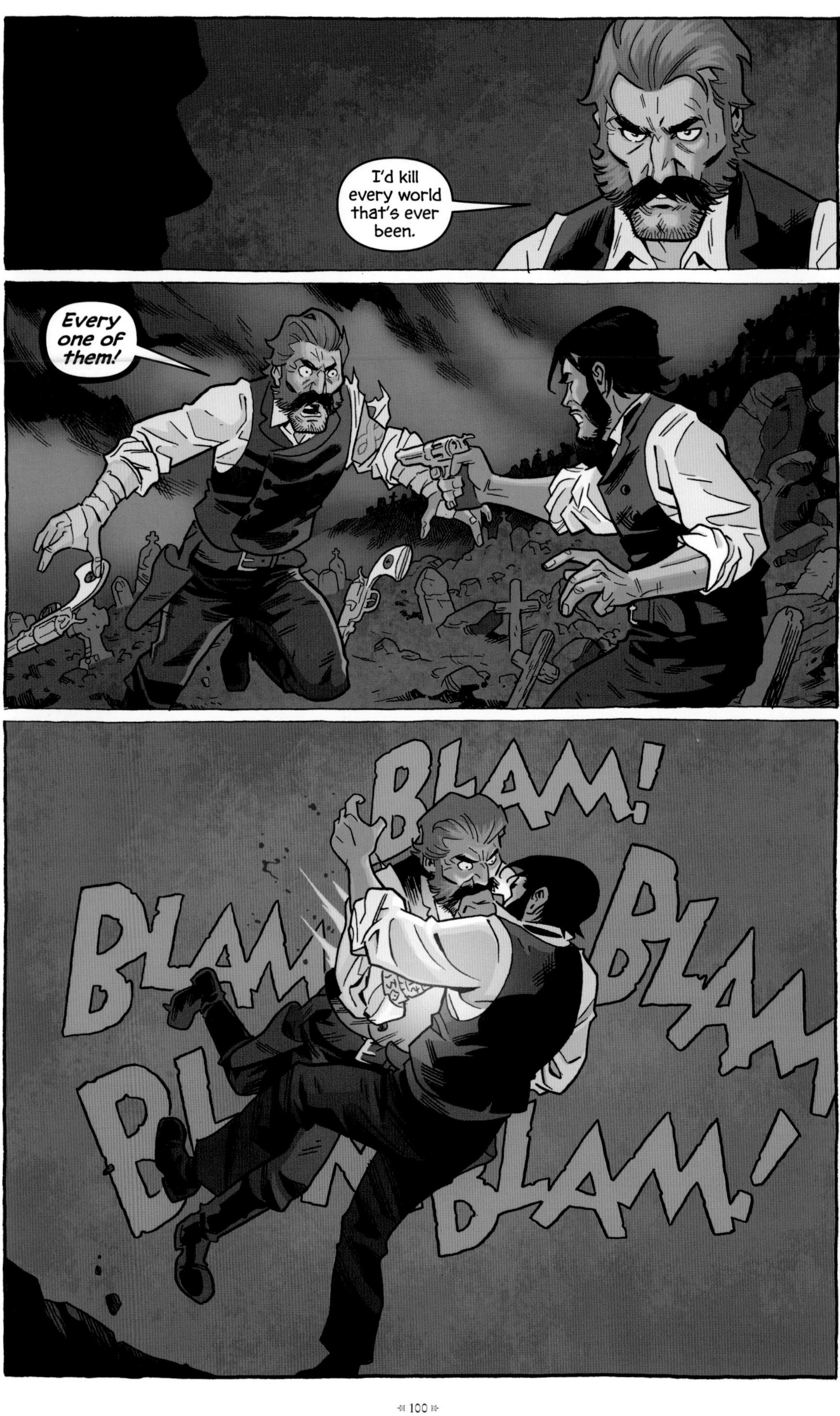
I'd kill every world that's ever been.
Every one of them!
BLAM!
BLAM!
BLAM!
BLAM!
BLAM!

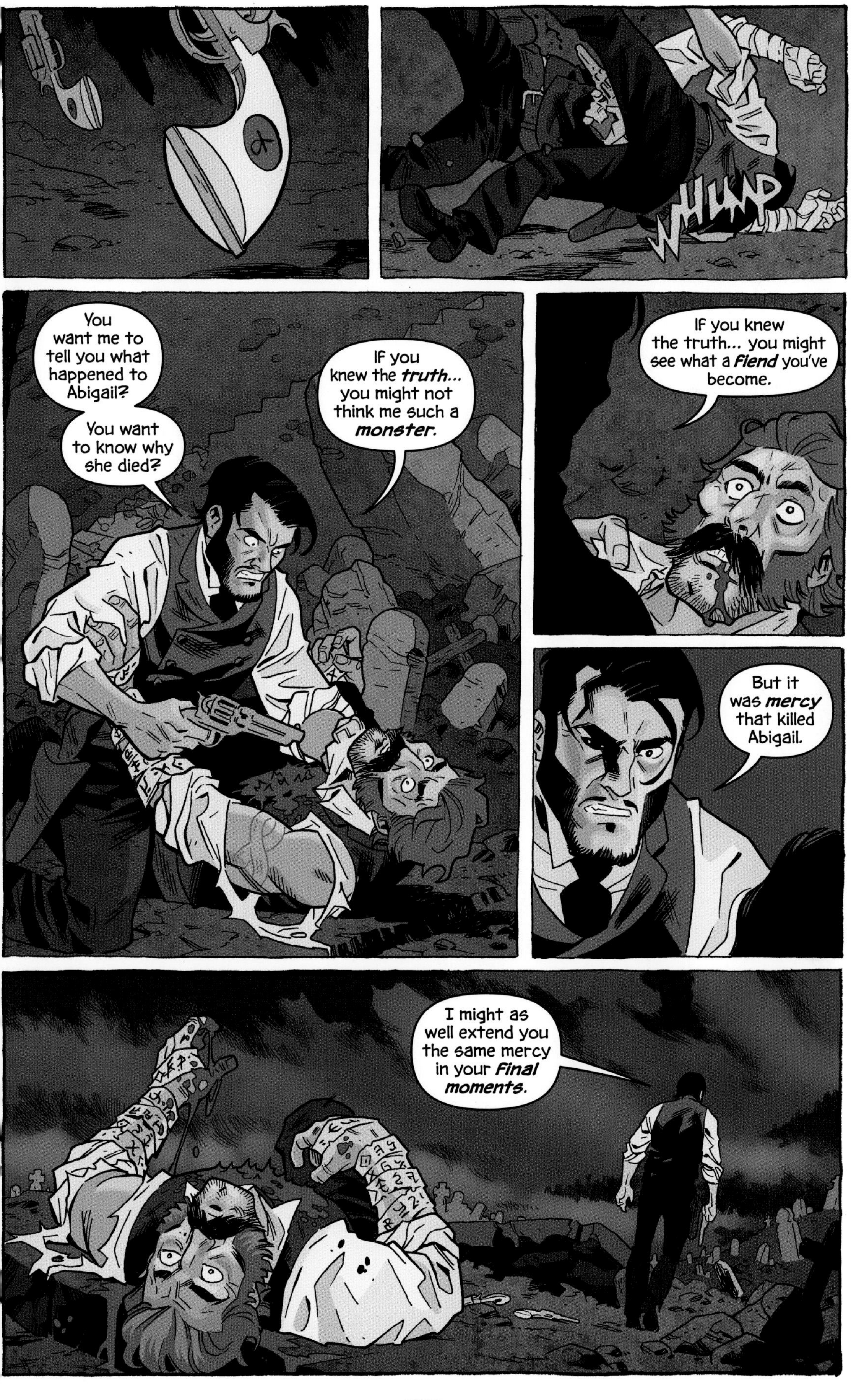

WHUMP
You want me to tell you what happened to Abigail?
You want to know why she died?
If you knew the truth... you might not think me such a monster.
If you knew the truth... you might see what a fiend you've become.
But it was mercy that killed Abigail.
I might as well extend you the same mercy in your final moments.

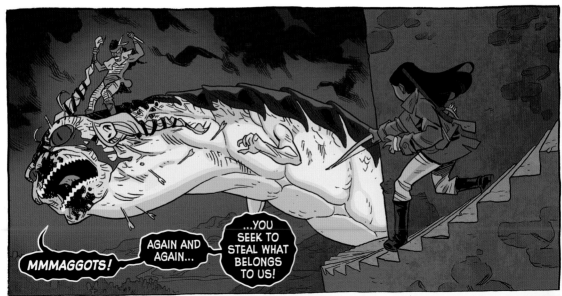

MMMAGGOTS!

AGAIN AND AGAIN...

...YOU SEEK TO STEAL WHAT BELONGS TO US!

AND NOW WE'LL BREAK OUR LONG FAST—

—UPON YOUR TREACHEROUS MEAT!

KRAK

THWP

Unnf!

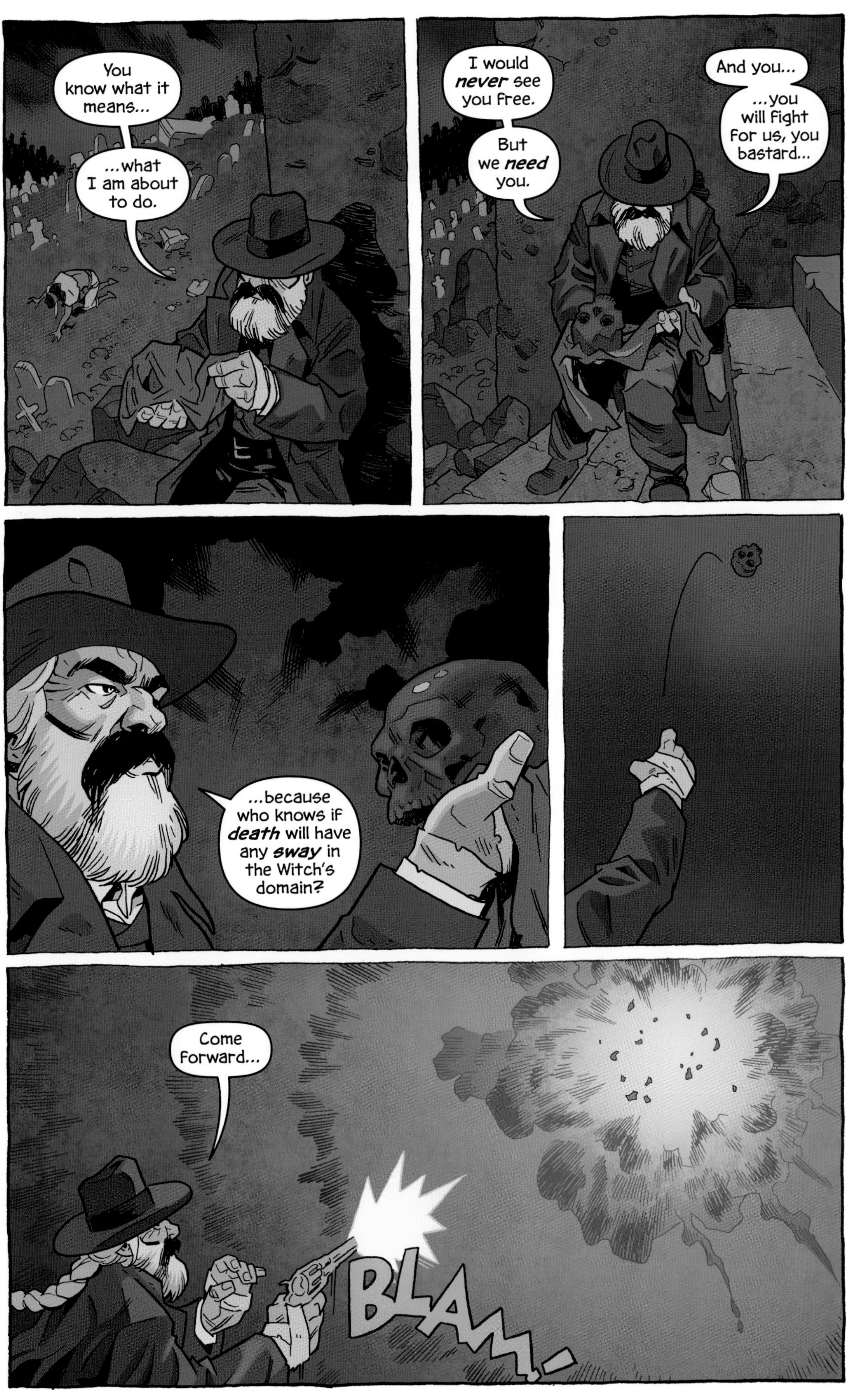
You know what it means...
...what I am about to do.
I would *never* see you free.
But we *need* you.
And you...
...you will fight for us, you bastard...
...because who knows if *death* will have any *sway* in the Witch's domain?
Come forward...
BLAM!

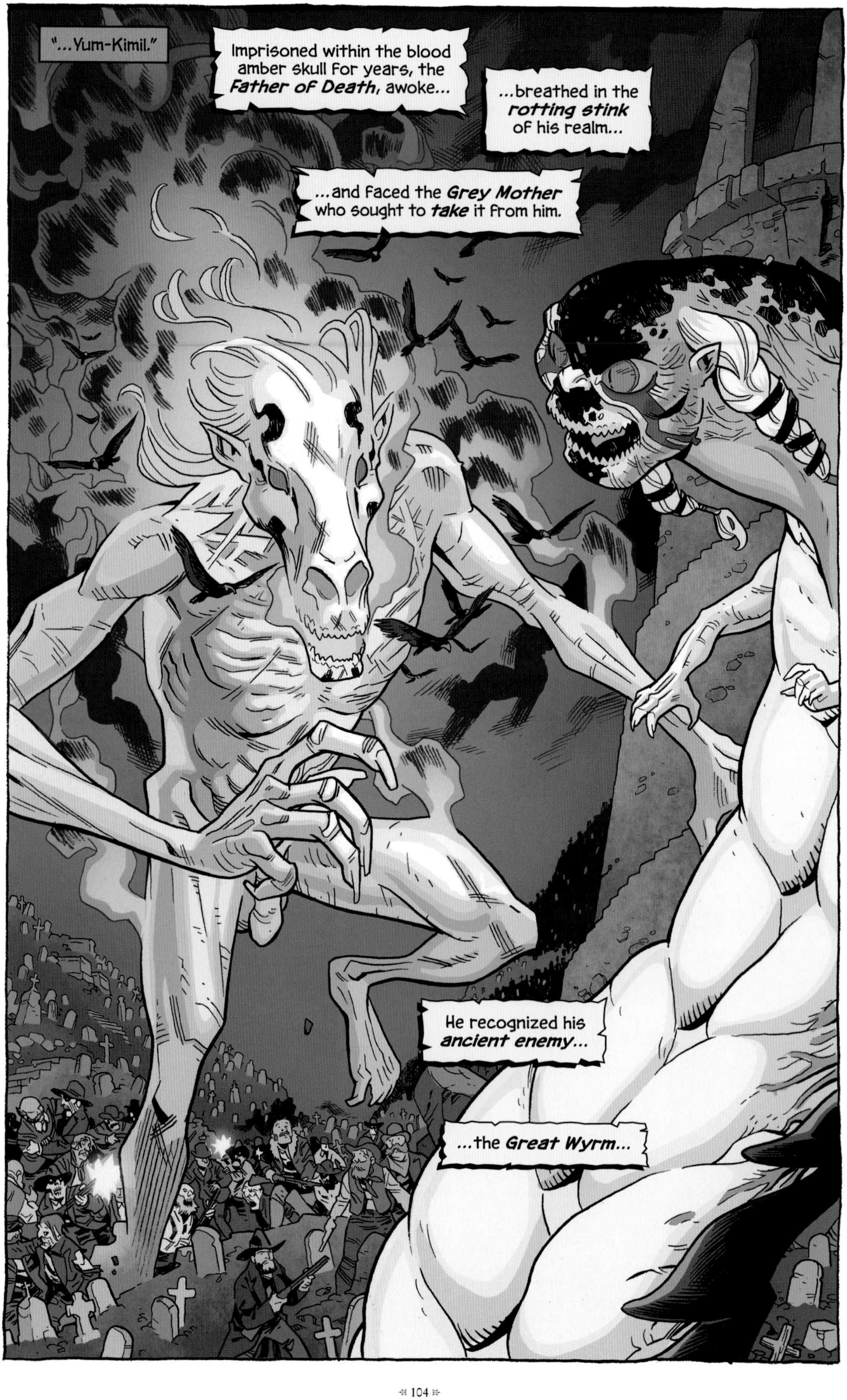
"...Yum-Kimil."
Imprisoned within the blood amber skull for years, the *Father of Death*, awoke...
...breathed in the *rotting stink* of his realm...
...and faced the *Grey Mother* who sought to *take* it from him.
He recognized his *ancient enemy*...
...the *Great Wyrm*...

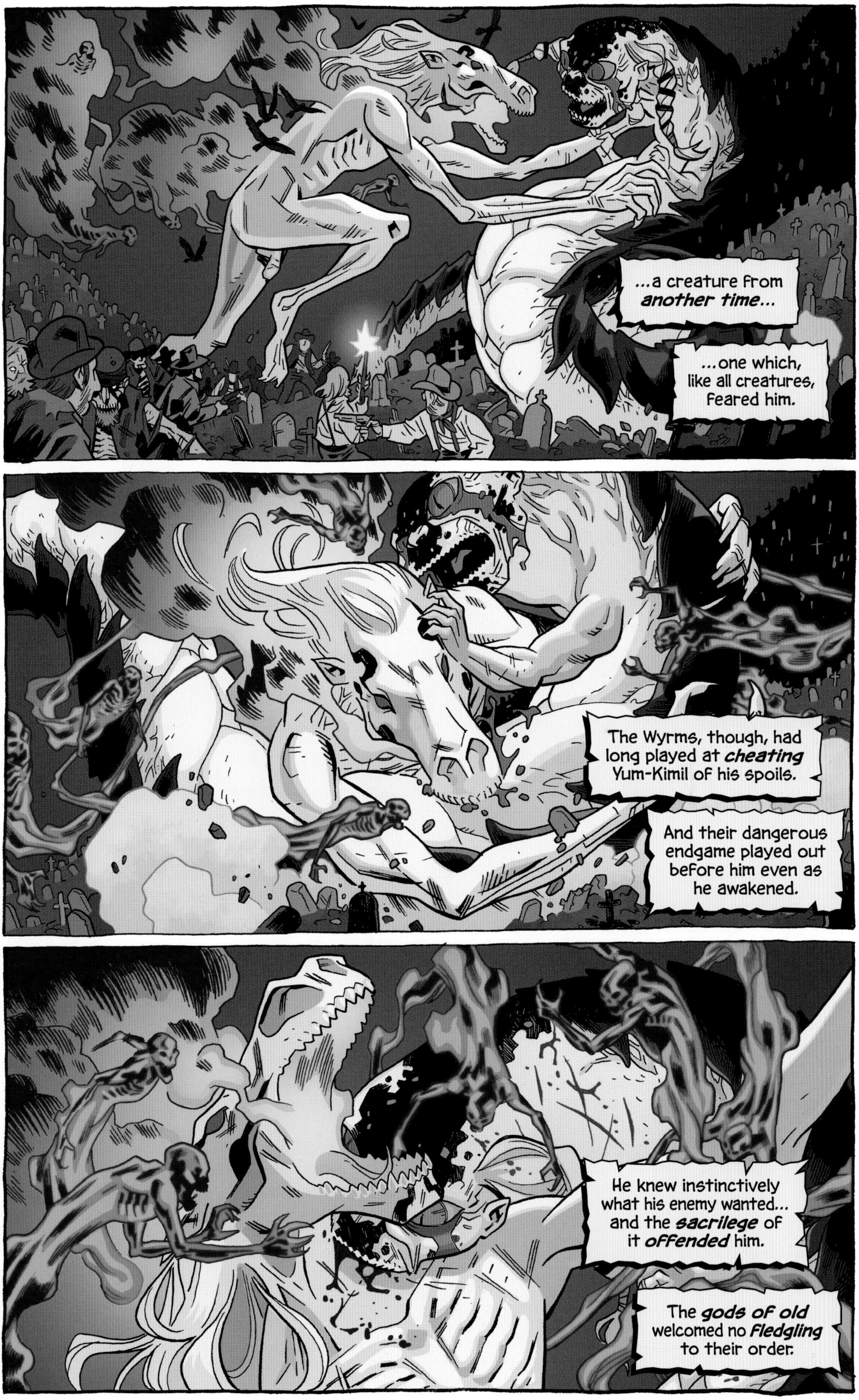
...a creature from *another time*...
...one which, like all creatures, feared him.
The Wyrms, though, had long played at *cheating* Yum-Kimil of his spoils.
And their dangerous endgame played out before him even as he awakened.
He knew instinctively what his enemy wanted... and the *sacrilege* of it *offended* him.
The *gods of old* welcomed no *fledgling* to their order.

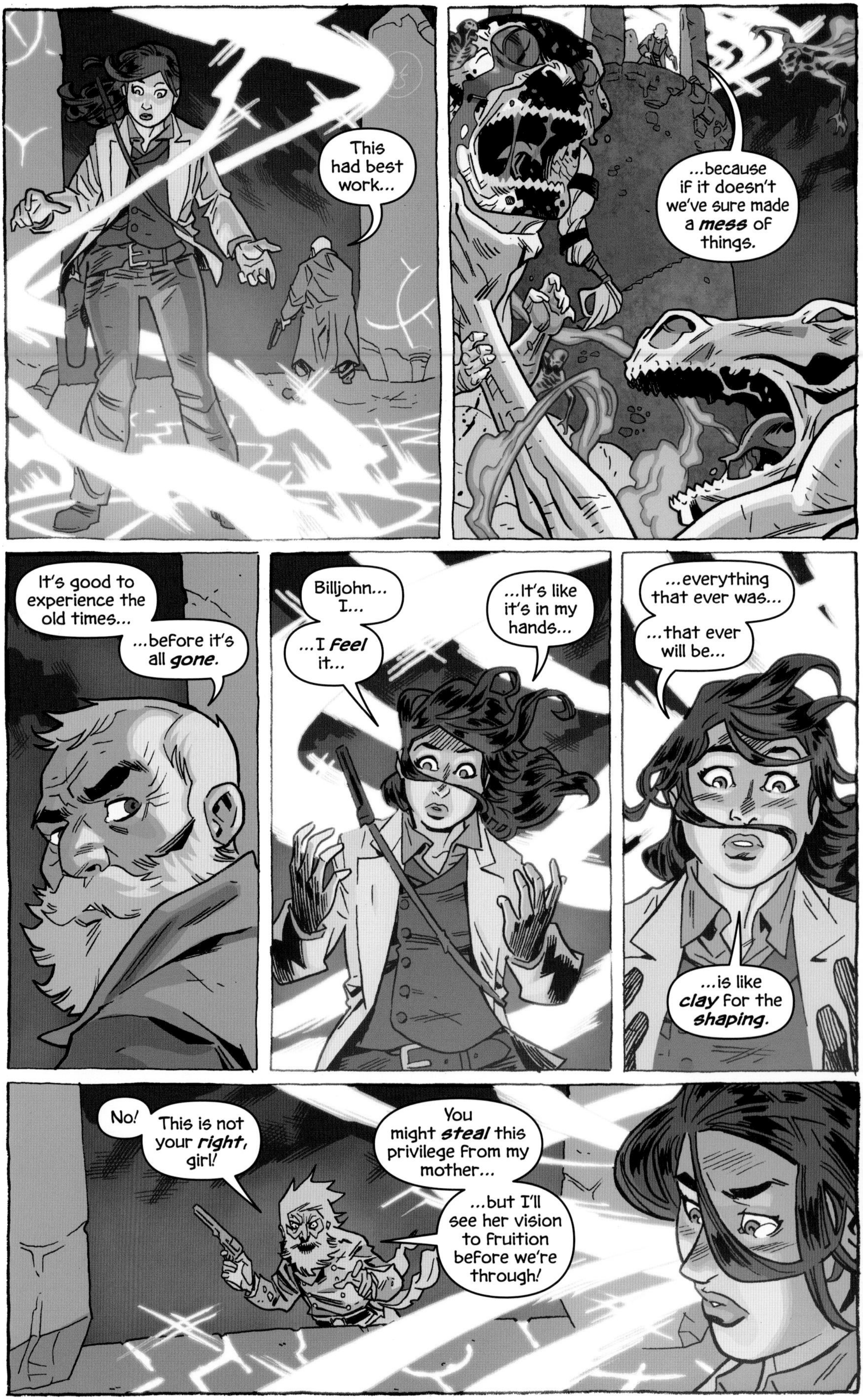
This had best work...
...because if it doesn't we've sure made a *mess* of things.
It's good to experience the old times...
...before it's all *gone*.
Billjohn... I...
...I *feel* it...
...It's like it's in my hands...
...everything that ever was...
...that ever will be...
...is like *clay* for the *shaping*.
No!
This is not your *right*, girl!
You might *steal* this privilege from my mother...
...but I'll see her vision to fruition before we're through!

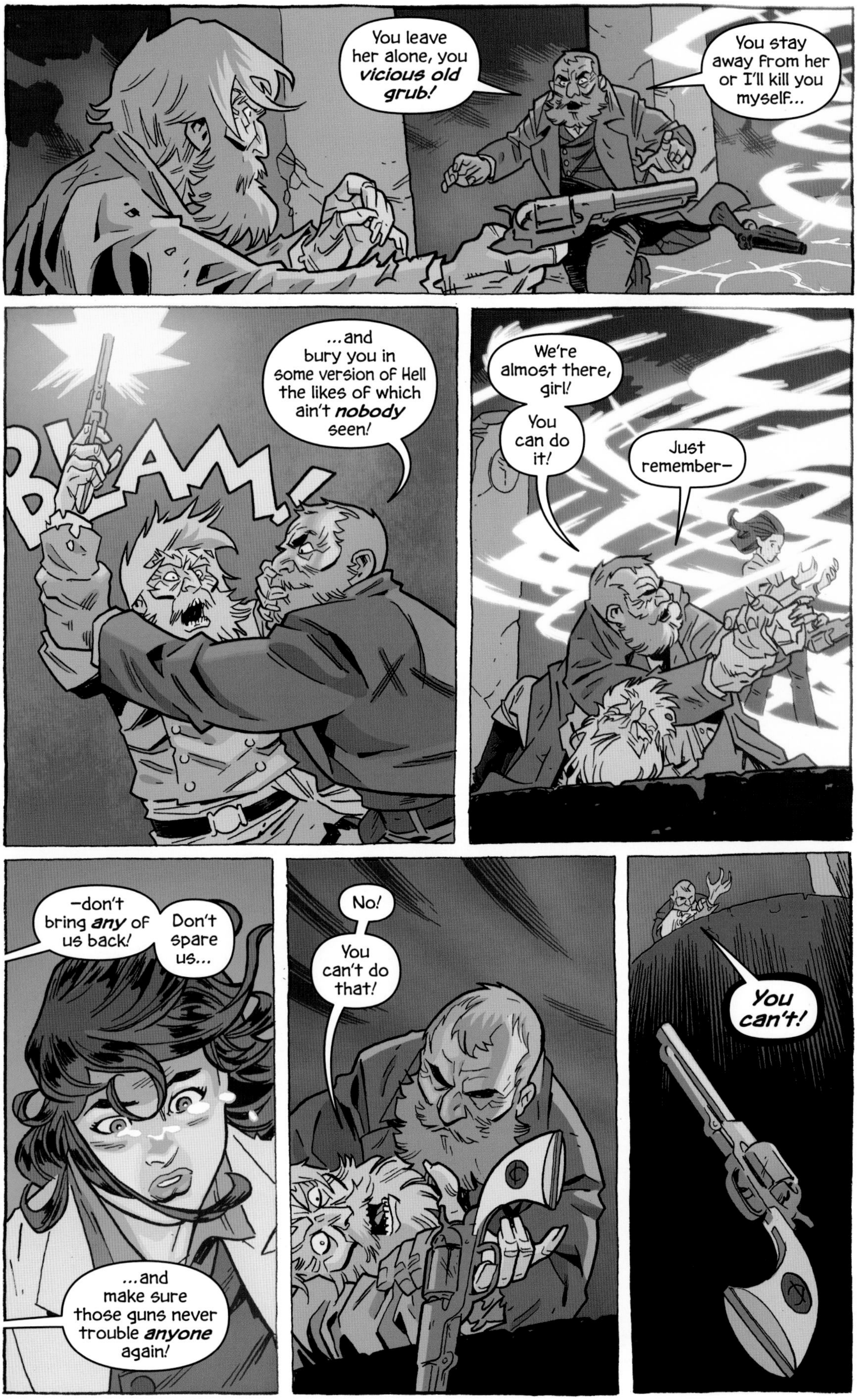

You leave her alone, you *vicious old grub!*
You stay away from her or I'll kill you myself...
...and bury you in some version of Hell the likes of which ain't *nobody* seen!
BLAM!
We're almost there, girl!
You can do it!
Just remember–
–don't bring *any* of us back!
Don't spare us...
...and make sure those guns never trouble *anyone* again!
No!
You can't do that!
You can't!

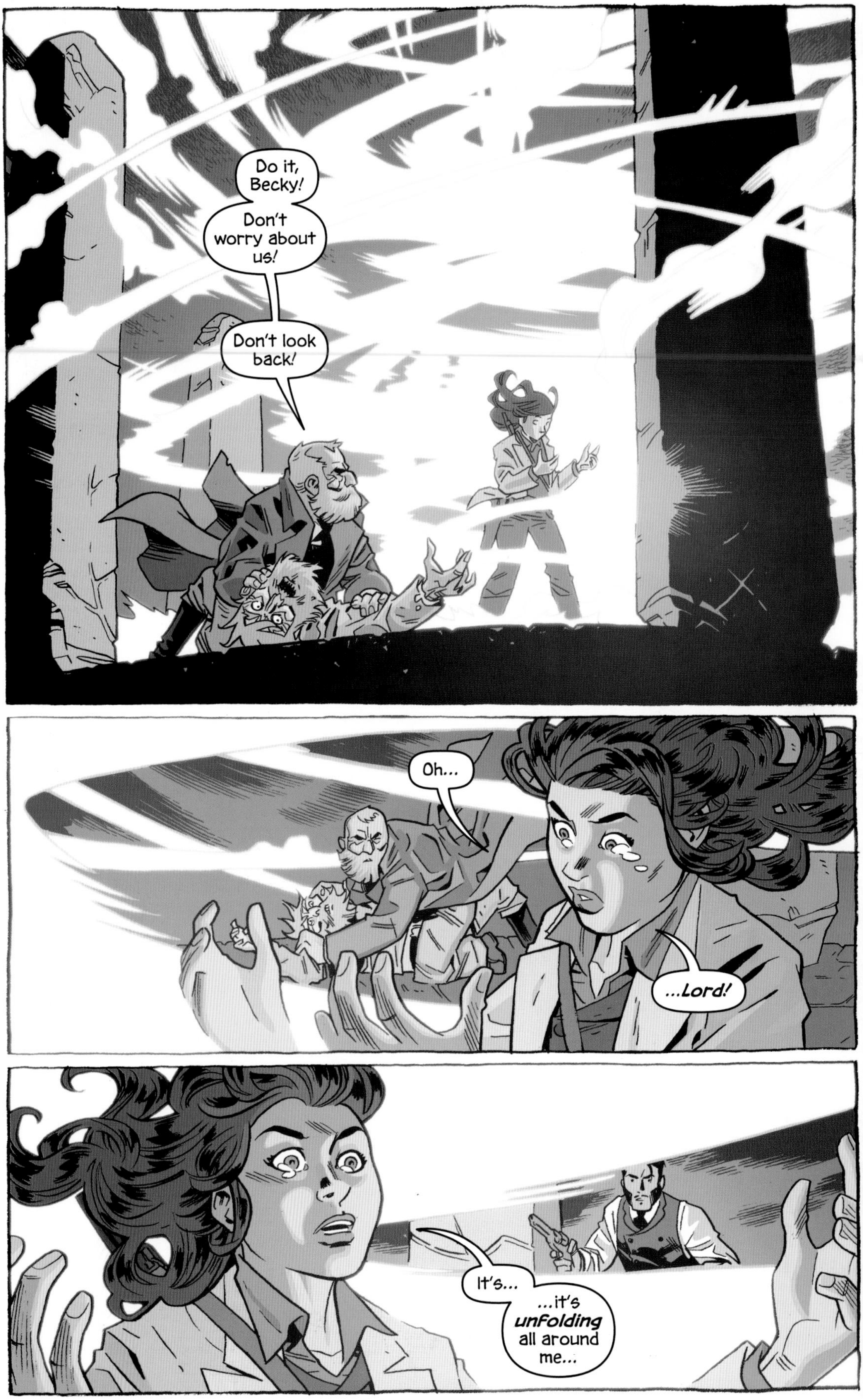
Do it, Becky!
Don't worry about us!
Don't look back!
Oh...
...*Lord!*
It's...
...it's *unfolding* all around me...

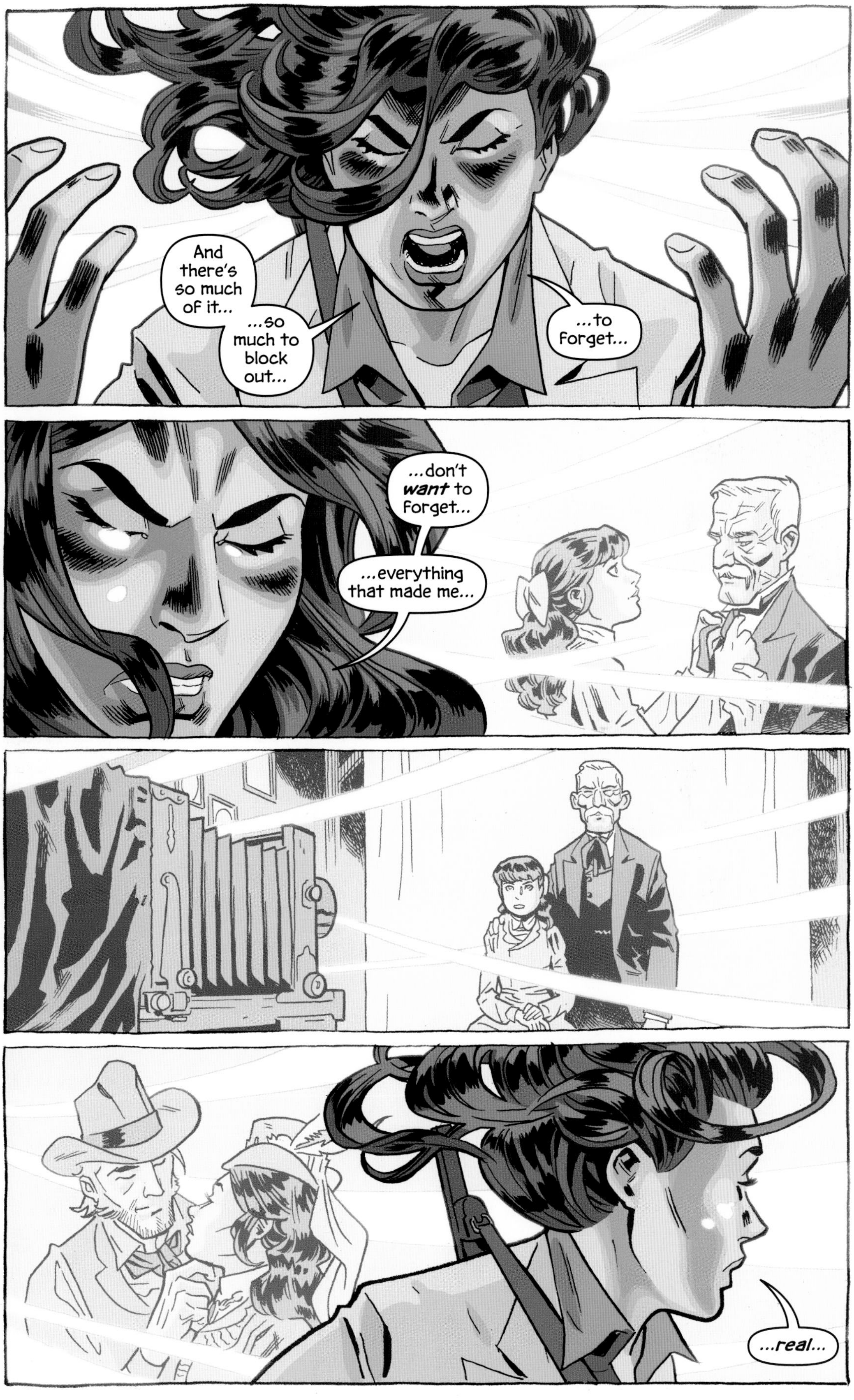
And there's so much of it...
...so much to block out...
...to forget...
...don't *want* to forget...
...everything that made me...
...real...

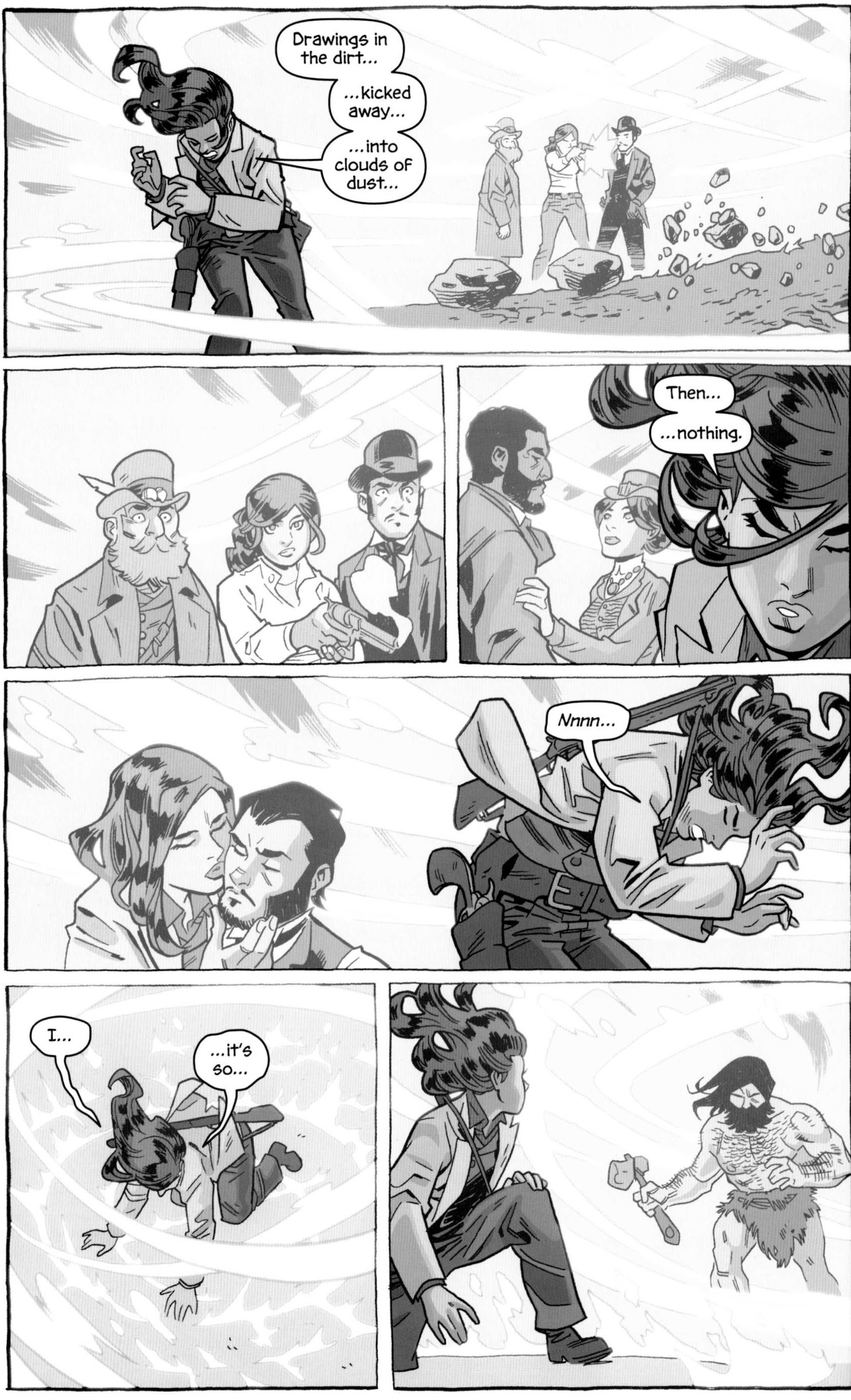
Drawings in the dirt...
...kicked away...
...into clouds of dust...
Then...
...nothing.
Nnnn...
I...
...it's so...

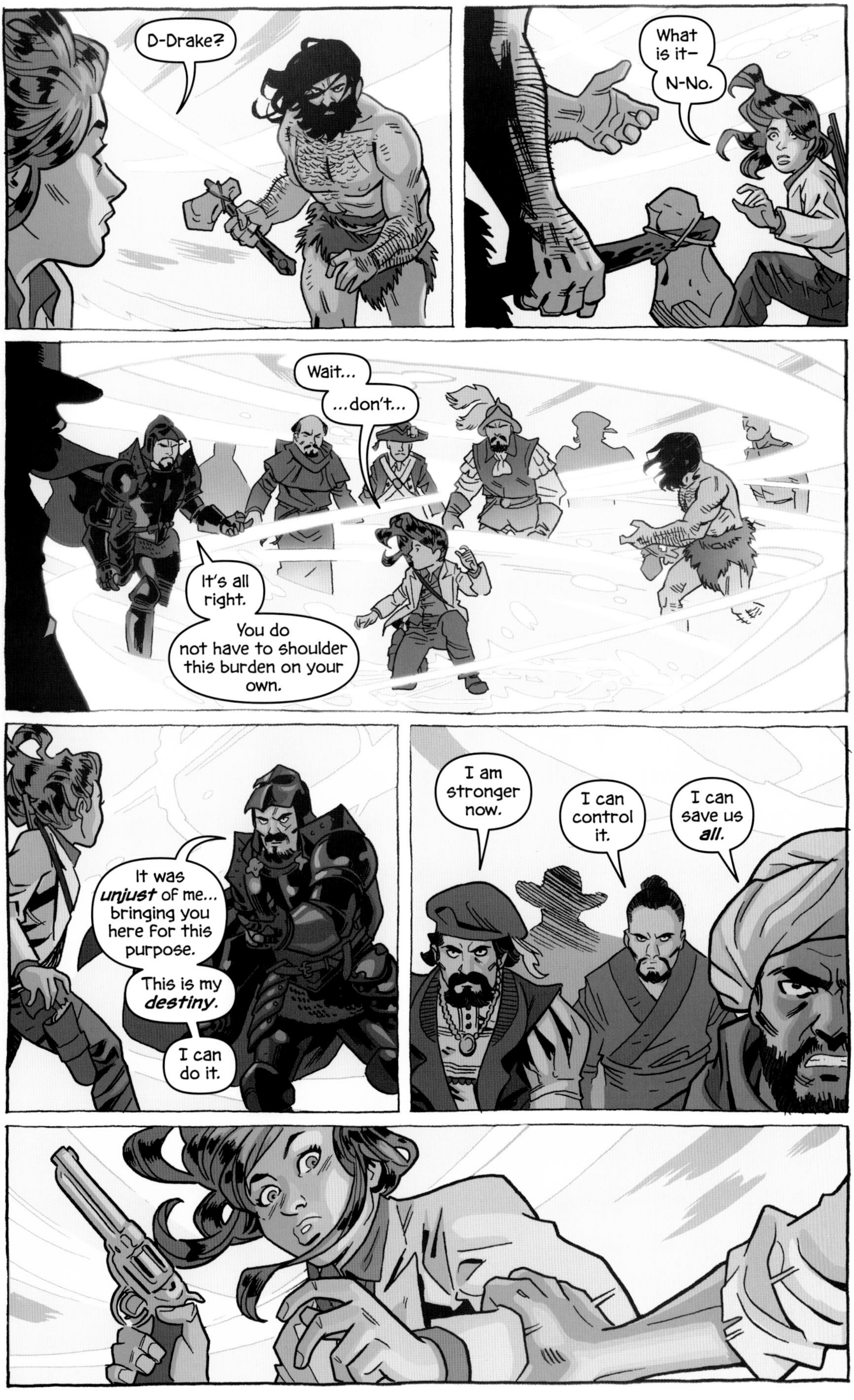
D-Drake?
What is it—
N-No.
Wait...
...don't...
It's all right.
You do not have to shoulder this burden on your own.
It was *unjust* of me... bringing you here for this purpose.
This is my *destiny*.
I can do it.
I am stronger now.
I can control it.
I can save us *all*.

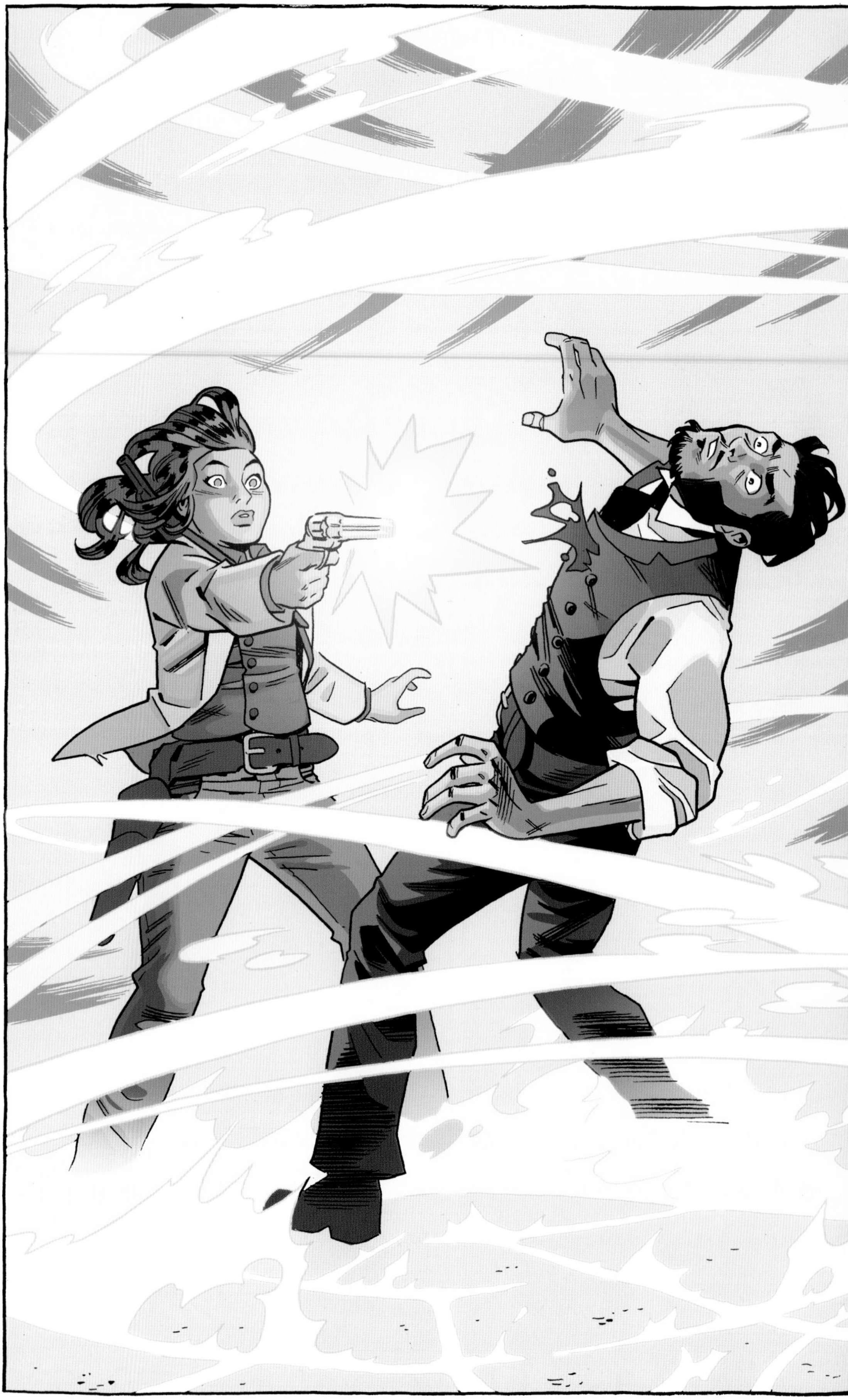

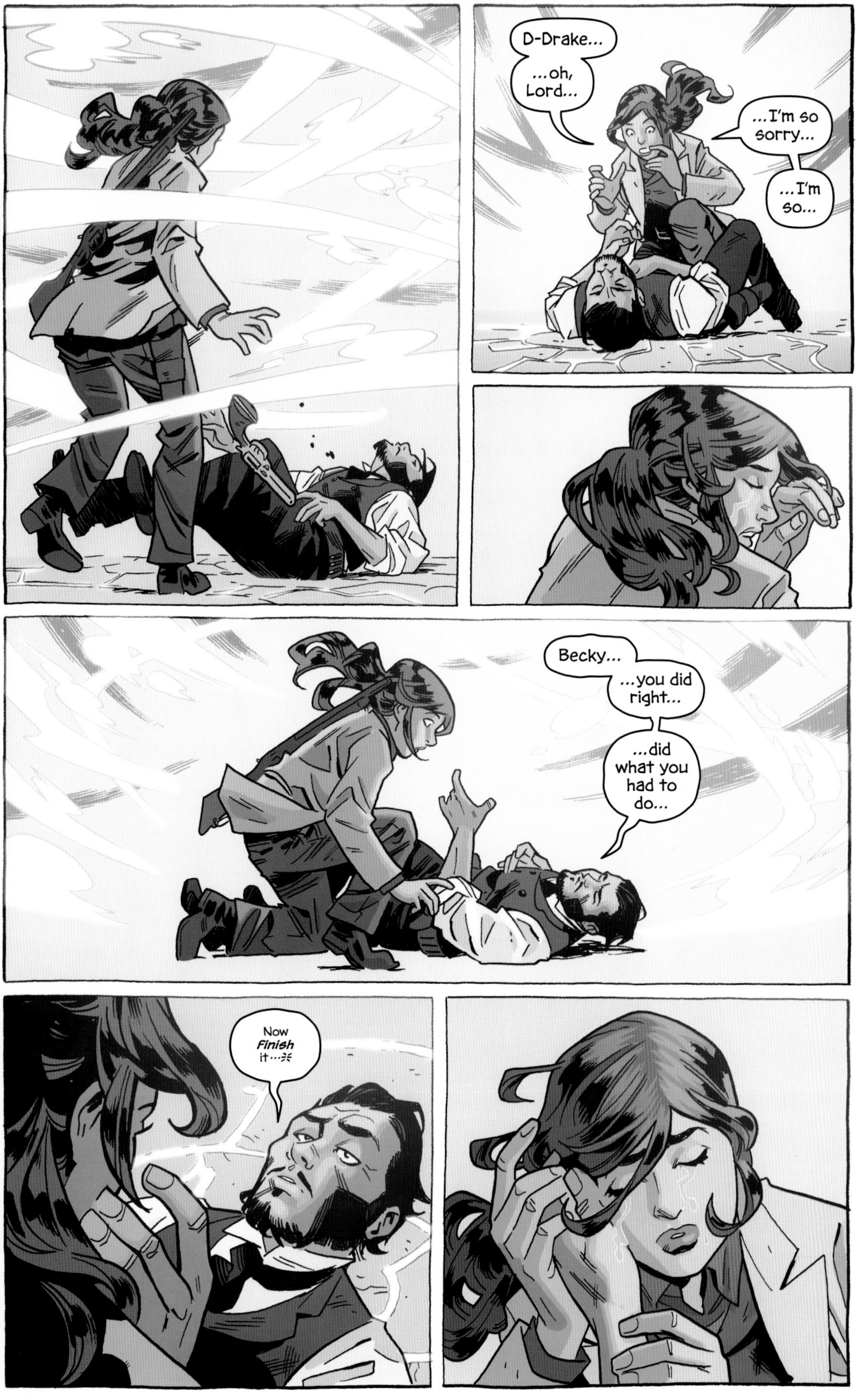
D-Drake...
...oh, Lord...
...I'm so sorry...
...I'm so...
Becky...
...you did right...
...did what you had to do...
Now *Finish* it...

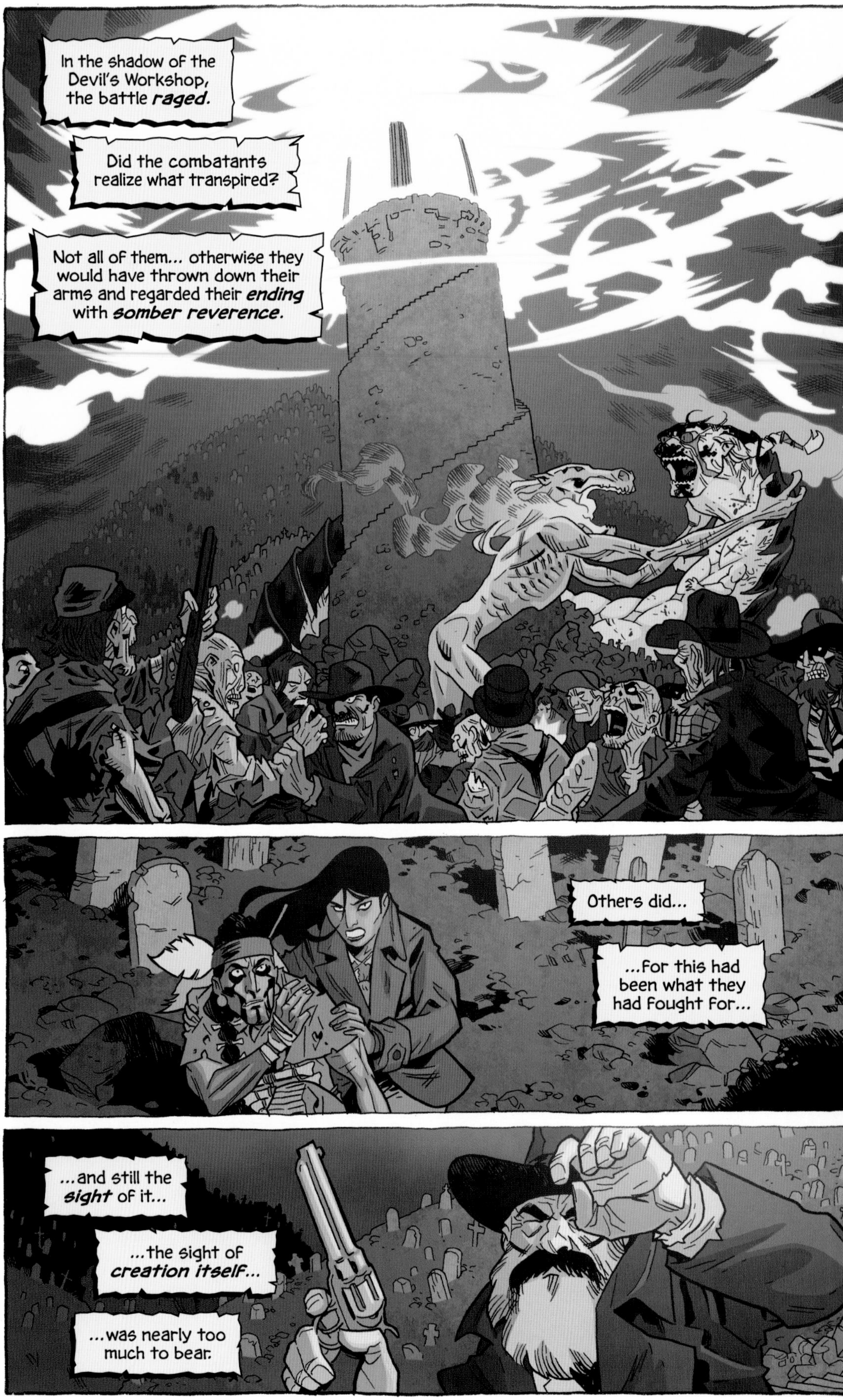
In the shadow of the Devil's Workshop, the battle *raged*.
Did the combatants realize what transpired?
Not all of them... otherwise they would have thrown down their arms and regarded their *ending* with *somber reverence*.
Others did...
...for this had been what they had fought for...
...and still the *sight* of it...
...the sight of *creation itself*...
...was nearly too much to bear.

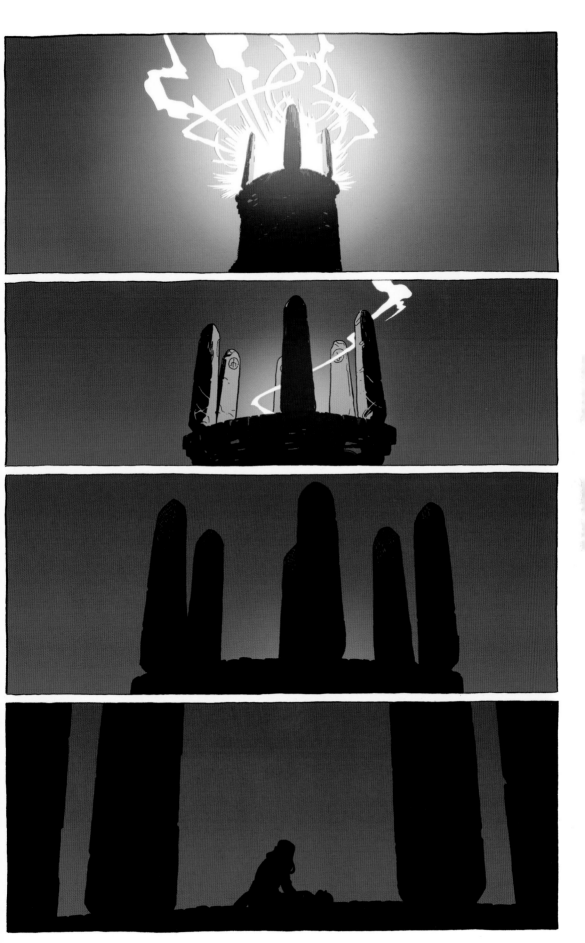

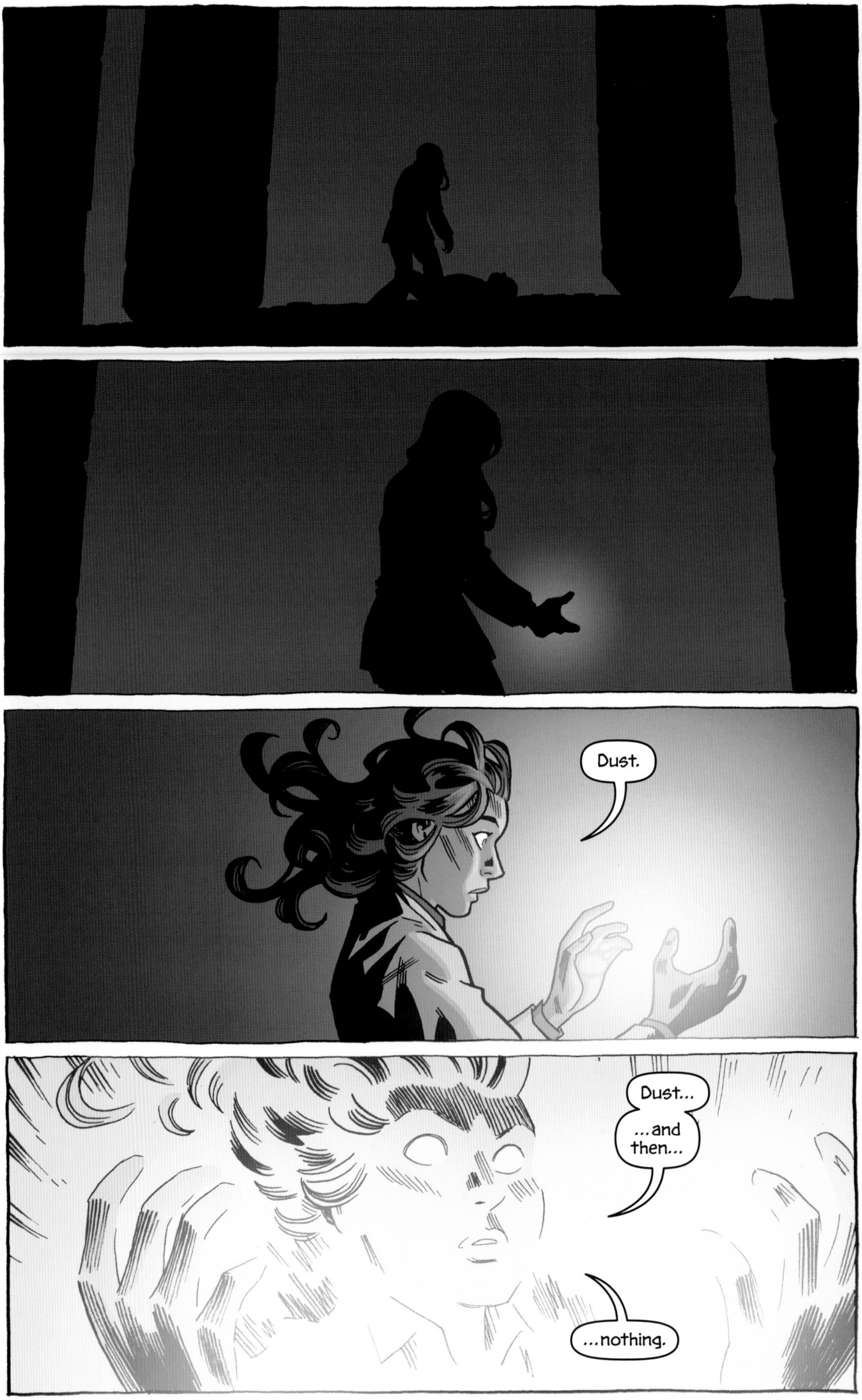
Dust.
Dust...
...and then...
...nothing.

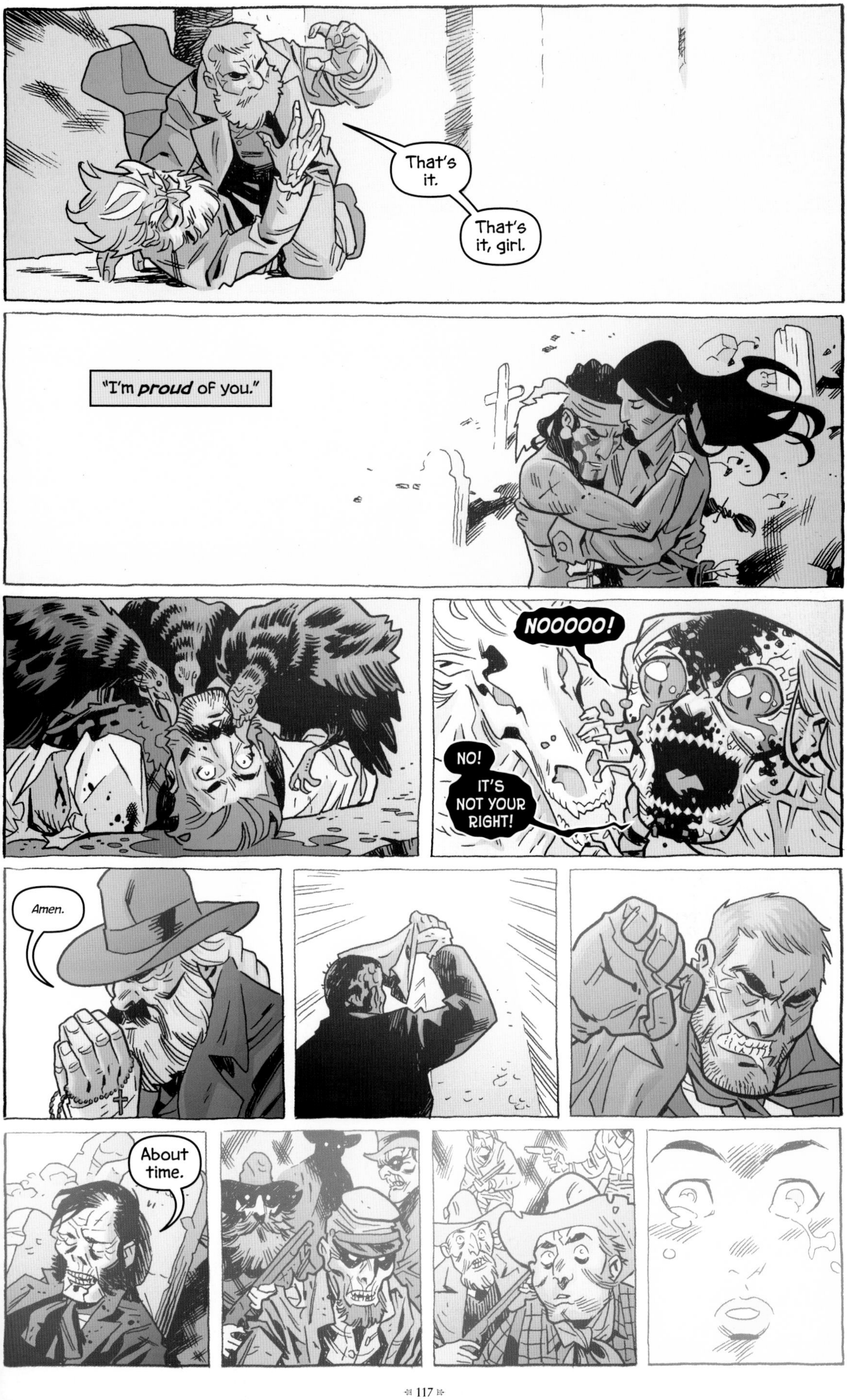

That's it.
That's it, girl.
"I'm *proud* of you."
NOOOOO!
NO!
IT'S NOT YOUR RIGHT!
Amen.
About time.

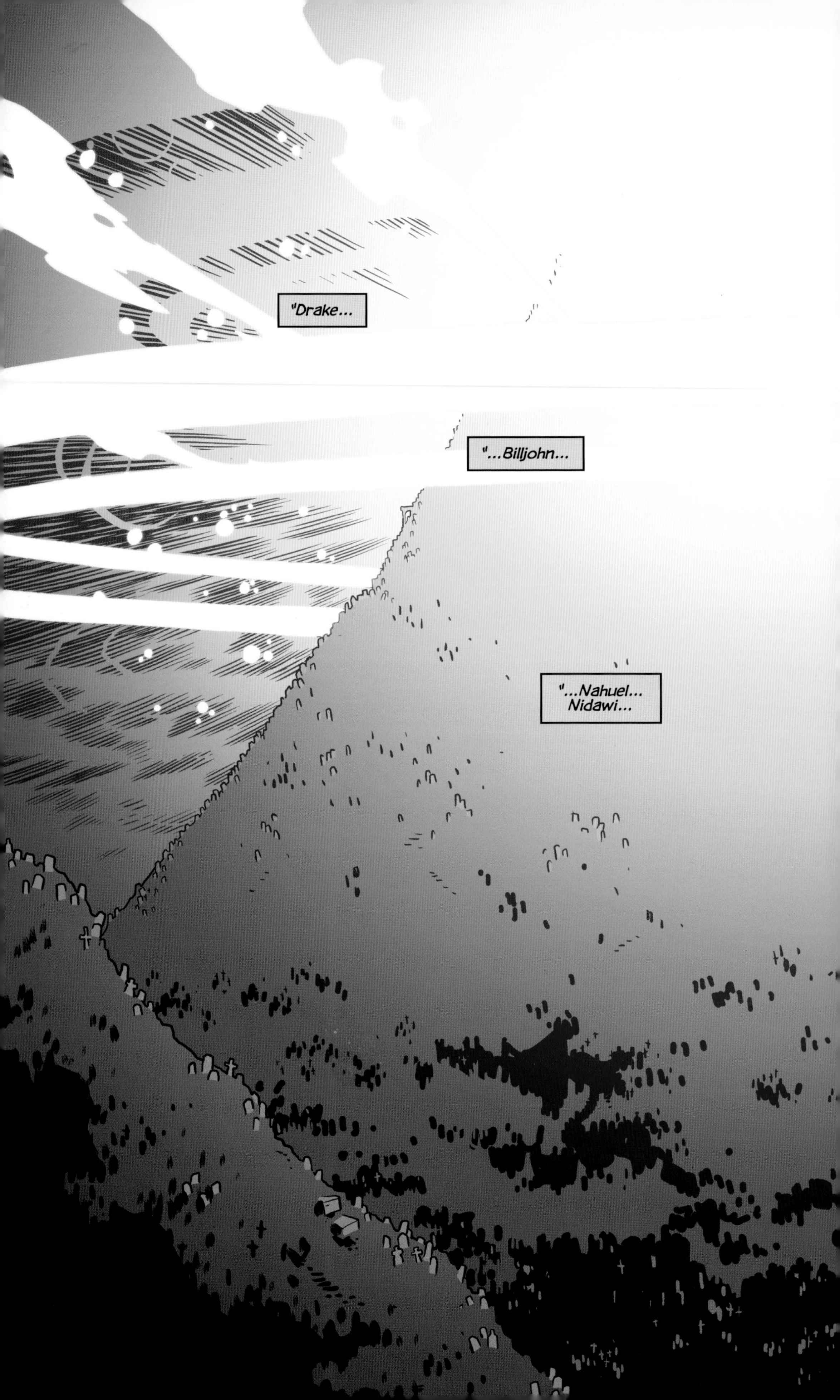
"Drake...
"...Billjohn...
"...Nahuel...
Nidawi...

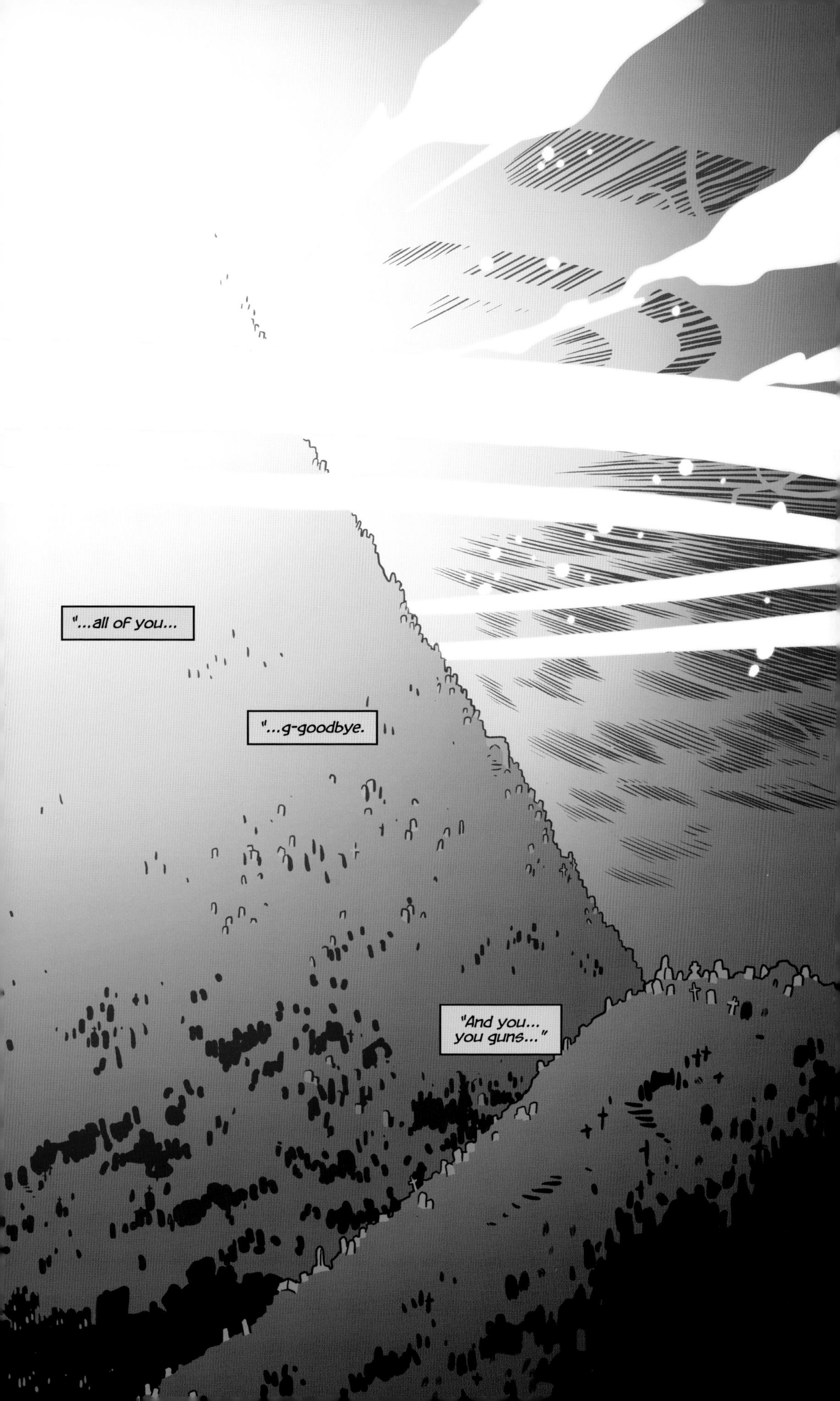
"...all of you...
"...g-goodbye.
"And you...
you guns..."

"...good riddance."

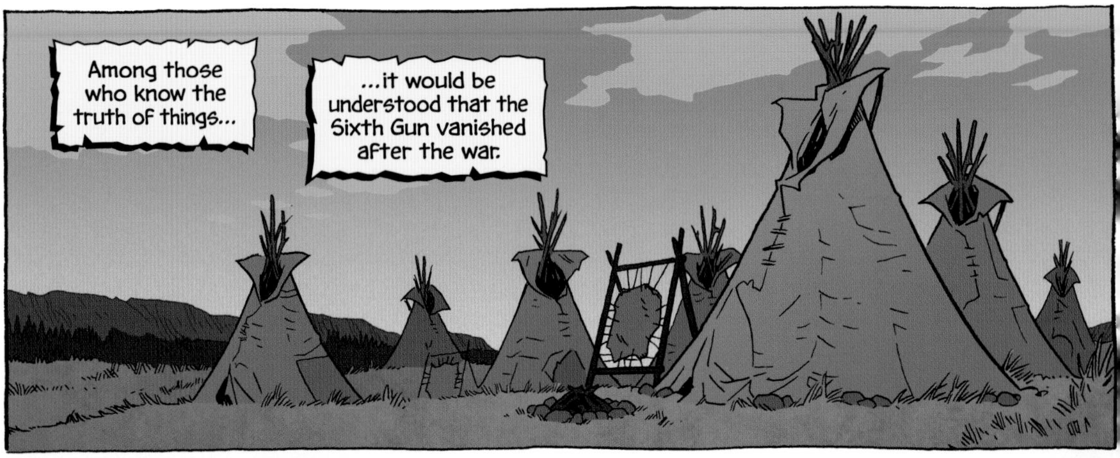
Among those who know the truth of things...
...it would be understood that the Sixth Gun vanished after the war.

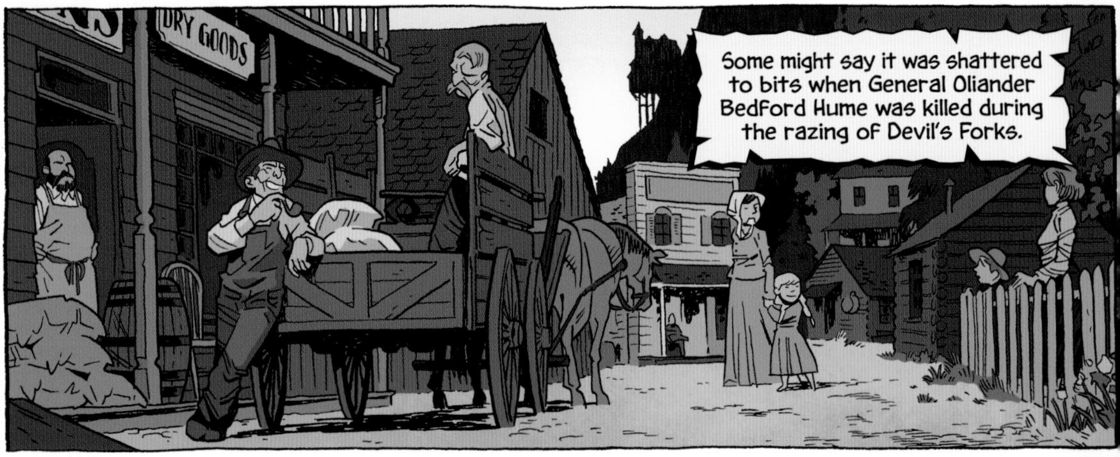
DRY GOODS
Some might say it was shattered to bits when General Oliander Bedford Hume was killed during the razing of Devil's Forks.

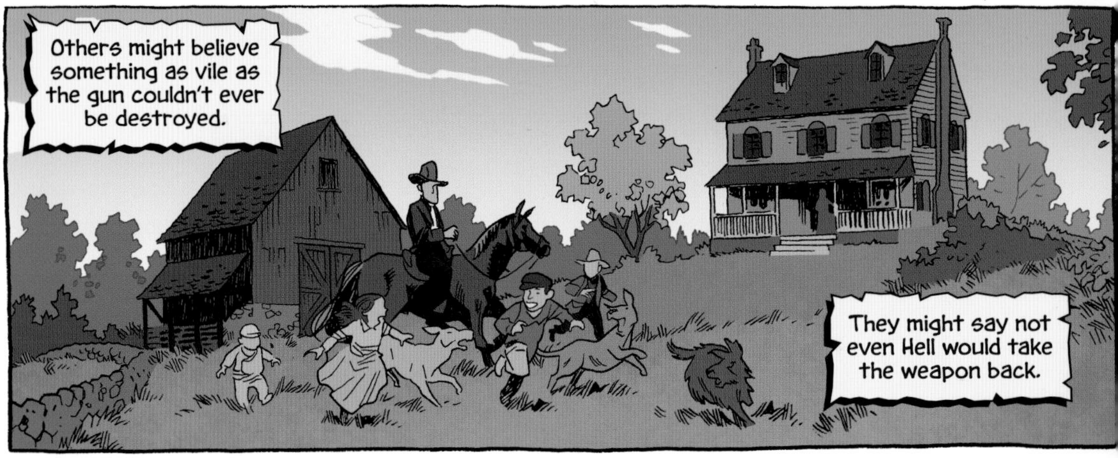
Others might believe something as vile as the gun couldn't ever be destroyed.
They might say not even Hell would take the weapon back.

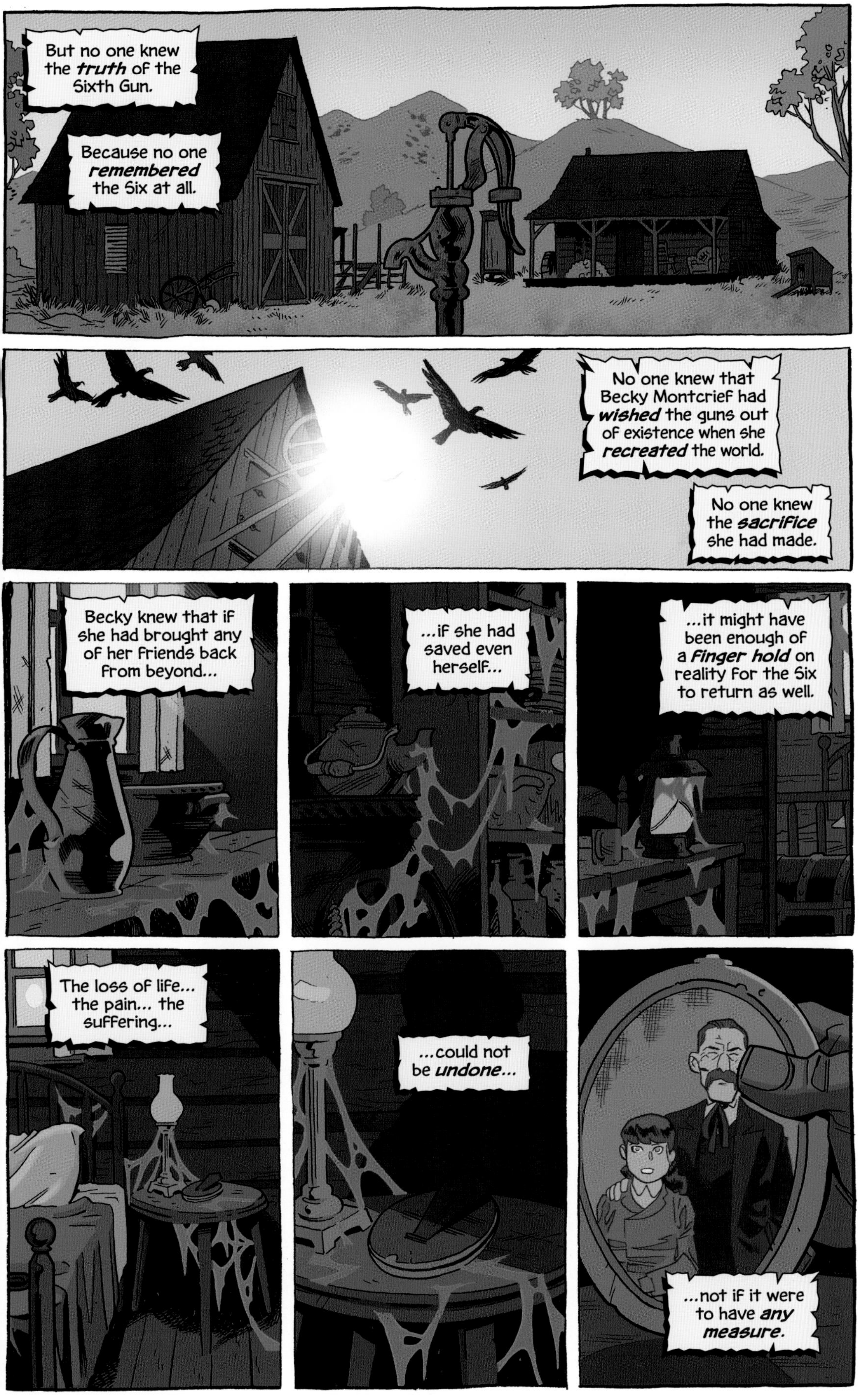

But no one knew the *truth* of the Sixth Gun.
Because no one *remembered* the Six at all.
No one knew that Becky Montcrief had *wished* the guns out of existence when she *recreated* the world.
No one knew the *sacrifice* she had made.
Becky knew that if she had brought any of her friends back from beyond...
...if she had saved even herself...
...it might have been enough of a *finger hold* on reality for the Six to return as well.
The loss of life... the pain... the suffering...
...could not be *undone*...
...not if it were to have *any measure.*

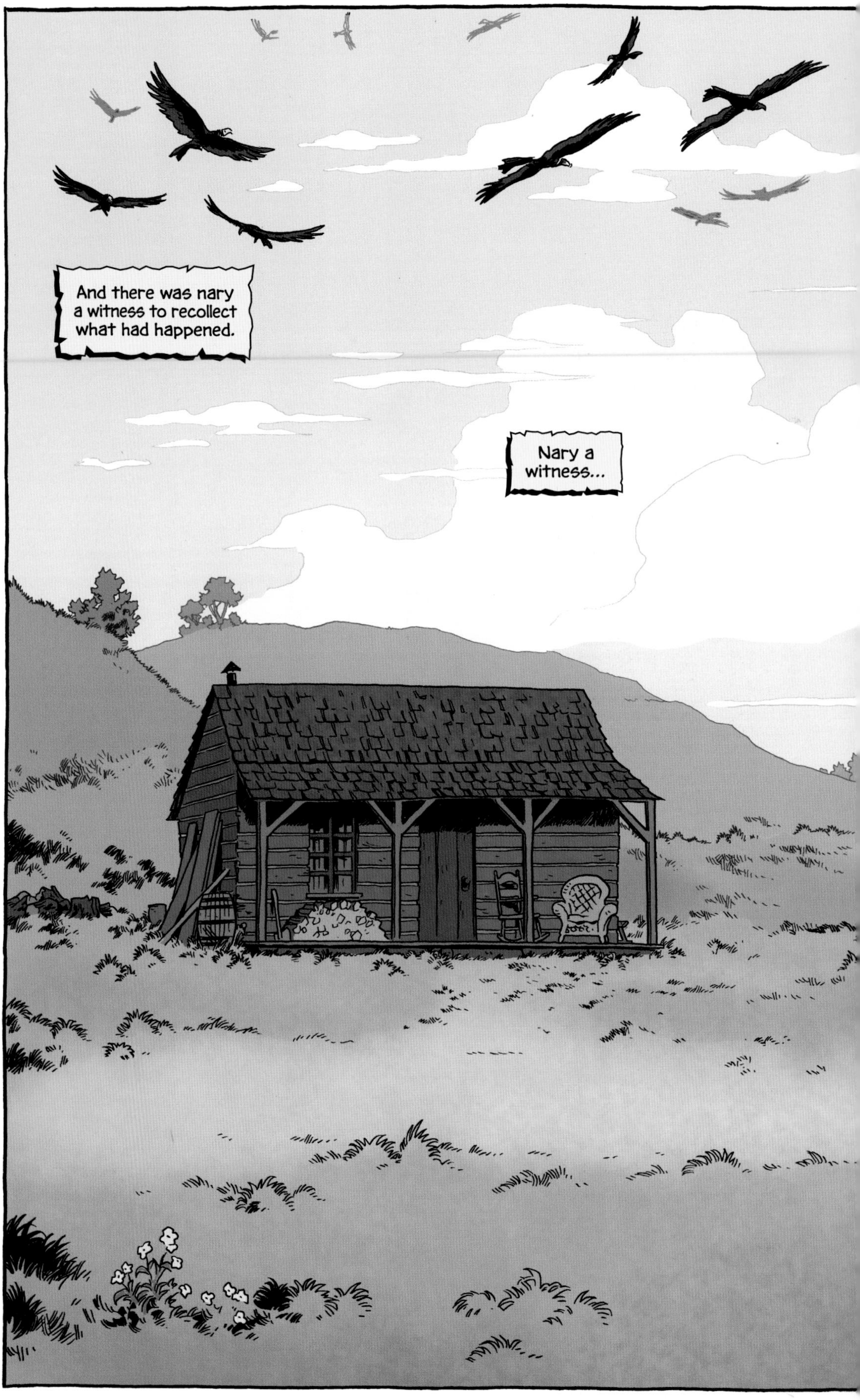
And there was nary a witness to recollect what had happened.
Nary a witness...

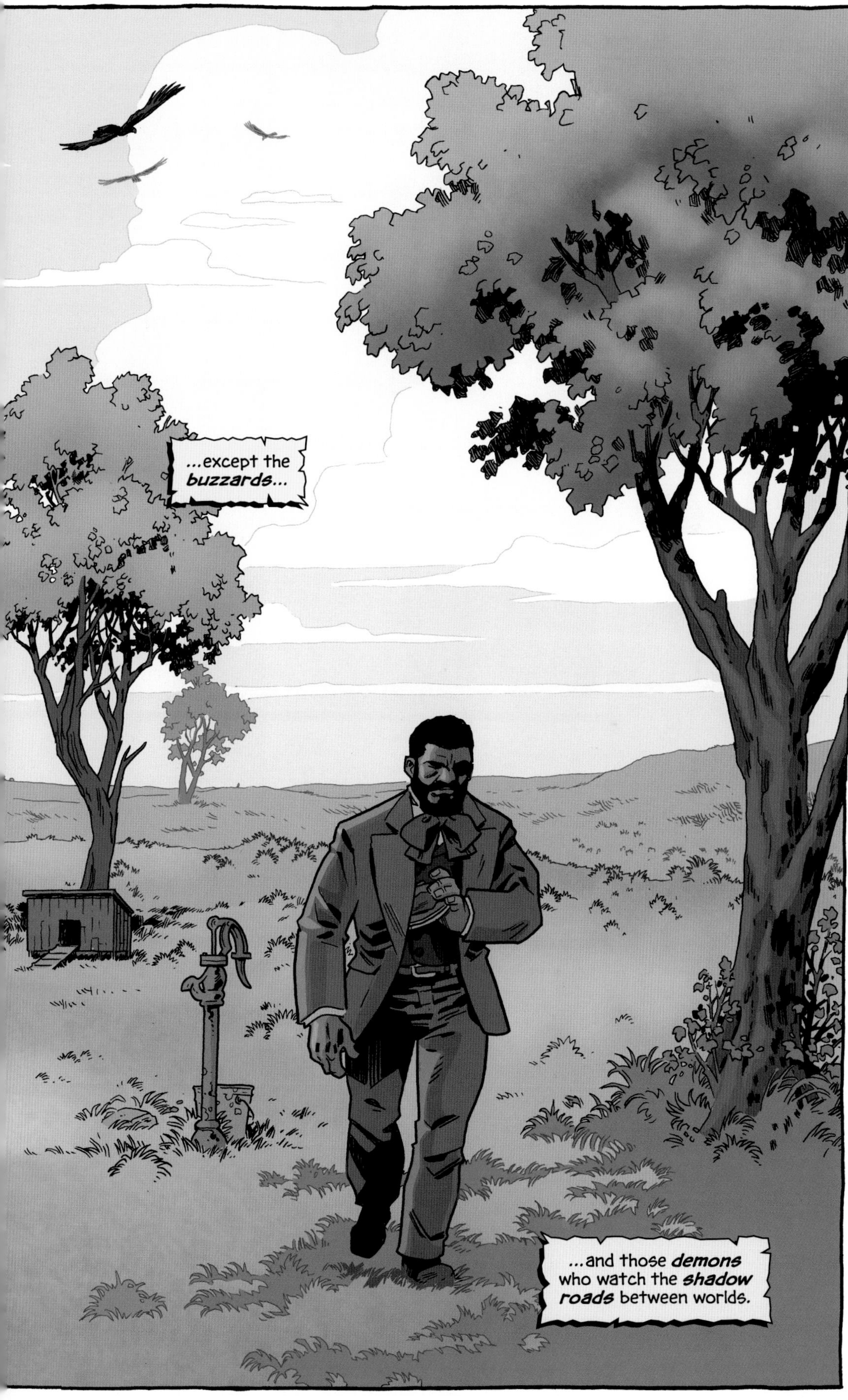
...except the buzzards...
...and those demons who watch the shadow roads between worlds.

C ullen Bunn is the writer of comic books such *The Damned,
The Sixth Gun, Helheim, The Tooth* and *Terrible Lizard* for
Oni Press. He has also written titles including *Wolverine,
Fearless Defenders, Venom, Deadpool Killustrated,* and *Magneto* for
Marvel Comics.

In addition, he is the author of the middle reader horror novel,
Crooked Hills, and the collection of short fiction, *Creeping Stones
and Other Stories.*

His prose work has appeared in numerous magazines and anthol-
ogies. Somewhere along the way, he founded Undaunted Press
and edited the critically acclaimed horror zine *Whispers From the
Shattered Forum.*

Cullen claims to have worked as an Alien Autopsy Specialist,
Rodeo Clown, Pro Wrestling Manager, and Sasquatch Wrangler.
He has fought for his life against mountain lions and performed
on stage as the World's Youngest Hypnotist. Buy him a drink
sometime, and he'll tell you all about it.

cullenbunn.com / @cullenbunn.

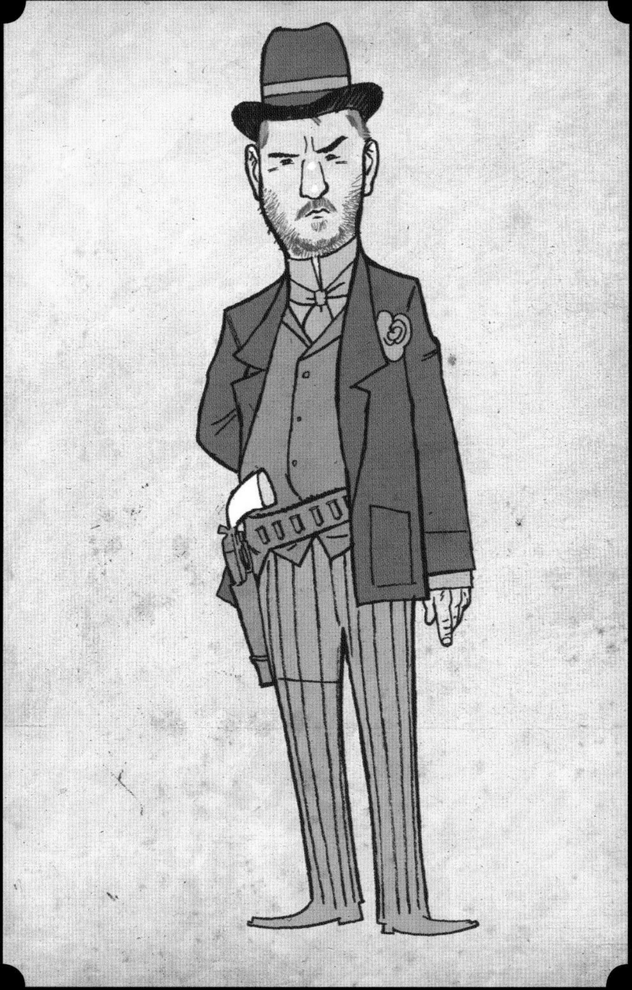

Author portrait illustrations by Jason Latour. jasonlatour.com

Brian Hurtt got his start in comics pencilling the second arc of Greg Rucka's *Queen & Country*. This was followed by art duties on several projects including *Queen & Country: Declassified*, *Three Strikes*, and Steve Gerber's critically acclaimed series *Hard Time*.

In 2006, Brian teamed with Cullen Bunn to create the Prohibition-era monster-noir sensation *The Damned*. The two found that their unique tastes and storytelling sensibilities were well-suited to one another and were eager to continue that relationship.

The Sixth Gun is their sophomore endeavor together and the next in what looks to be many years of creative collaboration.

Brian lives and works in St. Louis, Missouri.

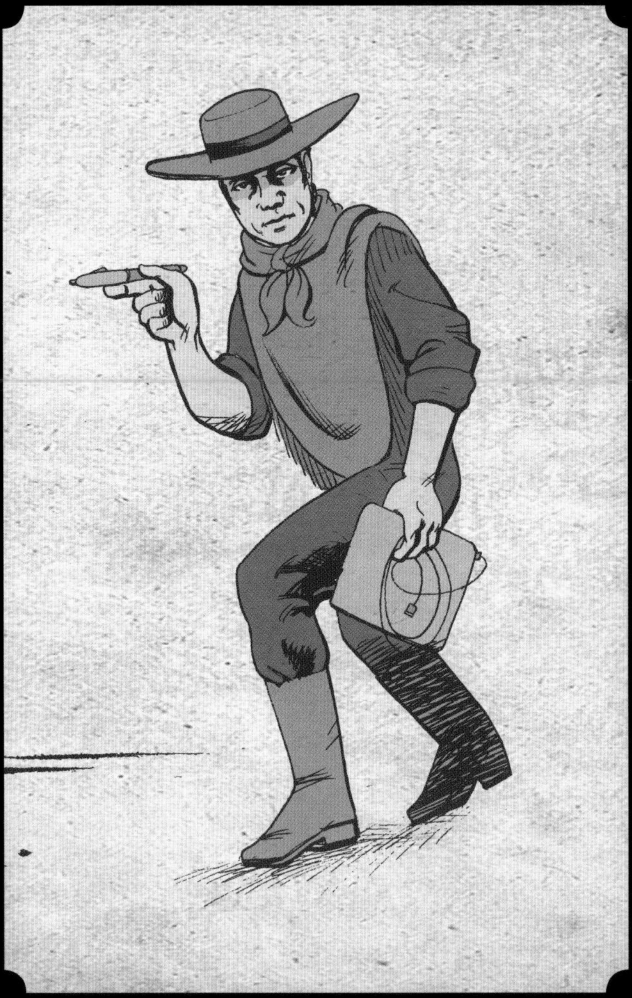

Illustration by Bill Crabtree.

Bill Crabtree's career as a colorist began in 2003 with the launch of Image Comic's *Invincible* and *Firebreather*. He was nominated for a Harvey Award for his work on *Invincible*, and he went on to color the first 50 issues of what would become a flagship Image Comics title. He continues to color *Firebreather*, which was recently made into a feature film on Cartoon Network, *Godland*, and *Jack Staff*.

Perhaps the highlight of his comics career, his role as colorist on *The Sixth Gun* began with issue 6, and has since been described as "like Christmas morning, but with guns."

@crabtree_bill